D1332986

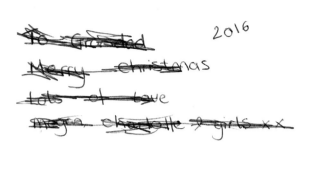

2016

To Grandad

Merry christmas

lots of love

Megan charlotte & girls xx

THE LAST BIG GUN

THE LAST BIG GUN

At War and at Sea with HMS *Belfast*

BRIAN LAVERY

This edition published in Great Britain in 2015 by
The Pool of London Press
A Division of Casemate Publishers
10 Hythe Bridge Street
Oxford OX1 2EW, UK
and
1950 Lawrence Road, Havertown, PA 19083 USA

www.pooloflondon.com

A CIP record for this book is available from the British Library

ISBN (hardback) 978-1-910860-01-4
ISBN (trade paperback) 978-1-910860-07-6
ISBN (ebook) 978-1-910860-08-3

Editing, cartography and design by David Gibbons
General arrangement drawings (pages 6–7) courtesy Ross Watton

Printed by Gomer Press Ltd, UK

POOLOFLONDON
The Pool of London Press is a publisher inspired by the rich history
and resonance of the stretch of the River Thames from London Bridge
downriver to Greenwich. The Press is dedicated to the specialist fields of
naval, maritime, military as well as exploration and cartographic history
in its many forms. The Press produces beautifully designed, commercial,
non-fiction volumes and digitial products of outstanding quality for a
dedicated readership featuring strong narratives, magnificent
illustrations and the finest photography.

To find out more please visit www.pooloflondon.com and to receive
regular email updates on forthcoming Pool of London titles, email
info@pooloflondon.com with Pool of London Updates in the
subject field.

For a complete list of Pool of London Press and Casemate titles,
please contact:

CASEMATE PUBLISHERS (UK)
Telephone (01865) 241249
Fax (01865) 794449
Email: casemate-uk@casematepublishers.co.uk
www.casematepublishers.co.uk

CASEMATE PUBLISHERS (US)
Telephone (610) 853-9131
Fax (610) 853-9146
Email: casemate@casematepublishing.com
www.casematepublishing.com

CONTENTS

HMS Belfast
General Arrangements 1942, after extended refit

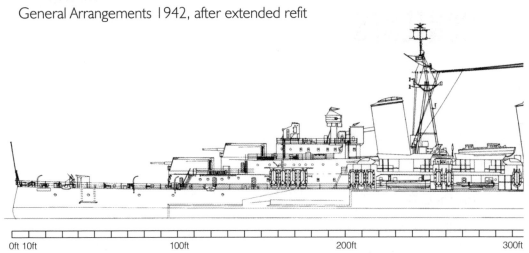

0ft 10ft   100ft   200ft   300ft

HMS Belfast
General Arrangements 1962, after refit

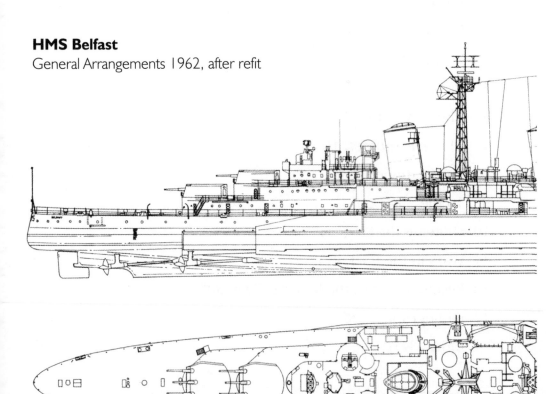

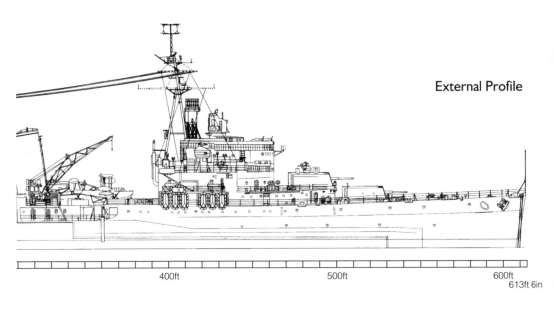

External Profile

	400ft		500ft		600ft

613ft 6in

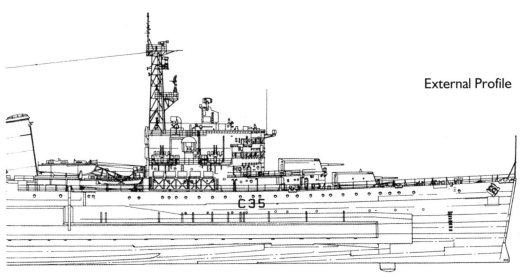

External Profile

C 35

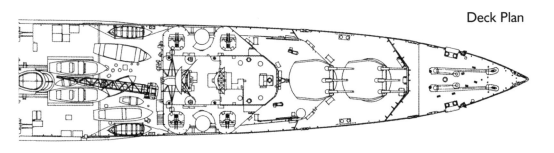

Deck Plan

PREFACE

HMS *BELFAST* HAS BEEN MOORED IN THE VERY CENTRE of the British capital for more than forty years now. She has perhaps the most prominent site of any preserved ship in the world, moored in the Pool of London, which was associated more with merchant than naval shipping – except that medieval warships belonging to the King were described as being 'of the Tower', that is the Tower of London, and of course the main job of the navy was to protect merchant shipping. She is by far the largest and most important representative of the country's oldest fighting service during perhaps its most dramatic and world-changing conflict. Despite this, when John Lee, now of Pool of London Press, suggested that I might consider some kind of book on the ship, I was surprised to find that there is no full narrative history of her. This volume hopes to fill that gap.

One of the great advantages of writing about the Belfast is the great range of material which as available. It is often vivid and informative, while other items are highly detailed but equally revealing. Unlike destroyers and smaller vessels, the logs of cruisers were preserved in the National Archives. They are not always easy to understand out of context, but as well as navigational data they provide information on matters such as leave and punishments; and they are invaluable in checking exactly what the ship was doing at any particular moment. There are numerous reports by captains and admirals in the same archive, which are far more revealing about the nature of the voyage and the commanders' instructions and intentions.

These items would be preserved for any ship of the period of cruiser size and above, but what makes the *Belfast* unique, apart from the existence of the ship herself, is the wide range of personal papers and oral history that is available. These range from senior officers such as Captain Dick, through more junior officers including George Thring and Brooke Smith, vivid midshipmen's journals by the likes of J. A. Syms and R. L. Garnons-Williams, petty officers including William Read, to junior seamen such as Richard Wilson and K. J. Melvin, and even Boy William Crawford. Between them they describe every level and department of the ship. It is a feature of naval history that quite ordinary men and boys might witness the great events of war, though as one of the *Belfast*'s men put it, each was only working to 'twiddle his particular knob and hope for the best'.

The accounts come in several kinds – manuscript autobiographies, oral history, papers collected at the time and letters to friends and family. The majority are in the Imperial War Museum, but others are to be found in the National Maritime Museum and Royal Naval Museum. The stock of personal papers is less rich after about 1947, but that is compensated for by the commission books for two of the voyages and the captain's order book and wardroom mess rules, which tell us much of the mores and practices of the age.

On a personal note, I see this book as a part of a study of many different types from the Second World War. I have already written on the 'River' Class frigates and Assault Landing Craft, which were very different in building and role from each other and from the *Belfast*. As such, the cruiser represents the 'big ship navy' of battleships and cruisers. In each case I have tried to provide an all-round view of the ship – its design and building, equipment and its operation, the social background, training and daily lives of its officers and crew, and its role in naval operations. I hope by these examples, as well as in more general works such as *Churchill's Navy*, *In Which They Served* and *All Hands* to help record and commemorate the varied experiences of those who served in the navy in very different ways.

I would like to acknowledge the help by the staffs of the National Archives at Kew, the National Maritime Museum in Greenwich, the Imperial War Museum in Lambeth, the Royal Naval Museum in Portsmouth and the London Library. Thanks are due to John Lee for the original idea and to David Gibbons for editing the text and pointing out errors.

Brian Lavery
September 2015

MINED

HMS *BELFAST* WAS READY FOR WAR as she steamed away from her anchorage outside Rosyth Dockyard in the Firth of Forth at 9.17 in the morning of Tuesday 21 November 1939. She was a brand new ship, commissioned just fifteen weeks earlier, a month before war was declared on Germany. She had had a few teething troubles, and it had taken several weeks for the catapult that launched her aircraft to be fully fitted, but now she was ready for almost anything. She had a fully professional crew of regular sailors, for wartime volunteers and conscripts had not had time to complete their basic training. To Lieutenant Commander George Thring, 'We were undoubtedly a very happy ship. The organisation ran smoothly, and people smiled.' Different branches such as seamen and stokers only mocked one another gently and did not clash seriously. The officers were not too 'pusser' or officious. Captain George Scott was popular, a 'nice man' according to one junior member of the crew. He had impressed them with his skill during an exercise when he played the part of a German raider and took the ship through the treacherous waters of the Pentland Firth in the dark. He took good care to inform the crew of events over the ship's Tannoy or loudspeaker system and with weekly briefings.

It was a 'lovely sunny morning' according to the master-at-arms, William F. Read, as 'members of the ship's company on the upper deck were going about their allotted tasks stripped to the waist and singing happily'. *Belfast* passed under the Forth Bridge in the wake of her fellow cruiser *Southampton*, which was flying the flag of Vice Admiral Sir George Edward-Collins, commanding the 2nd Cruiser Squadron. The two ships were to carry out gunnery exercises in the open waters outside the Firth. The tug *Krooman* (named quaintly after the native seamen often recruited on the African coast) was with them to tow a target. Thring and his colleagues 'could not help feeling that the navy was the only part of the nation that was actually doing anything'. The expression 'phoney war' was already in use. The armies in northern France were not pursuing the campaign with any vigour, and air forces on both sides were severely restricted in their choice of target. But it was different at sea, where many ships had already been lost to bombs, mines and torpedoes. The officers and men of the *Belfast* were well aware of the dangers from submarines – the ship had been present in Scapa Flow on the terrible night of 13/14 October when the great battleship *Royal Oak* was sunk by a U-boat inside a supposedly protected harbour. The *Belfast* had her own Asdic system to detect submarines, but most of her protection would come from the two escorting destroyers, which were better equipped for that kind of work. Air attack was another possibility. The *Southampton* herself had been bombed at anchor in this very Firth on 16 October, the day when the first enemy aircraft were brought down over British territory, and the officers of the *Belfast* had taken some advice from her experiences. Air attack could develop in seconds, so the crews of the anti-aircraft guns were 'closed up', or sitting at their stations. The director towers that would control the fire were all manned, along with the 4-inch guns, the 2-pounder 'pom-poms' and the .5 inch machine-guns. Radar, known as radio direction finding or RDF, was still very rare aboard ships and the *Belfast* had none. Instead six lookouts were posted to scan the sky with binoculars, being relieved every half hour to aid concentration. Others were detailed to look out for tracks of torpedoes. It was a clear day, but they could see nothing of any significance.

Apart from that, most of the crew were at their normal duties when not having a 'stand easy' on deck. The captain was on the bridge directing operations, and Lieutenant Commander Thring was up there with the chief telegraphist rigging up a microphone to give a running commentary to the crew in the event of an air attack. The twelve 6-inch guns, the ship's main armament, were as yet unmanned, though they would soon be prepared for the gunnery exercise. But for the moment Ordnance Artificer John Harrison and his two assistants were changing an air bottle at the top of a 20-foot ladder to the shell room under a gun turret. Below decks the engineers were running two out of the four boilers to conserve fuel, though the others were fired up so that they could be ready if needed. The steam from the boilers was being fed to the four cruising turbines that were used when the ship was sailing a moderate speed. Repair work was going on in the paint store, the main naval store, the cooling machinery compartment, the wardroom wine store and No. 6 store, so the doors to these compartments had to be left open. Otherwise all watertight doors were kept shut to prevent flooding in the event of a sudden attack, and two able seamen were employed to check this in each part of the ship. The ship's cooks were preparing dinner, the main meal of the day for the crew, with all of them except the chief cook in the servery or the preparing room.

At 1030 the two ships were well out into the Firth. The *Belfast* was four cables, or 800 yards, astern of the *Southampton*, her engines turning at 130 revolutions per minute and creating a speed of seventeen knots. On the bridge, Captain Scott followed the flagship and ordered an alteration of course to 295 degrees, then at 1042 to the exact opposite or reciprocal course of 115 degrees as part of a manoeuvre, then to 60 degrees at 1053. The turn was completed, and the helm was put amidships so that the ship could settle on her new course.

Despite several weeks of war and the trauma of losing the *Royal Oak*, what happened next was a shock in every sense of the term. There was a huge explosion in which the ship rose some feet in the air and then vibrated violently – was 'bounced up and down' according to a witness – for several seconds. The gunnery officer, with a good view high in the ship, saw a column of water 60 feet high abreast of the foremast, and then another one 100 feet high

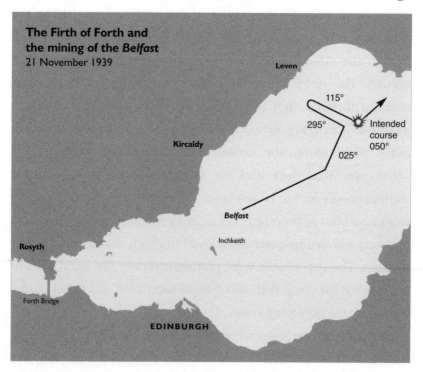

The Firth of Forth and the mining of the *Belfast*
21 November 1939

Leven

115°

295°

Intended course 050°

Kircaldy

025°

Belfast

Inchkeith

Rosyth

Forth Bridge

EDINBURGH

half a second or so later. He and his warrant officer were soaked as it came down again. Thring and the chief telegraphist held on tight to a rail and then found themselves 'garlanded' with wireless aerials. Thring noticed that the topmast was at an angle of 30 degrees. Forward in his store right in the bows, the ship's painter, H. Stanton, was thrown against the deck above and seriously injured in the head. Midshipman Syms reported, 'Suddenly there was an almighty bang and the ship shuddered as if being shaken by some giant hand. Standing at the back of the bridge to witness the shoot, the shock knocked me off my feet and my first reaction was that the other cruiser with us had somehow hit us rather than the towed target.' Able Seaman Lawrence Conlon was making his way along the corridor outside the chief petty officers' mess when he felt the shock. He picked up a key he found on the deck and continued on his way, noting that 'the passage seemed to be crumpled or bent', but he soon reached the open air. Boy 1st Class Peter McSweeney was coming from his mess and crossing the catapult deck when, as he said, 'I just went sliding.' From inside the turret Ordnance Artificer Harrison reported, 'I felt my spine going into my skull.' He thought the air bottle he was working on had exploded. He and his assistants climbed through an S-bend to get out and tried to go through a hatch between the centre and right-hand guns on the turret. At first it would not open, and water was rushing in. They feared that the ship had sunk, but eventually they forced it open. 'Much to our relief we got out and assessed the damage.' The galley was closer to the centre of the explosion, and all the cooks were flung to the deck. The range caught fire, but Petty Officers Brooker and Sadler shut off the fuel supply, which put it out. Nearby in the bakery, bags of flour were stored on the floor and apparently acted as sandbags to reduce the shock. The two ratings in there were unhurt but buried in flour.

Captain Scott ordered the stopping of all engines as soon as the explosion happened, then tried to move the ship forward with the order 'half ahead' – but there was no power. The ship still had enough speed to steer, and he had her turned on to a course back to Rosyth before she came to a standstill. At least the ship was not heeling to one side or the other, though she seemed to be deeper in the bows than the stern. No one knew what had caused the explosion, but it was natural to suspect a torpedo from a submarine, so the destroyers circled round looking for it. The tug *Krooman* abandoned the target she was towing and prepared to take up the tow of the *Belfast* instead. A line had been attached by 1140, less than 50 minutes after the explosion. Signals were sent out to get more help from the dockyard.

All the uninjured men headed for the upper decks, not knowing whether they would be ordered to abandon ship or to try to save her. It was fortunate the ship was not at full action stations because the ammunition supply parties might well have been injured if they were handling 6-inch shells weighing 112 pounds each, even if they were practice rounds containing no explosives. All the ship's boats had been damaged by crashing against the crutches that supported them except the two sea boats, which were hung on davits. The emergency life rafts, the Carley floats, were mostly intact, and a part of the crew got them ready in case they were needed. Boy McSweeney got to his feet on the catapult deck – 'we had to start sorting ourselves out and mustering.' They were assembled by their officers, while the boys' instructor went round and tried to account for his charges. The men did not stand still for long: soon they were found duties in an attempt to keep the *Belfast* afloat. Apart from the damage to the hull, the most immediate problem was that the electrics had failed, so the men below were in pitch darkness unless they could get hold of torches or miners' helmets. Telephones were out of action, and many other services were not working. The steam-operated generators were unserviceable, and the ship's ring main had fractured in many places, but a diesel generator was started and electrical parties carried out local repairs. Power was restored after about ten minutes.

The medical staff had been shaken by the explosion but were uninjured. The sick bay had to be abandoned as oil flooded in, and patients were lifted up on deck, squeezing wide stretchers though narrow passages. The three doctors set up medical stations in different parts of the ship, aided by the sick-berth attendants. Class distinctions no longer applied, and the exclusive territory of the officers' wardroom became a hospital ward. There were two severe head injuries including the painter, and others with concussion or fractures of the lower body, who were given morphine. The principal medical officer, Surgeon Commander E. J. K. Weeks, was pleased with how his team performed in their first emergency and was 'wreathed in smiles' by the end of the day according to Thring. In his white operating dress stained with blood he 'looked a bit sinister'. In all, 20 officers and men had sustained injuries that would need hospital treatment, and there were 26 more minor cases, including Captain Scott who had a small incised wound on the nose. He was regarded as 'highly strung and easily excited' by some of his superiors, but he kept his nerve in the circumstances.

Meanwhile the crew was fed using emergency supplies of corned beef and other tinned food, tin mugs and mess kettles of drinking water that were kept near the ship's boats. The domestic staff issued blankets for warmth. Later the men were given a meal of herring in tomato sauce, one of the least favourite items in the naval menu. The crew was calm, and there was no sign of panic. There were orders for dealing with underwater attack, but these were useless with the damage below the ship rather than in the side. However, the ship's organisation, prepared by the executive officer, Commander James G. Roper, held together well in difficult circumstances. There were no cowards and a few heroes, especially the ship's joiner, P. S. Davies, who ignored his own fractured dorsal vertebra to rescue two badly injured men, moving them over the raised coaming of a watertight door. The ship's pumps were now working and keeping the water at an acceptable level, for there was no large hole in the hull. Just after one o'clock the tug *Brahman* arrived from Rosyth and attached a line, to be joined by the *Grangebourne*, *Oxcar* and *Bulger* within the hour. Now the ship was making progress back towards Rosyth and passed the island of Inchkeith at 1411.

It did not take long for Captain Scott to work out that the ship had been damaged by some kind of mine. There was no sign of aircraft. Neither the cruisers nor the destroyers had made any Asdic contact with a submarine; no torpedo track had been seen despite numerous lookouts; and the ship had carried out major changes of course just before the explosion, all of which made a torpedo hit unlikely. The explosion had not been on one side of the ship as might have been expected, but underneath, causing a different kind of damage and casualties. In fact, the *Belfast* was the first major casualty of 'Hitler's secret weapon', the magnetic mine. It could be laid in relatively shallow water, in this case 16 fathoms or 29 metres, and was set off by a ship's magnetic field. This was one of several laid by a U-boat five weeks earlier. There had already been warnings with the loss of many merchant ships off the east coast and severe damage to the liner *City of Paris* by an underwater explosion in September. Exactly 24 hours before the *Belfast* explosion the First Lord of the Admiralty, Winston Churchill, had presided over a meeting in his office 'to consider steps to meet the enemy's magnetic mine'. On 23 November, two days after the *Belfast* explosion, Lieutenant Commander J. G. D. Ouvry recovered an intact magnetic mine off Shoeburyness in Essex, and countermeasures could be devised. The magnetic mine made it necessary to maintain a large fleet of minesweepers to clear the shipping lanes and for every ship to have its magnetic field reduced by 'degaussing', but it was not the war-winning weapon its inventors had hoped.

By five in the afternoon of the 21st the crippled cruiser was secured in the lock at the entrance to Rosyth Dockyard, and casualties were landed by crane to be taken to local hospitals. Stanton the painter eventually died, the only fatality. Later in the day the ship was taken further in, to a dry dock where the damage could be examined. Thring watched as the water was slowly pumped out: 'The ship started to rest on the chocks. This caused her to creak and groan like an animal in pain. Rivets were sheered, and the deck itself began to crack. Pumping was therefore stopped, and the ship was left floating, just clear of the chocks.' Most of the crew were sent to the dockyard canteen for the night, but the officers remained on board. 'It was an eerie feeling on board a nearly deserted ship, with all the usual machinery stopped. Continuous groans from plates and frames prevented most of us from sleeping, although we were very tired.'

Most of the crew were given a week's survivor's leave. Thring returned from his on an overcrowded night train where a party of drunks kept the others awake until they fell into 'a state of torpor'. They arrived four hours late in Edinburgh, and he refreshed himself in the North British Hotel before the last leg of the trip. By Christmas, 'there was a strong rumour that our happy party would have to break up'. Captain Scott tried hard to have the men transferred to a similar ship under construction, but to no avail. Special trains were laid on for the men, and Thring and some of the officers 'stood on the lines watching one of the finest ships companys [sic] drive out into the night, bound for Portsmouth barracks whence they would be scattered to the four corners of the earth'. He was initially told he would become first lieutenant of an aircraft carrier – assistant to the commander and 'just another cog in the machine', but he was delighted when that was changed to the command of the sloop *Deptford*. Lawrence Conlon went to the old destroyer *Wrestler*, a 'home for cockroaches'. His colleague, W. M. Crawford, was one of many sent to the ill-fated battlecruiser *Hood*. Most of them regretted the loss of a happy ship and the separation from good comrades, but this they had to accept: it was the way of the navy and the fortune of war. To Master-at-Arms William Read, the *Belfast* was the happiest ship he served in during a 23-year career.

Many thought that the life of HMS *Belfast* was over after less than four months in service. Among them was the German radio propagandist 'Lord Haw-Haw', who announced that the ship had been sunk with heavy loss of life. Peter McSweeney was on leave at his sister's at the time, and they could laugh over it. It was more serious for John Harrison, who was one of the technical staff kept behind at Rosyth. He desperately needed to phone his wife to tell her it was not true, and he had to light matches to operate a blacked-out phone box in Inverkeithing. Meanwhile the experts were assessing whether the *Belfast* had any future.

THE BIRTH OF A CRUISER

HMS *BELFAST* WAS A CRUISER, launched in the city of Belfast in 1938. The type was recognised as second in the naval pecking order, below the battleship, which had much bigger guns and thicker armour. The cruiser was versatile and could perform several functions. It might scout for the battlefleet, though that was becoming less important in the days of air reconnaissance. In the past it had been used to lead squadrons of destroyers, but that function became obsolete as specialist 'destroyer leaders' were built. It could police the British Empire with its dominions and colonies on five continents, deterring aggression or revolt and 'showing the flag', or it could patrol the seas against enemy commerce raiders in wartime. It was much cheaper to construct than a battleship, so larger numbers could be built; they did not necessarily have to be concentrated in a large fleet, so they could be dispersed as necessary. A cruiser's 6- or 8-inch guns were powerful enough to take on enemy ships of the same type, while its armour would hopefully keep out their shells. And, like all good fighting ships, it was able to run away from an enemy it could not hope to fight, so it was designed to be faster than a battleship.

Battleship development had tended to 'move in a straight line' since the famous *Dreadnought* of 1906 set the pattern. Ships became ever larger and faster with heavier main guns – though in that sense the new ships of the *King George V* class were a throwback with only 14-inch guns compared with the 16-inch armament of the *Rodney* and *Nelson*. Cruisers, however, had more varied functions, and so their development was more complicated. During the First World War there were no less than five distinct types. Armoured cruisers were made obsolete by battlecruisers, which matched the gun-power of the battleships. Protected cruisers had only light armour, but their coal was arranged to absorb shot. Scouts were designed to lead destroyer flotillas and carried only light armament. The 'Town' class cruisers were much larger and intended for long-range operation. Armed with a small number of 6-inch guns and with long, narrow hulls, they provided the basis for the new light cruisers that were built in some numbers during the war. They were very suitable as a scouting force for the battleships of the Grand Fleet in the North Sea, but less useful for world-wide deployment. This led towards the end of the war to the larger *Hawkins* class with 7.5-inch guns and able to operate with either coal or oil throughout the British Empire; they represented a great increase in gun-power compared with the early war 'C' class, from 500 to 1400 pounds.

After the war, the disarmament treaties of Washington in 1922 and London in 1930 altered the picture. The United States Navy was recognised as equal to the Royal Navy, and both were allowed to build up to 525,000 tons of capital ships. Japan was allowed three-fifths of that tonnage, 315,000 tons, while France and Italy had 175,000 tons each; Germany was still out of the naval race, tightly restricted by the Treaty of Versailles. Two types of cruiser were now accepted – heavy, with 8-inch guns (slightly larger than the *Hawkins*), and light, with 6-inch. Cruiser size was limited to 10,000 tons.

The British were highly sensitive about their position. During the negotiations they always insisted that they needed a large cruiser force, on the grounds that both their merchant shipping fleet and their empire were bigger than those of other nations. In addition, the homeland had to be protected against invasion. The country was determined to maintain a fleet bigger than that of any potential enemy, a category which excluded the United States in most people's minds. At the same time, Britain took the treaties far more seriously than other powers. A secretive and militaristic nation like Japan could build its ships largely under cover and saw no shame in exceeding the tonnage. The United States, on the other hand, was happy for the moment to be recognised formally as first-equal among naval powers, while a largely isolationist Congress did not always vote the money to build up to the tonnage limits. But in Britain the legalistic minds of the civil service made sure that the figures were not exceeded, either generally or for individual ships, while the navy was determined to squeeze the last ounce of value from its allocation. The naval constructors who designed the ships and supervised their construction had to resolve this conflict by building almost exactly to the limit. One solution was to use a special type of steel known as D-quality. It was lighter and stronger than normal steel, but it needed special equipment to work it. In a supreme irony, it was very difficult to weld, a process that would have saved much more weight as compared with the more traditional riveting.

* * * * *

Naval constructors were the product of a rather cruel and wasteful system dating back to Victorian times, by which about half the dockyard apprentice shipwrights were weeded out every year. According to one of their number:

In 1927 only 50 apprentices were accepted at Portsmouth. At the end of each [school] year an examination was held and apprentices who

British Cruiser Designs: Antecedents of the *Belfast*

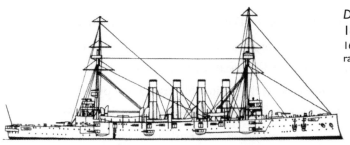

Diadem class protected cruisers, 1898–1903
16×6-inch guns; 1,600lb broadside; range 14,600 yards; speed 20 knots

Monmouth class armoured cruisers, 1903–1904
14×6-inch guns; 1,400lb broadside; range 14,600 yards; speed 23 knots

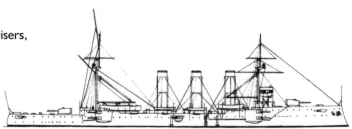

Boadicea class scout cruisers, 1909–1910
6×4-inch guns; 186lb broadside; range 11,600 yards; speed 25 knots

Weymouth class light cruisers, 1911–1912
8×6-inch guns; 800lb broadside; range 14,310 yards; speed 25 knots

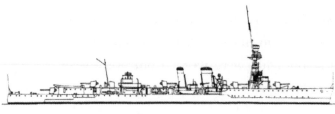

C class light cruisers, 1914–1918
5×6-inch guns; 500lb broadside; range 14,310 yards; speed 29 knots

Hawkins class cruisers, 1919–1925
7×7.5-inch guns; 1,400lb broadside; range 21,110 yards; speed 31 knots

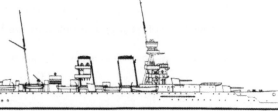

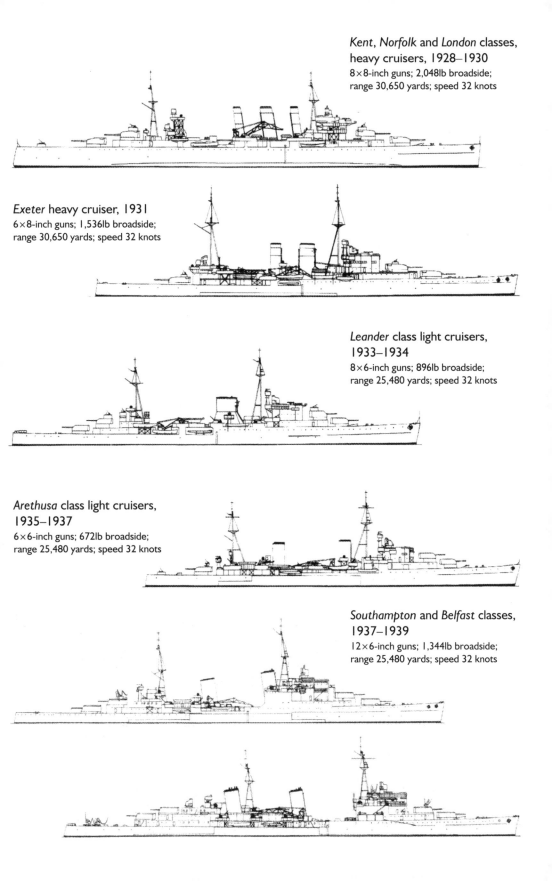

Kent, Norfolk and **London** classes,
heavy cruisers, 1928–1930
8×8-inch guns; 2,048lb broadside;
range 30,650 yards; speed 32 knots

Exeter heavy cruiser, 1931
6×8-inch guns; 1,536lb broadside;
range 30,650 yards; speed 32 knots

Leander class light cruisers,
1933–1934
8×6-inch guns; 896lb broadside;
range 25,480 yards; speed 32 knots

Arethusa class light cruisers,
1935–1937
6×6-inch guns; 672lb broadside;
range 25,480 yards; speed 32 knots

Southampton and **Belfast** classes,
1937–1939
12×6-inch guns; 1,344lb broadside;
range 25,480 yards; speed 32 knots

failed to qualify had to leave. So after four years only a dozen of the original fifty survived and these, together with the fourth year students of Plymouth, Chatham, Sheerness … had to compete for one only constructor cadet post and one only electrical engineer cadetship.

The successful youth was already well grounded in shipyard work before he went to the Royal Naval College at Greenwich to study naval architecture to degree standard. After he qualified he might be sent to work in the Admiralty Office in Whitehall, where lighting conditions were not ideal for drawing office work. Starting in the grade of Assistant Constructor Second Class, he would work as part of a team perhaps designing a new class of ship:

> … the Constructor had his desk in the middle of the room with his team around him [Constructors were then usually in their early-middle forties having had to pass through Second and First Class AC stages] … Constructors were always addressed as 'Sir' by all members of the team … Christian names were very seldom used except between equal grades or personal friends.

They worked hard at the drawing board to produce the outline and then the detail of the new designs and to carry out the numerous calculations involved.

In the late 1920s and early1930s the British built three-funnelled, high-sided cruisers of the 'County' classes, heavily armed with eight 8-inch guns to meet big enemy cruisers. They introduced twin turrets for cruisers with a further increase in gun-power to 2,048 pounds. To create larger numbers of cruisers to deploy around the world they also built smaller and cheaper ships with six or eight 6-inch guns, such as the *Leander* and *Arethusa* classes. In 1931 the Japanese began to build the *Mogami* class, large ships with fifteen 6.1-inch guns, and the Americans laid down the *Brooklyn* class with a similar armament. The British had never been keen on the 8-inch gun – their design was overweight and there were persistent mechanical problems – but now they agonised about its value compared with the 6-inch. On the one hand, the 8-inch had greater penetrating power through armour and a longer range (28,000 yards compared with 20,000), which would be vital in the early stages of an action. On the other hand, more 6-inch guns could be fitted in a given size of hull, and they could fire much faster – six or eight rounds per minute compared with two. However, studies showed that in wartime hits were rare in the range between 28,000 and 20,000 yards, so one of the main advantages of the 8-inch was nullified, and in 1933 the Royal Navy began the design of the *Southampton* class. The hull was almost as big as a 'County' (though with much less freeboard) but armed with twelve 6-inch guns in triple turrets.

As a further complication, the Anglo-German naval treaty of 1936 attempted to set limits on the sea power of Nazi Germany after Hitler renounced the Treaty of Versailles. U-boats, the great threat of the last war, were recognised as part of the new German navy, and a reduced limit of 8,000 tons was placed on new cruisers, but this did not come into force until the last day of 1936. By a quirk of the treaty process the Royal Navy had some spare cruiser tonnage during that year, and it was decided to begin two of them to the old limit of 10,000 tons before the treaty took effect. These, which would be the *Edinburgh* and the *Belfast*, were to be slightly larger than the *Southampton* class, and there was great debate about how the extra tonnage should be used. The first favoured solution was to build them with three quadruple turrets, which was feasible but would involve a new design, while another idea was to have five triple turrets, three forward and two aft. By the spring of 1936 they had settled on the now conventional armament of 6-inch guns in four triple turrets. The extra weight was to be taken up with stronger deck armour, but the constructors pointed out that 'the change from quadruple to triple turrets is not in itself sufficient to provide for the additional protection desired ...' However the ship could be shortened by 10 feet as the new turret arrangement took up less space, and that would save on armour. It would also be necessary to reduce the arc of fire of the turrets from 145 to 140 degrees on each side, which was considered acceptable.

The constructors already had a hull design from the *Southampton* class, which was based on previous experience. It had been tested by the usual means of numerous calculations and towing a model through a water tank, but it was not yet tried at sea, as the ships would not enter service until 1937. The design could be modified slightly to fit the dimensions of the new ships. They were to be long and narrow like most cruisers, with a total length of 606 feet and a beam of 63 feet 4 inches. In midships the hull was mostly rounded below the waterline, and flat and angled slightly outwards above it. This form was maintained for the middle third of the ship, which included the main machinery. The area forward of that was dominated by the 'knuckle': the hull just above the waterline was flared outwards, and that increased towards the bows. This flare would help keep spray off the decks and would produce a righting motion if the bow was buried in a heavy sea. At the level of the lower deck, the knuckle, the sides became far more vertical to give a more convenient interior shape. Seen in profile, the bow was straight and set at an angle of ten degrees. Aft, the underwater shape was arranged to allow water to reach the four propellers and the single balanced rudder in sufficient density. Above that, the ship was designed with a rounded and elegant shape known appropriately as the 'cruiser stern'; though sceptics suggested it would be far cheaper and no less convenient to use a flat stern. Below the waterline, bilge keels were fitted on both sides of the ship in the curved part of the bottom. They were of proven value in preventing rolling. The hull was low compared with the 'County' class, and later it was observed that they made only one degree of leeway, or sideways movement, in a storm, whereas a 'County' class ship would have made three or four degrees. The bridge was rounded, and wind tunnel tests on a detailed model showed that because of that and low freeboard the *Belfast* had less wind resistance than most ships of the time.

The navy already had a successful 6-inch gun, and a triple turret to hold it was designed from 1932, after which it was fitted in the *Southampton* class. The two new ships were to use an improved version, the Mark XXIII, in which the shell hoist rotated with the turret and extended all the way down to the platform deck where the shells were stowed, and the cordite hoist went even lower into the hold. This increased weight and depth slightly, and the aftermost guns in 'X' and 'Y' turrets had to be fitted a deck higher to make room for it, but it reduced the need for manual handling of the shells and became standard in later ships.

The engine arrangement followed the latest practice of alternating the two boiler rooms and the two engine rooms and allowing any boiler to feed any engine, so that a single hit would not put the whole system out of action. It was much less conventional in that the engines were placed further aft than usual. This had the advantage that the propeller shafts would be shorter and therefore less likely to be damaged, any distortion of which would seriously affect the ship's performance, something regarded as highly likely in the event of bombing. Moreover, the new arrangement moved the fore funnel well away from the bridge and gunnery directors, eliminating the problems of smoke and heat that had dogged British battleships earlier in the century. The funnels were raked backwards, which is difficult to explain. It was usually seen as a way of taking the smoke away from the bridge, but it was unnecessary in the circumstances, and it was believed that an enemy could measure the rake to calculate the angle at which the ship was sailing. The whole arrangement gave the ships a unique appearance, which many sailors found rather odd and unattractive. Joining the *Belfast* in 1939, Midshipman Syms thought, 'With her two funnels disposed clumsily towards the stern, she was no beauty and presented a somewhat ungainly if purposeful appearance.' But there was a far more serious problem, in that the main anti-destroyer and anti-aircraft armament of 4-inch guns was situated in midships, above the engine and boiler rooms, so that its ammunition had to be transported from a magazine further forward, by means of the 'shell conveyor', or 'scenic railway', exposed on the deck. Viewing one of the ships after her completion in 1939, Admiral Dunbar-Nasmith expressed his horror: 'The gear takes up a great deal of space on the upper deck and is extremely vulnerable from hostile aircraft, etc., as it is completely unprotected.'

Nevertheless, the design proceeded in the spring of 1936. A sketch design was circulated, and the Assistant Chief of Naval Staff thought that it would produce 'a very fine ship', though he wanted increased anti-aircraft armament and more protection for the steering gear. On 28 May the Board of Admiralty approved 'the Sketch Design of the 10,000 ton 6-inch cruiser of the 1936 programme'. The constructors went back to their offices to elaborate on this, and next month they came up with the 'legend and drawings' for the new ship. In the absence of the Director of Naval Construction, Mr F. Bryant wrote that calculations had been made 'in sufficient detail to satisfy me that the design is satisfactory in all essential matters', though the full calculations were still proceeding. All the Admiralty departments concerned in the design had been consulted, though he did not make it clear if they had agreed. The 'legend' outlined the particulars of the ship in standard form, listing dimensions, weight, armament, engines and equipment. There was a fairly simple drawing showing the layout of the main features. The Board discussed it on 21 July and approved it with its stamp.

Drawing office work and calculations continued as Bryant had suggested. Weight was still very important, and not just because of the treaty limitations. If the hull and its contents were too heavy the ship would float low, reducing speed, increasing draught and making the decks wetter in bad weather. If the weight was set too high the ship would become unstable, but that was difficult to resolve as heavy items such as guns in their turrets and armoured bridges had to be high enough to be effective. Everything was carefully calculated by the constructors in their notebooks, which might occupy several volumes and hundreds of pages for an individual design. They were so important that they were retained as records, and no deletions could be made – any changes had to be noted in red ink. The work had to be meticulous, and things could go wrong. While the two ships of the 1936 programme were building, a junior constructor made a serious error in the design of the 'Hunt' class of destroyer escorts, and his superiors were too hard pressed to check it. It was only when the first ship was tested that the mistake was discovered, and drastic changes had to be made.

* * * * *

There were only fourteen established warship builders in the country with the equipment to use D-quality steel, some of which were too small to build cruisers. Work was scarce and shipbuilding had not fully emerged from the Great Depression, when unemployment rates in the industry had reached 62 per cent. Nine firms were interested enough in the 1936 project to send senior draughtsmen to London to look at the plans. Among them was Harland & Wolff, by far the largest shipbuilder in Northern Ireland and the biggest employer in the city of Belfast (though it contributed to the city's notorious religious sectarianism by favouring Protestant employees over Roman Catholics). Founded in 1861, the yard was most famous for building the liner *Titanic*, the loss of which was paradoxically less prominent in the public consciousness than it is now, and the yard had also produced many more successful ocean liners. Its yard along the south of the River Lagan to the north-east of Belfast had eight building slips facing into the river of the Abercorn Basin with space along wharves to fit out ships that had been launched, supported by offices, drawing offices and workshops, with cranes including two famous gantries to lift materials and fittings.

The company had barely survived the Great Depression in the early 1930s. It had built no major warships since the last war apart from the small cruiser *Penelope*, which was nearing completion and offered hope for the future. In July when the Naval Estimates projected two additional cruisers, the *Belfast Telegraph* commented, 'The addition to the naval programme makes it certain that Messrs. Harland & Wolff will obtain a share of the work.' The directors of the company were certainly interested and gave some assurances to the Admiralty as they submitted their tender on 6 August 1936. Their electric welding equipment was adequate, and they had enough skilled workmen to use it. They would take great care 'to provide the maximum space and facilities for manipulation, examination and repair of machinery in all its parts'. They were a respectable firm, inscribed in the King's National Roll of Employers (for commitment to employ a certain proportion of disabled men); and there would be enough water in Belfast Lough to sail the ship away when she was completed, though only just, with two feet below the keel. They were awarded the contract for one ship on 21 September, while Swan Hunter on Tyneside had the other.

Just over a month later the Admiralty allocated the names *Belfast* and *Edinburgh* to the two ships. As one admiral would put it at the *Belfast*'s launch, 'The idea of naming vessels of the new cruiser class after the great cities of the Kingdom was to draw contributions to the personnel of the Navy from their vast populations and also to establish special interest between each city and a particular vessel of the fleet.' The name *Edinburgh* was already well established in the Royal Navy, with three predecessors over the centuries. There had never been a *Belfast* before, though there was several *Dublins*. That was because the city had only recently taken on the status of capital of Northern Ireland, when the rest of the island left the Union in 1922. It recognised a parallel with Edinburgh as the Scottish capital and was generally taken as a compliment to the city of Belfast, or at least by the Protestant two-thirds of it. According to one of her officers the ship was 'known as THE CRUISER; in Belfast's eyes, none other counted. The Lord Mayor himself was very anxious that the ship should be worthy of the silver bell presented by the City ...'

The contract and specification were about a thousand pages long, with separate sections on the hull, materials and testing, electrical equipment, the main machinery (that is the engines and boilers that would power the ship), and mechanical appliances such as capstans, winches and cranes. The work would be supervised by the principal (ship) overseer, Constructor Bogie of the Admiralty, who was already based in Belfast. A full-size plan of the ship was drawn out on the mould loft floor, and patterns were taken off it to form the actual components.

The keel plates of the *Belfast* were laid on blocks in the building slip on 10 December 1936 to mark the start of construction – rather late in the day to meet the deadline at the end of the year but not as late as Swan Hunter, who laid the keel of the *Edinburgh* on 31 December. The obsession with weights would continue as the ship was built. Each section of the contract started with the injunction in bold type: 'Economy of weight in this vessel is of utmost importance. The Contractors are required to keep this continually in view, and when detailed drawings are prepared for submission to the Admiralty all proposals are to be closely analysed with a view to economy of weight.' Down in the yard, an official known as the Recorder of Weights was employed to be 'responsible for obtaining the duly certified weight of each such article …' After the keel plates were laid, the vertical members that formed the backbone of the ship were riveted above them running fore and aft. Then came the frames, which were placed at three-foot intervals in the vital areas of the engine room and magazines near the centre of the ship, increasing to four feet towards the bow and stern. These formed the main structural members of the ship – some suggested that their place should be taken by longitudinal members running fore and aft instead of across the ship, but this idea was resisted by conservative shipbuilders especially on Clydeside, and the *Belfast* used the traditional method. Frames were cut out in several sections of flat steel, reinforced with angle-iron brackets around the edges. In midships the ship had a double bottom to minimise damage from grounding or underwater explosions. Some of the lower frames were watertight to prevent damage spreading; others were oil-tight as the double bottom was used for fuel stowage. There were fourteen watertight bulkheads rising to the level of the main deck to contain damage, and these were penetrated only by watertight doors, which would be kept closed in action.

Armour plate was fitted to sides and deck. The bows and stern were unprotected to save weight, and no danger was anticipated from directly underneath, but the main belt, three to four inches thick, was arranged to cover the machinery spaces, magazines and control positions in midships. Deck armour protected against bombs and plunging shells in the same area and was three inches thick over the magazines and two inches over the machinery. The side armour protruded as it was thicker than the normal plating, and there was no attempt to fair it. The decks were pierced with large, round holes to take the barbettes for the main armament when it arrived.

At the bow and stern, a cast-steel frame formed the main outline of the more complex shape. Each was to be interchangeable with other ships of the class, though at the moment only one more was planned. Once the frames were erected, the plates were fitted on top of them after being cut and rolled to shape and drilled with holes. Each plate overlapped with and was joined to the ones above and below and fore and aft of it, which gave rigidity to the hull. The plates were joggled near their edges, and the rivets were countersunk to provide a smooth surface on the outside. The lower part of the stern used the new technique of welding, which needed no overlap, but the rest was held together by rivets. Each was driven through pre-prepared holes and then hammered flat – the sound of riveting dominated a large area of a shipyard town on any working day.

Various naval officers began to arrive in Belfast to supervise the construction, put forward ideas of their own for the details and learn about the working of the ship. An accountant officer such as Paymaster Commander A. M. Piggott was expected to make contact with naval officials and yard management down to overseers and foremen, 'who can do much to help, but they should not be asked to make alterations or additions without the consent of the Principal Ship Overseer'. An accountant officer was advised to look closely at desk accommodation, racks and cupboards, lighting, the position of telephones and many other items.

Lieutenant Commander Stuart Ferguson arrived in October 1937 to deal with the engines. The machinery consisted of four boilers and four sets of turbine engines, which operated with a circular motion rather than the up-and-down, or reciprocal, motion of older engines. Turbines needed a great deal of skill in their manufacture and gearing to reduce the revolutions to a suitable number for the propellers, but they took up less space than reciprocating engines, were more efficient at high speed and each had only one moving part, the turbine itself. They were used on fast passenger ships like ferries and liners, and on practically all modern warships except submarines.

Turbine engines needed high-pressure steam to operate efficiently, and this was provided by four Admiralty three-drum boilers in two separate boiler rooms, arranged side-by-side in the forward space and one behind the other in the after one. In each boiler the lower drums were filled with water and linked to the upper one by tubes to form a tent-shaped structure. Oil fuel was burnt inside it to boil the water, with the steam collecting in the upper drum. A superheater consisting of more tubes was fitted between the other tubes; the superheated steam created this way was 'dry', with no moisture content. It was passed to the engines to provide the power.

Each of the four engines came in three units. At high speed the steam went into the high-pressure turbine then to the low-pressure turbine to get the maximum use out of it. There was also a cruising turbine in each system, geared through the high-pressure unit and used at normal cruising speeds to save fuel. Using either system, gearing was needed to slow the revolutions down to an efficient speed for the propellers, while under each engine there was a condenser that returned the steam to water to go back to the boilers to begin the process again. The engines and boilers were made by Harland & Wolff to patterns provided by the Parsons Company, which held the licence. Each boiler could be linked to any of the engines, so that various combinations were possible, to suit either peacetime economy or wartime damage.

When Ferguson got there, the drums of the boilers had been drilled, the tubes had been fitted, and the blades were on the turbines. Castings for the main machinery had just arrived from the Clyde, and various types of auxiliary machinery were coming in from sub-contractors. He now had to supervise the assembly and installation. There were water pumps, air compressors, distilling machinery for water, electric generators, refrigeration and ventilation equipment, capstan and crane engines and steering gear as well as more domestic items such as galley ranges, cabin radiators and later even shirt presses. Ferguson was soon joined by a commissioned gunner, a warrant shipwright and a commissioned electrician, all of whom had risen from the ranks and could be expected to be familiar with the detail of their respective departments. The senior rating was Chief Engine Room Artificer Tom King, 'a quiet, even-tempered man in his early forties' who was 'nevertheless a good disciplinarian …'

* * * * *

By March 1938 the hull was largely complete, but without guns and most of its fittings. It was now supported on cradles that were placed on launch ways ready to slip into the sea, and Mrs Anne Chamberlain, wife of the Prime Minister, was invited to launch her on 17 March, St Patrick's Day. She broke a bottle of champagne over the bows with the traditional words 'God bless her and all who sail in her', and the ship slid gracefully into the water. A future mayor of the city stood on the 'unofficial side' of the river with his cine camera, 'and when I saw the ship slowly move towards the sea and finally settle in the water, the picture of the massive hull created in me a feeling of joy.' After the launch, Mrs Chamberlain was presented with a bouquet by riveter's catch boy Robert McBride, and at a dinner later she was given a diamond bracelet. Acknowledging the gift, she told of her husband's long association with the yard, back to the days when he was unknown and was kept waiting by one of the directors. She said she would never forget the sight of the huge crowd gathered in the yard for the launch. Mr Rebeck, chairman of Harland & Wolff, took the chance to stress the need to build more merchant ships, which happened to be the company's forte. And Lord Craigavon, Prime Minster of Northern Ireland, announced that he was going to accompany Mrs. Chamberlain on her journey back to London, 'where he hoped to impress upon the government Belfast's earnest hope that more Government work would be given to the yard, which was the most important business concern in Ulster'.

Fitting out the *Belfast* continued alongside the shipyard wharf, and Mrs Chamberlain's husband had his moment of triumph in September when he returned from the Munich meeting with Adolf Hitler announcing that it was 'Peace for our time'. But it was short-lived. The Germans broke the agreement by occupying the whole of

Czechoslovakia in March 1939, and war seemed almost inevitable as the *Belfast* prepared for her sea trials.

The naval team in Harland & Wolff continued to grow with a torpedo officer (who was largely concerned with the electrical systems), a gunnery officer and then Commander James Gregson Roper, who would eventually be second-in-command of the ship and was in charge of duties and routine. The main armament arrived from Vickers and was installed by 18 March 1939. Early in April the ship's navigation officer, Richard Tosswil, was appointed, followed by the captain, George Scott, for the ship was almost ready to put to sea for trials. As a preliminary she was subjected to an inclining trial on 23 March. She was put into dock and weights were moved from side to side to test her stability; this could not, however, be definitive, as the secondary armament of 4-inch guns had not yet been installed. There was a party of naval officers and skilled engineers from the ship's complement and the department of the engineer-in-chief of the navy. The stokers (who did not actually shovel coal in the days of oil-fired ships but worked as semi-skilled mechanics) were provided by the shipyard. At 0915 on Monday 22 May she sailed for the first time with three separate teams on board. The Admiralty officials, according to Lieutenant Commander George Thring, who had joined the ship two days before, showed an 'impersonal interest'. The shipyard representatives were quiet but concerned: 'Theirs was the great responsibility to the Country, the Admiralty, and above all to the City of Belfast.' The naval officers were even more involved – 'To us the ship … meant much, our future home and our friend.'

The ship went into Belfast Lough to 'swing the compasses', which would correct them for magnetic deviation by turning the ship through every heading. After that the trial did not go well. A test of the capstan engine showed it could only raise the anchor at a speed of 28 feet per minute instead of the 40 feet specified, and eventually it was found that a connection had broken. The engines were worked up to full power for a one-hour trial, and that was completed successfully by 1700. But during the next test the ship suddenly came to a stop and the lights went out. The engineers had not checked the amount of oil in a suction tank. Some of the engineer-in-chief's staff had pointed this out, but the warning was ignored, for command was always difficult when so many different groups were on board. As a result the ship was stationary and out of control for an hour and a half until the fault was rectified. Fortunately the weather was calm, and she was in open water.

Next day the ship sailed across the North Channel to Greenock on the River Clyde. The capstan gear had been repaired and was tried successfully, though it was not the last time it would give trouble. On Wednesday the 24th, in dull weather and slight winds, the various trials of the engines in every possible condition were begun – this time it was a six-hour consumption trial with the engines at 3,000 horsepower using both main and cruising turbines. The ship anchored off Lamlash on the Isle of Arran overnight, and next day the engines were run at 14,000 and then 20,000 horsepower for six hours. She went to the well-known measured mile, which was one of the reasons why the Clyde was used for such trials. Marks on shore were lined up in transit to show each end of the mile, and unlike other sites round the country the water was deep enough to allow a fair test without interaction with the sea bottom. The *Belfast* made four runs starting at 1300 and then prepared for perhaps the most dramatic test for those on board. The ship was proceeding forward with 196 revolutions on the engines when the telegraph was suddenly put over to 160 revolutions astern. The ship was stopped in 3½ minutes and then went astern at 15 knots. Performance was satisfactory, and it was noted that 'the quarterdeck remained dry during this trial'.

There were more engine and steering trials over the next week and an even more severe reversing test on the 31st, when the engines were at full power and put into reverse so that the ship stopped in 2¼ minutes. Next day the guns were tested off the Scottish coast. The 4-inch guns had yet to be installed, but apart from that the gunnery officer, Lieutenant Commander Hardie, 'fired every barrel'. It was impossible to aim accurately, as the main gun directors had not been fitted, but it was noted that there were 'no abnormal deck deflections' during the shoot. The engineers objected to an instruction from the Admiralty that the ship should be turned at full power using the engines instead of the rudder. They claimed that there was 'a grave possibility of damage to the engines' but agreed to do the test at a maximum of 250 revolutions. This was done: the ship turned through 360 degrees but rather slowly in a diameter of two or three miles. The area was crowded with shipping, so it was decided not to repeat the test. Next day the ship returned to Belfast. The different teams had bonded after initial difficulties, and they jokingly awarded themselves the 'Harpic Medal', named after a well-known cleaning fluid. The 'citation' was full of in-jokes largely incomprehensible to the outsider, but it is clear that the Admiralty overseer, Mr Bogie, was mocked by Commander Roper, while Commander (E) Lister was accused of 'only surfacing at meal times', and Mr McCuag, the fierce disciplinarian of the shipyard, produced 'order out of chaos'. On a more serious level, Engineer Commander F. B. Secretan, on the staff of the Commander-in-Chief at Portsmouth, was commended by his admiral for showing 'tact and ability on trials of new construction'. Thring commented, 'Trials were marvellous, everyone returned to Belfast with the feeling that she was a fine ship …' The ships officers were 'well pleased with the ship generally'. Their only objection was a rather trivial one – 'The good appearance of the cabins resulting from the fitting of modernised furniture was spoiled by these uncovered washbasins, which looked like sinks.'

* * * * *

When not at sea the naval party made the best of rather disappointing summer weather – they formed a mixed hockey team, incorporating wives and fiancées, against the 'Mighty Shipbuilders', braving a rather dangerous level-crossing to find the pitch, even though there was 'no reputable pub within miles'. Commander Roper captained the cricket team, taking precedence over Captain Scott. They attended a dinner held by the Ulster Division of the Royal Naval Volunteer Reserve on the old First World War cruiser HMS *Caroline*. They also visited the Giant's Causeway and the Mountains of Mourne with the yard management, and formed lasting friendships – after the ship had finally sailed, Atholl Blair, head of the engine department, wrote to Roper and Lister to ask how the engines were doing and regretting that the departure of the *Belfast* had 'left a gap in our surroundings on the Queen's Island!'

Commander Lister noted down the system of operating the engines with maximum efficiency and especially economy, which was vital in the peacetime navy. The economical speed was 13 knots, which could be attained at 106 revolutions per minute. In fact, the ship could operate at up to 18 knots with only one boiler in use, feeding the four cruising turbines, which were more economical and could be used at up to 23 knots. Two boilers were needed for speeds between 18 and 24 knots, or when getting under way, anchoring or manoeuvring, and the main turbines would have to be engaged. Three boilers were used to reach up to 28 knots, and all four for the planned maximum speed of 32 knots – the *Belfast* actually attained 32.98 on the measured mile. It was calculated that the ship could steam for 7,950 miles at her most economical speed of 13 knots, using 3.5 tons of fuel per hour 'under war conditions at half an hour's notice for full speed allowing 5% fuel remaining, ship six months out of dock and paravanes not in use'. If ordered to proceed 'with moderate dispatch' she would use 8.2 tons per hour for a speed of 20.5 knots, but her range would be restricted to 5,350 miles. There were figures for 'all convenient dispatch' using two-fifths power, 'with dispatch' using three-fifths and 'with all dispatch', which used nine-tenths power to attain a speed of 30.2 knots and a range of 2,540 miles. 'Full authorised' speed was 31 knots using 28 tons per hour, exactly four times the economical consumption, with range reduced to 2,370 miles.

William F. Read, a 35-year-old former stoker petty officer, was appointed Master-at-Arms, the head of the ship's police and the senior rating on board. He left Portsmouth on 17 July as part of a group of six key ratings to join 30 or so already in Belfast. The train was overcrowded with holiday traffic, and the steamer *Duke of Atholl* from Heysham was no better. In Belfast the party found they were not expected, and they had to contact the yard to send a lorry to collect them and their kit. There was no accommodation on board, so four of them found good lodgings with a Mrs Crowe. Next day they went to see the ship, which was 'something of a shock as she was not nearly so advanced as we imagined in view of the fact that she was due to leave in just over a fortnight'. There was little for them to do as the 'nominals' giving the names and ratings of the crew had not been sent up by the hard-pressed drafting staff in

Portsmouth. They spent their evenings in the sergeants' mess of the East Lancashire Regiment while a ship's writer used personal contacts to get a list of the new crew from Portsmouth. There was 'great excitement' when it finally arrived on the 28th, but it varied in many ways from the ship's official scheme of complement. There were around a hundred boys instead of the 42 officially allowed because of a shortage of experienced men. The chief gunner's mate produced a 'flood of invective' when he found that his carefully laid plans would have to be altered. Master-at-Arms Read looked over the list with an experienced eye for good men or 'fouls' with whom he had served before. Meanwhile, the captain presented the Long Service and Good Conduct Medal to Leading Stoker Rimington – Read commented on 'the lucky recipient … I use the term lucky in the fullest sense of the term as it is generally accepted that one has to be very lucky to keep his misdemeanours hidden for fifteen long years. Furthermore I knew Rimington very well.'

* * * * *

The long-awaited 4-inch guns and their mountings had arrived in July and were installed. There was another inclining test on 29 July when the hull structure was almost complete except for some non-stick material known as Semtex to be fitted on the decks, and a certain amount of painting. The controversial 4-inch ammunition conveyors were only half assembled, and the naval officials complained that 'there was a considerable amount of lumber and plant on board for a ship in such an advanced stage of completion'. Nevertheless, the test was successful. There was a farewell dance for the officers at the Craigavad golf course, when they changed into uniform for the first time during this assignment. On board the *Caroline* the honorary captain of the RNVR division, addressed them:

'While we rejoice that yet another ship – an Ulster one at that – has been added to the Fleet – we at the same time are very sorry that the time has come to say goodbye to those officers … whose genial presence amongst us will be greatly missed.'

A 'steaming party' of 300 men was sent up from Portsmouth to take over the ship. Among them was George E. Finch, an Engine Room Artificer. As such, he was one of the most privileged members of the lower deck with the status of a chief petty officer, but that did not free him from the vagaries of naval life, especially on the verge of war: he was pulled out of his work at Portland and forced to cancel a visit to his mother in Worthing to go north with the party. When the men arrived in the shipyard at 1030 in the morning they could not go on board as the ship was still being inspected by the Admiral Commanding Contract Built Ships, who had to dodge the wet paint to avoid ruining his uniform. The men were given lunch, and according to Read, 'In the afternoon we embarked with our kits and found our respective messes.' Almost uniquely among the crew, he had a small cabin of his own in a corner of one of the seamen's messes with a settee to sleep on. They were given leave that evening and many of them tested the advertising slogan 'Guinness is good for you'. This caused several defaulters, but the master-at-arms and his staff were lenient on them for now. There was not much sleep that night as the shipyard workers were still painting.

Next morning the ship sailed for her final acceptance trials including two hours at full power. She was now considered to be 'in all respects ready for sea', though three lists of relatively minor defects were made out. Ten naval officials signed the certificate of acceptance including the captains of the gunnery, signal and torpedo schools, along with Captain Scott and six of his specialist officers, down to the Boatswain and Warrant Shipwright. Naval officers and ratings paraded on the quarterdeck at 1815, but the red ensign of the merchant navy had wound itself round the flagstaff in the variable winds: to the amusement of the rest of the crew, a signalman had to climb up to free it, after which it was replaced by the white ensign of the Royal Navy. Superstitious sailors might regard that as a bad omen, but at eleven minutes past seven that evening the anchor was weighed and the ship began her journey to the naval base at Portsmouth.

2

PREPARING FOR SEA

CAPTAIN GEORGE ARTHUR SCOTT had been the commanding officer of the *Belfast* since 24 April 1939. A 50-year-old native of Bath, he had started as a cadet in the training ship *Britannia* at Dartmouth in 1903, two years before the school came ashore to form the Royal Naval College. His marks were not spectacular with second or third class passes in the main subjects, but in 1913 he was commended for an essay in naval history. In the meantime, he served in cruisers and battleships and was promoted to lieutenant in 1910. With the coming of the First World War he found his niche as a destroyer officer. He was awarded the Distinguished Service Cross for his service in the *Severn* in 1914–15 and took command of the *Nymphe* in 1916, followed by the *Mons*; in 1918 he was censured for causing a collision due to excessive speed. He survived the 'Geddes Axe' by which up to a third of naval officers in some ranks were made redundant, and in 1923 he was in command of the destroyer *Whitshed*, in which he 'maintained very high state of efficiency, ship's company very happy one, and ship model of cleanliness and good order.' But again he fell foul of the authorities, being blamed by the Admiralty when his ship failed to retrieve a practice torpedo fired by the battlecruiser *Repulse*. Nevertheless at the end of 1923 he had the crucial promotion to commander at the age of 35. He spent much of the next decade and a half in staff duties with the occasional sea command, but he was still accident-prone. In 1929 his destroyer *Watchman* collided with the *Velox*, and he was blamed for failing to stop his engines in time. Despite this he was promoted to the rank of captain in 1931, as distinct from the courtesy title held by the commanding officer of any ship, however small. Soon another side of his personality began to emerge in reports by his superiors. One wrote: 'A curious, independent, somewhat impetuous and somewhat intolerant character. Always dashing from one thing to another: apparently he can never be still ... A little too self-confident, but this may disappear in time. A good disciplinarian and a good seaman. He brought his ship to a high state of efficiency and cleanliness in a very short time ...' Another wrote: 'His declamatory manner is somewhat fatiguing.' It was generally agreed that he was an excellent staff officer – 'Very accurate and tireless. Knows battle instructions and manoeuvring orders from cover to cover. Full of resource and imagination. Always ready to take responsibility.' His superiors were divided about whether he was suitable for higher command, and he lacked recent sea experience. Perhaps he was given command of the *Belfast* to compensate for this.

For many officers a cruiser, especially a brand new one, was the ideal command. It might spend a great deal of its time working in a squadron which in turn was part of a fleet, but it was capable of independent service if needed – unlike the more glamorous destroyers, which had not quite outgrown their dependence on depot ships. *Belfast*'s twelve 6-inch guns could project shells weighing a total of 1,344 pounds, or 610 kilograms, containing up to 384 pounds of explosives, over a range of more than fourteen miles, and do so at a rate of eight rounds per minute per gun. The ship seemed to be well defended against air attack, with twelve 4-inch guns, two eight-barrelled 'pom-poms' and four machine-guns. The complement was made up of 761 officers, men and boys, mostly highly trained and resourceful. The ship carried its own air detachment with two Walrus amphibians and a military force of 82 marines, who could carry out amphibious operations or be landed to police the British Empire. Its vitals were protected with up to four inches of armour plate. For underwater warfare, it could fire torpedoes that might wound an enemy ship far larger than the *Belfast*. It had an Asdic system to detect submarine attack and paravanes that could be streamed from the bows to deal with mines, though only of the old-fashioned 'contact' type. It had a strong medical team with three doctors and a dentist. There was an instructor with good academic qualifications to teach the midshipmen and a schoolmaster for the ship's boys, as well as petty officers to train them in subjects like gunnery and seamanship. The ship had an Anglican and a Roman Catholic chaplain. The Royal Marines provided a band of fifteen musicians. There was a team of four commissioned engineer officers, three warrant officers, 26 highly skilled engine room artificers and 130 semi-skilled stokers to run the engines, with ordnance and electrical artificers, shipwrights, joiners, plumbers and painters for maintenance of the great range of equipment. A battleship ranked higher in the naval pecking order, and the long-range guns of a new ship of the *King George V* class were nearly twelve times as powerful as those of the *Belfast* and had fifty percent greater range. But a battleship or battlecruiser was far more restricted in its operations. It was too precious to risk on dangerous missions, and the loss of one, such as the *Royal Oak* in 1939 or the *Hood* in 1941, was a national calamity. A cruiser like the *Belfast* was largely self-sufficient, equipped for diverse tasks and available for service anywhere in the world.

Officers lived in the stern of the ship as they had done in the days of sail, when they had easy access to the command position on the quarterdeck. This was no longer relevant now that control was exercised from the bridge, but it was 1942 before the navy began to change this for new-built destroyers. There were strict divisions even within the officers. The admiral (if carried) and captain lived in their own cabins at the stern. Since there was no admiral on board *Belfast* at this time, Captain Scott probably settled into the admiral's quarters, with an odd-shaped 'day cabin' right aft, almost triangular in plan and with sides curving inwards to reflect the form of the cruiser stern. The occupant would conduct his business there, while forward of that he had a dining cabin with a table that could be extended to seat up to fourteen people. Forward of that on the starboard side were his sleeping cabin and a private bathroom, with staff officers' cabins on the other side. A captain was allowed two stewards and two cooks for his own service. With Scott in his spacious apartments, Commander Roper might take up the captain's quarters, with a day cabin on the starboard side of the ship plus a sleeping cabin and a bathroom. The other officers, from lieutenant to commander, had their own small cabins and used the wardroom as a communal space. This was in the after superstructure with two tables to dine up to 35. There was an ante-room next door. In addition to four stewards and three cooks, the officers were served by a dozen Royal Marine wardroom attendants under a corporal. They were to muster at 6 each morning, to lay the table and clean up after every meal, as well as washing the officers' clothing. When waiting at table, each man was to 'keep alert, and try to anticipate officers' wants without waiting for instructions'.

In 1939 the ship was commanded by regular career officers who had nearly all trained in the Royal Naval College at Dartmouth,

Devon. Well-intentioned schemes to promote men from the lower deck provided only a trickle: most potential officers joined the service as cadets at the age of thirteen after an interview and a competitive examination, and had had a largely technical education. The training was 'primitive, sordid and sadistic' according to Louis Le Bailly who attended in 1929–32: 'The first ring of the firebell at 6 am sent us naked down the dormitory through an icy, over-chlorinated plunge bath and out again before the ringing stopped. Betowelled but still wet we stood at attention in front of our basins awaiting the order to wash necks, followed by wash teeth … After early morning studies life was conducted at the double.' The training was also expensive – in the 1930s it cost about £850 (about the price of a good suburban house) to put a boy through the course of three years and eight months. There were concessions for the sons of naval personnel, but in general a Dartmouth education was for the affluent and the privileged. A young man was likely to be promoted midshipman at the age of fifteen, but his training was not finished, for he had to spend a good deal of time at sea before being commissioned. His education was excellent in places, according to Charles Owen:

> For the most part what emerged was a definite breed of fit, tough, highly trained but sketchily educated professionals, ready for instant duty, for parades or tea parties, for catastrophes, for peace or war; confident leaders, alert seamen, fair administrators, poor delegators; officers of wide interests and narrow vision, strong on tactics, weak on strategy; an able, active, cheerful, monosyllabic elite.

The second-in-command of the ship, 'the commander', the 'executive officer' or more colloquially 'the bloke', was far closer to the crew than the captain. He was the head of the executive branch and responsible for organising the numerous lists of duties for different evolutions, as well as maintaining discipline and morale. James Roper took up the post at the beginning of November 1938. Thirty-seven years old, he had served most of his time in submarines since being commissioned in 1921, and he had commanded four of them since passing the submarine commanding officers' course in 1930. His current appointment was very different from the adventurous spirit and free-and-easy discipline of the submarines, but a successful term as commander of a battleship or cruiser was almost essential as a path to the higher ranks of the navy. He was keen to do this, and Scott would later commend his 'untiring devotion to duty' and saw the value of 'the personnel whom he has trained and the organisation which he has perfected'. To Midshipman Syms he was 'a benevolent and understanding man'. According to the master-at-arms who had to work closely with him, he was always quick on the scene of any mishap, and 'he had the interests of the ship's company at heart'. Since neither he nor the captain had any recent experience of cruisers, Roper may well have been guided by Commander Russell Grenfell's *A Cruiser Commander's Orders* and Captain Rory O'Conor's recent book *Running a Big Ship*, based on his time as a commander of the battlecruiser *Hood*. Certainly a section in the *Belfast*'s orders on handling high-speed powerboats lifted large passages from O'Conor's book, though they may have shared a common source in the writings of Lieutenant Commander Peter du Cane.

The standard among the other officers was very high. The next senior in the executive branch was the torpedo officer, Lieutenant Commander W. Smith, who was responsible for the ship's electrical equipment as well as the torpedoes. Lieutenant Commander George Arthur Thring shared his patriotic Christian names with the captain but was a very different character. He was universally noted for his 'pleasing cheerful personality' and his 'good social qualities'. He had done well at Dartmouth after entering in 1917, with three firsts out of five subjects, but he remained a 'salt-horse', or non-specialist, seaman officer. Richard Gibson Tosswil was the navigation officer, with five firsts at Dartmouth. He was 'quite exceptionally promising', a 'good leader of great personality and high character'. The gunnery officer, C. Hardie, had qualified at HMS *Excellent* in Portsmouth Harbour in 1934. As the principal maintainer and operator of the ship's main armament, he was an influential figure on board. Newly promoted Lieutenant Commander Alan Seale was another submariner, who had passed the commanding officers course in 1938 and wore a beard in the tradition of the service.

At the beginning of the century Admiral 'Jacky' Fisher had supported the 'Selborne Scheme', which tried to integrate seamen and engineer officers with a common system of entry. All midshipmen would learn a good deal of engineering, and specialist engineer officers would be selected later in the same way as gunnery, navigation or torpedo officers with equal chance of reaching high rank. Frederick Lister, now the chief engineer of the *Belfast*, had therefore started as a cadet in the ordinary way in 1916 and went to sea as a midshipman in 1919. His marks in engineering were no better than those in seamanship, navigation or 'torpedo', though he was weak in gunnery. The engineering branch was not popular with ambitious officers as it offered poorer promotion prospects despite assurances from Fisher and his supporters; nevertheless Lister was moving towards an engineering career by the early 1920s. Perhaps it was because his father had been an engineer rear admiral, or it was just a way to survive in the peacetime navy when non-specialist junior officers were most vulnerable to the 'Geddes Axe'. He was sent to the battleship *Ramillies* to learn duties in the stokehold and engine room, then to the Royal Naval Engineering College at Keyham, Plymouth, where he passed sixth in a class of 24 as a lieutenant (engineering). He was a commander (engineering) by 1936, and Captain Scott wrote that he was 'a very zealous officer, thorough, reliable' who 'brought his department to a high pitch of efficiency'.

Meanwhile the Selborne Scheme failed, though the position of the engineers improved slightly. They now had the 'executive curl' above the rank stripes, which increased their status, and their rank titles were slightly less discriminatory – 'Lieutenant (E)' instead of 'Engineering Lieutenant' for example; but purple cloth between the gold stripes was used to keep them apart from the executives, and they did not have any 'military' authority or status – serious offences by stokers would have to be referred to officers of the executive branch. Louis Le Bailly was forced to transfer to the branch after his eyesight began to decline, and he described a kind of ritual humiliation: 'I had to discard my dirk and telescope, sew purple stripes on my sleeves and officially become a 'civilian' in the Royal Navy.' But despite everything, many high-quality officers chose engineering in the 1930s, partly because the discipline was less severe and also because it offered some kind of career on the 'outside' if there was another 'Geddes Axe'. They were trained at Keyham and Manadon, in and near Plymouth, where they learned scientific subjects like mathematics and thermodynamics, workshop appliances and electrical engineering, marine engines and boilers, and ship construction. But there was a perpetual conflict between the technical skills of an engineer and officer-like qualities. In 1943 Rear Admiral Ford attempted to define what was required: 'It is considered that Naval Engineer Officers must first be leaders and secondly engineers. This definition does not by any means imply that all officers are required to be cast in the same mould, but it does imply that leadership and decision and officer-like qualities is one of the primary requirements for a Naval Engineer Officer.'

When the ship was commissioned, the four engineering officers, including Lister and Ferguson, transferred from the staff of the engineer-in-chief of the navy to become part of the ship's complement. It was 'a team of first class engineers' according to Engine Room Artificer Finch, who served under them. They too lived in the wardroom, where the other officers included a captain and two lieutenants of marines, the medical officers (known as surgeons for historical reasons), two 'paymasters' in charge of finance and administration, the two chaplains and the midshipmen's instructor lieutenant who had, according to Cadet Macdonald, an obsession with 'endless and apparently pointless spherical trigonometry'; he was also the ship's meteorologist.

The warrant officers' mess was situated just across the passage from the wardroom, a smaller version with a dining room and lounge. Its eleven members (some of whom, paradoxically, were commissioned) wore officers' uniform with only a single thin stripe. They were mostly specialists who had been promoted from among the ratings, especially from the artificers, who provided two warrant engineers, an ordnance officer and a warrant electrician. The main exception was the schoolmaster, who was recruited direct from civil life to educate the ship's boys. The warrant officers were in an awkward position, having risen to a certain level by ability but were now restricted by class from rising any further. According to a petty officer of the time they were 'those most forlorn and pathetic of creatures ... neither real officers nor lower deck men, they sat in their cabins darning their socks.' The most junior officers, the sub-lieutenants and midshipmen, lived in the gun room in the same area, with an optimistically titled midshipmen's study. But for the moment it was spare, as the midshipmen had not yet joined the ship.

* * * * *

Belfast had a quiet voyage south then east to Portsmouth, and according to Read she did not encounter any 'roughers' that might test whether she was a good sea boat. They were overtaken by the new Atlantic liner *Mauretania* in the English Channel, with much waving from both sides. Early in the morning of 5 August the *Belfast* passed the familiar landmarks of Portsmouth, watched by Bank Holiday crowds that were already gathered on the pebbly beach at Southsea. At 0814 she tied up alongside the Pitch House Jetty in the dockyard, close to Nelson's ship *Victory*, which was now restored to her condition at the Battle of Trafalgar in 1805. Lorries carrying the crew's kit were standing by, while a party of ratings to make up the bulk of her complement had already been detailed in the naval barracks nearby, and they came on board with their kitbags and hammocks at 0930. Nineteen-year-old Laurence Conlon of Leeds had already served on a destroyer and qualified as a seaman torpedoman, but he was impressed: 'Cor! … When I walked aboard I thought, good grief, look at this … This is the real navy.' That afternoon Captain Scott formally commissioned the *Belfast* as a ship of the Royal Navy and addressed the hands. According to Read, 'He told them of the manner in which he proposed to run this fine new ship which we had just joined. One of the points he stressed was that the less defaulters he had to see the better he would be pleased and that we should all be happy together.' He described the planned working up process, but Thring wondered how much of it would be completed, with war looming. That evening the captain sent a telegram to Mrs Chamberlain to tell her that the ship she had launched was now commissioned, and she replied next day, 'Please accept and convey to Officers and Ship's Company my warmest thanks for your message which I deeply appreciate, I send my best wishes for the auspicious opening of *Belfast*'s career.'

Settling the crew into its duties and maintaining morale was not always straightforward. The navy was expanding rapidly for the first time in decades. It had reached a low point of 90,000 men in 1933, but 118,167 were voted in the 1938–9 Navy Estimates. It was not too hard to recruit these numbers while unemployment remained high, but Thring worried that so many of the *Belfast*'s crew were very young and inexperienced. There was also a difficulty in the supply of suitable petty officers to lead them. Officers joining HMS *Hood* in 1938 were told by Captain Pridham, 'Do not expect too much of your Petty Officers. We cannot expect that their standard shall be a very level one; large numbers are being made up and many are of very limited experience.' Fast-tracking promising men did not always help: 'It is well known that few men on the Lower Deck regard special promotion with any enthusiasm. Trade Unionism and an innate fidelity to their own kind limit their aim to one of general security, i.e. equal opportunity to rise steadily on a pay scale.' Officers were warned, 'The young Petty Officers and Leading Seamen have a difficult job. They find themselves in charge of men older than themselves (to whom the young seamen defer) and some of these will endeavour to trip them up.' One problem was the 'threebadge AB'. In the navy, chevrons indicated long service rather than rank, and a man who had served for thirteen years with reasonably good conduct was entitled to three, whether he rose to leading seaman or petty officer or not. Pridham wrote, 'Keep an eye on the older Able Seamen, in these days the fact that an Able Seaman is wearing three badges, or ought to be, is in many cases proof of his unsuitability. Their influence with the younger men is considerable and frequently bad.'

On 11 August, nineteen boys from the training ship HMS *Caledonia* joined the ship, followed by eight more from *Wildfire* in Kent, then others from *Ganges*, near Harwich, and the local training base, *St Vincent*, to make up more than a hundred seamen boys and boy signalmen and telegraphists. They had just completed a very rigorous training. Most ratings had joined as boys and signed on for twelve years after the age of eighteen, though recently a scheme of 'special service' had been introduced by which men served seven years with the fleet and five in the reserve. Before he was drafted to the *Belfast*, Peter McSweeney had spent 14 months training in HMS *Caledonia* at Rosyth, actually the old liner *Majestic*, which was moored inside the dockyard and commissioned in 1937 as a static training ship for 1,500 seamen boys and 500 artificer apprentices. The boys did seamanship in the morning and gunnery, which included marching and foot drill, in the afternoon; or vice versa. They learned knots and splices, gun drill, rowing and sailing, and took part in sports in the evenings. Other training bases were actually ashore, such as HMS *St Vincent*, near Portsmouth, and HMS *Ganges* near Harwich, which had already gained a reputation for brutal treatment. One inmate described a life

> of marching and counter-marching, of saluting to the left and saluting to the right, of moving at the double and moving at the slow march, of marking time and turning about, until Ginger remarked to the P.O. that he thought he'd joined the Navy and not the blasted Army, and was rewarded with a slap across the backside from the petty officer's stonickey: a twelve-inch length of rope with a large manrope knot at the end.

After this it was often a relief to be drafted to a real ship. In the *Belfast*, according to Thring, they were under the care of 'an excellent Chief PO, with the patience of a fisherman and the kindliness of a Father, and above all with a hearty laugh'.

Once on board, the men and boys were allocated messes according to rating and function, and the class system of the navy was integrated with the design of the ship. The crew lived forward of the engine room, an area that tended to be less comfortable in a rough sea. Certain rules were applied in the allocation of messes. Seamen were kept separate from stokers, who had joined the navy as adults rather than boys and worked in very different conditions so had different standards of discipline and cleanliness. The next large group, the Royal Marines, were also segregated. They too had joined as adults but were fiercely proud of their neatness and parade-ground discipline. The tradition that their role was to protect the officers in the event of a mutiny was still well known in the navy, for example by Ordnance Artificer John Harrison; but it was greatly exaggerated and had very little relevance in 1939. However, the marines were indeed messed furthest aft of the non-commissioned ranks, just forward of the administrative and control area under the bridge. Seamen's messes were placed forward on the upper deck with the circular barbette of 'A' turret taking up the centre of the second one. The seamen petty officers were on the starboard side of 'B' turret, with the officers' cooks and stewards to port – they were kept apart to prevent too much spreading of gossip from the wardroom, and they took their meals in the pantry there. Chief petty officers and stoker petty officers were situated further aft on the port side, with the sick bay, the engine room artificers and more petty officers to starboard. On the lower deck the seamen's messes alternated with the stokers, with the boys in the middle and the marines aft. Every

mess had its own wash-place and toilet, often some distance away –
only the boys had the wash-place inside their mess, for the authorities
were anxious not to expose them, though that was difficult to
maintain with so many on board. The stokers' and engineers' wash-
places were between the messes and the engine room to allow them
to wash after coming off duty.

Each man had an average of about 15 square feet of space,
though there was one advantage in that the deckhead was 8 feet 6
inches high in midships and up to 9 feet 10½ inches towards the
bows. The seamen's mess on the lower deck around 'B' barbette was
designed for 55 men in an area of 820 square feet. There were three
or four portholes on each side, but the mess relied largely on electric
lighting. There were three tables on the starboard side and four to
port, varying in length to fit around the guns. Each was supported
by two hooks engaging a small angle-iron at the outside end and by
galvanised steel legs. It could be stowed by hanging from the deck
beam above. The long stools had folding legs, and they could be
stowed on the tables. There was supposed to be a minimum space
of 21 inches per man on each table. Hammock hooks or bars were
fitted from the deck above, also 21 inches apart and 10 feet 6 inches
long, to allow room for the ropes, or nettles, from which a hammock
was suspended. New seamen were instructed:

> Sling the hammock between two hammock bars by passing the
> lanyard over the bar, back through its own ring and form a sheet
> bend over the nettles. Then distribute the bedding evenly over the
> length of the hammock and tauten up the slack nettles if necessary.
> To keep the head of the hammock apart a stretcher can be used, but
> this is optional. It consists of a length of wood two feet in length with
> a V cut at both ends.

In the daytime the hammocks were stowed in a rack forward on the starboard side. The spaces on the bulwarks fore and aft, and around the barbette, were fitted with kit lockers in two or three tiers, one for each man, but each had to be stowed very carefully to get all his gear in. The messdeck was the centre of the seaman's life while he was on board, and comradeship was forged in the crowded conditions. This was encouraged by the officers, and it was generally accepted that if an officer passed through with his cap off, the men did not have to pay the usual respects.

Roper drew up a detailed list of duties to be performed in harbour. Each day started at 0505 when men under punishment were called – though the *Belfast* was a happy ship, and there were few if any of these. Hands were called to stow their hammocks at 0530, then the cooks of the messes began their duty. The signal 'G' was sounded on the bugle to signify that the men had to be ready to take up stations within the next ten minutes, and they fell in to clean the ship at six o'clock. They had breakfast an hour later and at 0753 there was the signal 'out pipes' – though the great majority of seamen smoked cigarettes in those days. It did not mean instant readiness, just that they should finish their current smoke and be ready to go back to work. At 0820 'requestmen and defaulters' went before the commander, asking for privileges or facing punishment. At 0905 the men paraded in 'divisions' to be inspected. In the *Belfast*, as on most ships, the seamen were in three divisions, with names dating back to the days of the sailing ship – quarterdeck, or QD; topmen, or 'top'; and forecastle, or FX. The stokers were in two groups, and there were separate divisions for Royal Marines, boys, signallers, artificers and artisans and the Fleet Air Arm.

Routine work and training resumed with the occasional 'stand easy'. At 1200 the hands were called to dinner, the main meal of the day, which lasted until 1315 to allow some relaxation. The pattern was similar in the afternoon, until 1550 when the order 'secure' was given, and after 'evening quarters' ten minutes later there was 'tea', after which most of the men were off duty. For those who could not or did not want to go ashore there was supper at 1900. Boys were expected to turn in at 2045, other ratings at 2200 and chiefs and petty officers half an hour later as the ship bedded down for the night. There were different routines on Saturday, when work finished early, and on Sunday, when there was a church service.

During the next few days, according to Engine Room Artificer (ERA) Finch, there was a 'mad scramble' to get the ship ready. In the daytime the men worked hard at loading provisions and ammunition – already as she arrived in Portsmouth on 5 August there were seventeen railway trucks of supplies waiting to be loaded. The crew had to handle '20 tons flour, 5 tons potatoes, half ton onions, four tons beef and carcasses of mutton, one ton mutton legs, half ton of fresh pork, one and a half tons of bacon, half a ton of cheese, a quarter of kidneys, a quarter of a ton of liver, a quarter of a ton of sausages, one hundred and sixty stone of cod, seventy stone of kippers, eight cwt rolled oats besides tons of tinned foods, preserves, etc.' According to Read, a few tins of pineapple disappeared, but the operation was generally successful. He was in touch with the crew's feelings, and they were beginning to think they were in 'a general cargo ship'. The ship was allocated 2,040 'common pointed ballistic capped' rounds for the 6-inch guns, which could penetrate light armour, plus 360 high-explosive rounds, which had higher explosive content and would detonate on impact, as well as 432 practice rounds. The 4-inch secondary armament needed 3,000 rounds of high-explosive time-fuse rounds plus 200 starshells to light up the sky at night, 810 for high-angle or anti-aircraft practice and 120 for low-angle. The 2-pounder 'pom-poms' had 28,800 rounds, plus practice ammunition. All this had to be manhandled carefully and stowed in the various magazines. The crew worked willingly – 'the ship's company quite realised the necessity for all this hectic rush as apart from the fact that war was likely to break out shortly the ship had to be ready to sail for exercises with the fleet on Monday the 14th.'

The crew familiarised themselves with new equipment and carried out exercises such as fire stations and launching the sea boat to pick up a man overboard. Captain Scott was generous with leave while the ship was in Portsmouth. Only half a watch, a quarter of the crew, had to remain on board overnight. Men were allowed ashore at about 1600 after the day's work had finished and did not have to be back until seven the next morning. They could leave the ship at midday on a Saturday and at 0915 on a Sunday. Each ship was attached to one of the three home ports – Plymouth, Chatham or in this case Portsmouth. Its men would be drafted from the barracks there, they would undergo training courses locally, and in peacetime the ship would return there, as far as possible, for major repairs. The married men could settle down in the area, though the navy did not provide married quarters and they mostly lived in rented flats and houses. The men of the *Belfast* were able to spend some time with their families in the area, which was looking increasingly important as war began to threaten again. Portsmouth was a long-established naval base, and for single men it offered a full range of cinemas, dance halls, hostels, pubs, music halls and brothels. Scott gave weekend leave to one watch on the 12th and the 13th, but it was three weeks since the last pay-day, and some of the men had run out of money. They were not particularly politically aware, but they could not help notice developments that might affect them as Germany and the Soviet Union suddenly became closer and Britain and France warned Germany against any more aggression. There was no way of knowing how long they would enjoy the blessings of peace.

3

WAR WITH GERMANY

THE HAPPY DAYS OF LEAVE IN THE HOME PORT did not last long. *Belfast* was now complete, except that she was unable to operate aircraft because part of the catapult had not yet been delivered. Commander Roper had worked out the stations for the men on entering and leaving harbour. Hands fell in at least twenty minutes before the manoeuvre started. 'Special sea duty men' were picked hands to carry out key tasks. A skilled quartermaster stood by the steering wheel under the bridge. Two boatswain's mates were stationed beside him to operate the telegraphs that relayed orders to the engine room, and there was another quartermaster in the after steering position near the stern in case the usual one failed. Four seamen stood by in the 'chains' on the side of the ship, ready to cast the lead line to find the depth of water. Others were ready to hoist the cones or flags that might indicate the ship's speed and movements to other vessels. If the anchor had to be raised, a cable party of an officer, petty officer, leading seaman, twelve able or ordinary seamen, a blacksmith, a shipwright and a signalman was posted on the foredeck. In this case, on orders from the bridge, men simply had to release the mooring lines holding the ship to the jetty. The marine band was stationed aft of 'Y' turret, buglers were positioned on the lower bridge, while the bulk of the men paraded in their divisions. Those on the forecastle and quarterdeck were 'sized' with the tallest men closest to the extremity of the ship, and all hands had the chinstraps of their caps down, as it was not the moment for one to blow away. At 1140 on Monday 14 August 1939 the lines were slipped and the ship turned around to head out to sea for the first time as a commissioned warship.

They sailed out of the harbour between the historic Round Tower and Fort Blockhouse, the headquarters of the submarine service. They reached the anchorage of Spithead just outside the harbour but protected from the worst winds by the Isle of Wight. There the ship manoeuvred for an official photograph then headed east out of the Solent, while 'the crowd on Southsea beach seemed to sit up and take notice as we passed'. The crew was still unaware of their destination, though there were 'vague whispers' about a rendezvous off the mouth of the River Humber. There was still plenty to do to turn the *Belfast* into an efficient fighting machine, and exercises were carried out as she steamed towards the North Sea. That afternoon the men practised 'general quarters' or action stations, followed by an abandon-ship drill. By the end of the first day, according to Read, 'we began to realise that we were really in a man of war and not in a general cargo ship …' On Tuesday the 15th, off the east coast of England, the ship slowed down and the order 'hands to bathe' was given over the Tannoy. According to Ordnance Artificer Harrison, two men dived over the side before the ship had stopped properly, and a boat had to be sent to rescue them as they were left behind. Then the ship exercised taking up a tow forward, followed by training for night action. On the 16th they prepared for steering breakdowns, followed by evening quarters and 'away lifeboat's crew', while most of the hands bathed. By 1800 they were in sight of the Horns Reef Light Vessel off the coast of Denmark. It was a significant place for anyone interested in recent naval history, like

George Thring, for it was just there that the German High Seas Fleet had finally escaped from Admiral Jellicoe's Grand Fleet after the Battle of Jutland in 1916, an event that rankled within the navy for decades.

Now the daily sea routine was in effect. Life was dominated by the need to keep watch, to ensure that enough men were on duty or on call at any given moment to meet any emergency. The day was divided into four-hour periods known as watches, except between four and eight in the afternoon when there were two two-hour 'dog watches' to create variety. The seamen were divided into two watches, so that in normal circumstances half were on duty at any given moment. Work in the engine room was more intense, and the engineers and stokers were in three watches.

The morning watch was called at 0345 to take up its duties a quarter of an hour later. At 0535 the hands were called to begin scrubbing decks. Traditionally this was supervised by the commander in person, to the horror of visiting army officers, but as O'Conor wrote, '"Carry on Sergeant Major" is not good enough.' The hammocks were rolled up and stowed at 0640, and breakfast began at 0700. Both watches fell in for duty again just before eight. Some of the seamen had special tasks during their watch, including the quartermaster who supervised the steering, the duty helmsman (chosen in rotation) who actually operated the wheel, and two telegraphmen who transmitted orders to the engine room. In peacetime there were two lookouts on the bridge at night and one by day, along with a boy to carry messages. Two men stood by to operate warning flags and cones, while the boatswain's mate of the watch, a leading seamen, was based in the wheelhouse and was responsible for routine. There was a seamen gunner of the watch who stood by to release a rocket as required, a range-taker who

67

might be called to the bridge to measure the distance from an object for navigational purposes, a torpedoman for emergency repair work or to operate a crane or winch, and the shipwright of the watch. There was a sea boat's crew of a leading seaman and five men ready to launch in emergency, with five more in the handwheel party who would take over the manual steering if the power system failed. They might also be detailed to act as leadsmen, sounding the depth in shallow water. The marines provided the corporal of the watch, who reported routines to the commander on the quarterdeck. Another marine was the lifebuoy sentry, who stood by in case a man fell overboard. The rest of the crew carried out routine duties, with a combination of physical drill, painting, cleaning and training.

'Divisions' were called at 0905, when the men paraded in their groups for inspection. There was a break, or 'stand easy', at 1030, but ten minutes later the bugler sounded 'out pipes'. By 1150 the ship was preparing for dinner, the main meal of the day for the lower deck. 'Cooks of the messes' did not have to do much actual culinary work in a modern ship, but they were expected to fetch the crew's rum ration and food and take it below. The meal began at noon and it was 1315 before both watches had to fall in again, though helmsmen, lookouts and others stayed on duty and ate at a different time. At 1600 the first dog watch began, and the ship started to wind down for the night.

Belfast had been 'pitchforked' into her first naval exercise according to George Thring. 'Someone had to be the "enemy"; and we were the choice … presumably because we were not sufficiently efficient to be anything else!' Captain Scott lectured the men on the coming exercise. With the old cruiser *Dunedin* and the new destroyer *Javelin*, they were 'to represent a ship of a certain power with which war at that time seemed imminent'. Read commented, 'It all sounded very exciting and naturally everybody was anxious to see how this game of wits between ourself and the defending forces would pan out.' Things were quiet on the Wednesday except for numerous calls on the loudspeaker for hands who had failed to report to their stations. Read was tolerant. 'Allowances had to be made as for one thing the men had not had a real opportunity to find their way round, furthermore a great many of them were aboard a man o'war for the first time and didn't even know what part of the ship the particular station they were required in was situated.' Even the highly experienced George Thring found that at night, 'We were finding our way round in the dark without a torch; and learning all the obstacles from cabin to bridge often by painful personal contact.'

Off Horns Reef the ship met a German liner carrying out the Hitler Youth 'Strength Through Joy' programme with a cruise to Norway, then she was photographed by a Luftwaffe seaplane, which circled her. In the exercise, she was to simulate the German cruiser *Hipper* and attempt to escape into the Atlantic through a British blockade. They were soon spotted by an 'enemy' aircraft, and the three ships parted. Captain Scott took good care to 'darken ship' and make sure that no lights could be seen. He headed north-east at speeds of up to 25 knots while the crew went to 'cruising stations', with half of the anti-aircraft armament manned by part of the watch. The Northern Lights provided good visibility ahead but poorer astern – an 'enemy' ship would be spotted from the *Belfast* long before she spotted the intruder. There was a delay the following evening as the ship had to slow down to ten knots due to fog, but Scott had conceived a plan to sail through the treacherous Pentland Firth between Orkney and the mainland in the dark, rather than go round the north of Orkney as might be expected. As a destroyer officer in the last war he knew the area well, but it was not easy and conditions were largely unpredictable even though the navy had been using the area for many years. The Admiralty *Pilot Book* warned,

> … overfalls and eddies occur over a large part of the firth and, in consequence, a small change in position may be accompanied by a very considerable alteration in both the direction and rate of the stream; further, the extent of, and even the existence, of races and eddies depends on the rate of the stream, the force of the wind, and the relative directions of wind and stream; the streams may therefore be very different at springs and at neaps, and during calms, westerly gales and easterly gales.

AB Conlon was on the upper deck as the ship passed through and could see the shore lights on either side – 'Oh, hell', he thought. The ship's log for the period between 0105 and 0150 on the 18th recorded more prosaically: 'Course and speed as necessary for passing through the Pentland Firth clear of shipping.' Soon the *Belfast* was through and just after four in the morning she crossed the finish line of the exercise in triumph. Scott's prestige was greatly enhanced in front of the officers and crew. 'All the lads were chuffed with him,' said Conlon. The hands had their fortnightly payment at noon that day, and Read noticed that there was often a queue of forty outside the canteen to buy small luxuries such as chocolate. He observed, 'Thus we ended our first fortnight in commission just as clean and efficient as if the ship had been in commission at least three months.' Morale was soaring as they looked forward to time ashore with money in their pockets and respect from other ships. It was less happy that evening when the guns were exercised. 17½-year-old Boy John Campbell was taking part in drill at one of the 4-inch guns when he was injured 'by allowing his right middle finger to become caught between the moving breech block and the base of the practice cylinder, thereby sustaining accidental traumatic amputation of the first two phalanges'.

After a call in the Humber Estuary, the ship was ordered south to Portsmouth, where married men might be reunited with their families and the others could enjoy the pleasures of the great naval port. She was off the coast of East Anglia around six in the evening of 21 August. Ordnance Artificer Harrison was in his messdeck using natural light streaming through a porthole to write a letter. Suddenly he noticed that the light shifted rapidly and thought, 'The sun doesn't move like that.' He looked out to see a great arc in the wake as the ship turned through 180 degrees. *Belfast* had been ordered to head north again to Invergordon to take up war stations. Two days later Neville Chamberlain announced that Britain would stand by Poland if Germany invaded, and war seemed almost inevitable. According to Read, 'The ships company on the whole had a philosophic view of this sudden turn of events.'

Invergordon had a resonance for naval officers as the scene of a mutiny in 1931, and perhaps Commander Roper was nervous about it when he heard reports that the crew was unhappy with the food. According to Read, 'the commander saw a representative body in his office and told them he had heard rumours that the food was insufficient; a state of affairs which he deeply regretted although the catering was outside his province. He said that he was satisfied there were grounds for complaint and that he had taken steps to have matters made satisfactory. His action was very much appreciated ...' Roper promised an improvement, but many of the potatoes loaded with so much effort at Portsmouth turned out to be rotten. The crew was often served with rice instead, for there was no time to replenish at Invergordon. Teams were just about to go ashore to play football when a signal was received to go further north.

The *Belfast* proceeded to Scapa Flow to join the Home Fleet under Admiral Sir Charles Forbes, who inspected the ship on Sunday the 27th. It was a bleak spot after the delights of Portsmouth, and from the destroyer *Tartar* Ludovic Kennedy wrote, 'The islands were treeless, just heather and grass, seabirds and sheep, and across the bare face of the Flow tempests blew, often for days on end. There were no women, shops, restaurants, just a couple of canteens that dispensed warm beer, a hall for film shows and the occasional concert party, and football fields that too often displayed the sign "All grounds unfit for play".' However, potatoes were on the menu again – they had acquired a few from another ship – and the first letters for six days arrived.

The *Belfast* was allocated to the 18th Cruiser Squadron led by Rear Admiral Ronald Hallifax flying his flag in the *Aurora*. The *Belfast* had exercised with her lighter guns, and carried out 'sub-calibre' practice with the 6-inch guns – where there was no space for full-calibre firing, or there was a need to save ammunition, a 3-pounder barrel was attached to the side of one of the main guns in each turret and 1,800 rounds were issued for practice. According to the then-current edition of the *Gunnery Pocket Book*, 'Practice with these guns gives excellent experience, and for a fair test for the control system and for layers and trainers; unfortunately the loading numbers obtain very little value from this form of practice and only a few of the men are required to take part.' At last, on the 30th, a 'very important day' according to the master-at-arms, she prepared for full-calibre firing just outside the Flow. Hatches were closed, boats secured, windows screwed up tight and skylights fitted with steel covers to protect against the blast. Then she trained her 6-inch guns at a target pulled by a tug, rather than the smaller ones used for sub-calibre practice, and fired for eleven minutes. Thring noticed the 'slow, stately, and simple' practice of the big-gun crews, who aimed carefully before firing. It was the opposite with the anti-aircraft crews, as the port and starboard sides competed to get off the maximum number of rounds without much regard to accuracy – so much so that the crew of the target-towing aircraft reported them as a public menace. Read thought that at least the battening down had gone well – 'there was very little damage caused between decks as a result of the shock.' Meanwhile a rumour spread round the messdecks that Hitler had 'chucked his hand in'.

Part of the function of a cruiser was to train young midshipmen to be commissioned as officers, for smaller ships such as destroyers did not have room for the instructional staff needed. J. A. Syms was one of a party of five who left Dartmouth to take the train to the far north. 'It all seemed so romantic; we had been brought up on the history of the Grand Fleet at Scapa Flow ... There was an air of urgency in our crowded carriage that was palpable and unforgettable.' After many hours in the train, 'In the early morning, tired, sticky and grubby, we were revived by a traditional Scottish breakfast in the hospitable hotel at Thurso ... A brisk passage from the tiny harbour at Scrabster ... across the Pentland Firth to Scapa Flow finally blew away the cobwebs of the night before.' They arrived on board the *Belfast* on 1 September, and Syms was not impressed with her looks.

The ship already had a few young men who were on a different route to a commission. The 'Special Entry' scheme was started in 1913 as a faster way of providing officers for the fleet during its great expansion period. It was aimed mainly at public-school boys who were entitled to apply between the ages of 17 and 18 years.

Clearly it had great advantages for boys who had failed to enter Dartmouth at 13, or who had not yet settled their choice of career. If successful in the examinations, they had eight months of training as cadets in a cruiser, then became midshipmen and were, in most respects, the equal of the Dartmouth cadets. The Special Entry scheme was to be a major factor in future expansion programmes and was enlarged in 1936 but numbers were still quite small compared with the Dartmouth entry, as so far few of them had reached the fleet. Five of them joined *Belfast* at the end of August 1939, having been recalled from leave on the threat of war and of missing their final voyage in the training cruiser. Among them were Terence Lewin (later to become Admiral of the Fleet Lord Lewin) of Judd School in Kent, who had taken part in the Public Schools Exploring Society expedition to Newfoundland in 1938, and Roderick Macdonald (later to become Vice Admiral Sir Roderick) from Fettes School in Edinburgh, who had captained the Scottish schoolboys Rugby Union team. In his own words he was 'only 18, ignorant and worse still terribly keen – typical (perhaps) of public school special entry and self-nurtured on Mahan, Taffrail, Keble Chatterton and the *Wonder Book of the Navy*'. Lewin remained on board while Macdonald, a 'keen volunteer to escape "big ship"' routine', was seconded to a steam drifter patrolling the entrances to the Flow. He and his colleagues noticed a gap that could be used by a surfaced U-boat at high tide and informed the authorities before sailing off.

Syms described life as a midshipman under the control of a sub-lieutenant who lived with them in the gunroom and was their 'lord and master'. Not yet fully-fledged officers, the 'mids' had to sling their hammocks in passages around the gunroom, but they had a full range of duties:

In harbour we kept watch on the quarter deck with our telescopes under our arms as a badge of office … Our duties included seeing that the ship's boat routine was run to time, that no-one boarded the ship without a proper welcome and generally acting as the slave of the officer of the watch or day …

Soon other officers arrived to make the ship up to a full war complement. Some were members of the Royal Naval Volunteer Reserve, amateur seamen from many different professions who had done some training in evenings, weekends and summer cruises. They were distinguished from regular officers by the 'wavy' stripes on their arms, and the navy had very low expectations of the seaman officers. For the moment they were only expected to supervise the crew in menial duties or assist the regular officers. In 1932, Derek Rayner applied to the captain of the Mersey Division to join a specialist navigation course. But he was told that 'the Navy would never allow a ship to be navigated by an R.N.V.R. officer; that I should end up nothing better than a 'tanky' (navigator's assistant)'. This attitude was still common in 1939. A surgeon lieutenant, two temporary sub-lieutenants and a paymaster sub-lieutenant from the RNVR joined the ship during the run-up to war in August.

* * * * *

The gunnery practice was none too soon, for next day Admiral Forbes took the fleet to sea to patrol the area between Shetland and Norway to prevent any German breakout in the event of war. It was an impressive force that left that day, including the battleships *Nelson*, *Rodney*, *Royal Oak*, *Royal Sovereign* and *Ramillies*, the battlecruisers *Hood* and *Repulse*, the aircraft carrier *Ark Royal*, three cruiser squadrons, seventeen destroyers and seven minesweepers. However, the *Belfast* had different duties, and after more exercises and bringing up ammunition and torpedo warheads to their action positions, she headed north to take up her patrol station between Mull Head and North Ronaldsay to the north of the Orkney Islands. Hands were at defence stations, which meant that half the armament was manned at all times; watertight doors were kept closed, and the ship was darkened at night. Taking a zig-zag course to avoid any surprise torpedo attack, she was in her war station half an hour before midnight and began patrolling. The missing parts for the catapult had arrived, but there had been no chance to install them.

Germany invaded Poland on 1 September, and the British and French issued an ultimatum that was due to expire at 1100 in the morning of the 3rd. At 1030 that morning Captain Scott addressed the crew in the port hangar. 'He said that in all probability the country would be actually at war and to the younger members of the ship's company to whom war would be a novel experience he stressed the importance of not getting fed up or casual on their duties as lookouts etc. when war did come.' He quoted a personal experience of the effects of laxity in the last war. The ship's company was 'piped down', and at 1100 George Thring and some of the officers listened to Neville Chamberlain's mournful and carefully articulated broadcast on the paymaster commander's radio in his cabin: 'This morning the British Ambassador in Berlin handed the German Government a final Note stating that, unless we heard from them by 11 o'clock that they were prepared at once to withdraw their troops from Poland, a state of war would exist between us. I have to tell you now that no such undertaking has been received, and that consequently this country *is* at war with Germany.' Thring recorded, 'Most people did not say much; but we all thought a lot.'

At 1117 the Admiralty sent out a signal to Admiral Forbes, and it was passed on to *Belfast* at 1140. Engine Room Artificer Finch was in charge of the after engine room at the time, when Lieutenant Moriarty, officer of the watch, 'came clattering down' and handed him a piece of paper without saying a word. It said, 'Commence Hostilities at once with Germany.' According to Master-at-Arms Read, 'The effect on the majority was barely perceptible.'

That afternoon there was a heavy ground swell, which made the younger members of the crew very uncomfortable. With no radar, lookouts 'relied perforce on the eye plus binoculars' according to Midshipman Syms. They spoke to a neutral Swedish ship but let her pass. Boy William Crawford kept detailed notes of the ship's movements, and on Tuesday 5 September he recorded, 'During the morning 5 ships were seen on the horizon but they turned out to be the battle cruiser *Renown*, cruiser *Edinburgh* and 2 destroyers. We were ordered to follow them as two German cruisers had been reported about 4 miles off the coast of Norway probably to assist the *Bremen*. A heavy mist came down and we missed them and started for Scapa Flow instead.' They arrived there next day and sailed on the 8th as Crawford noted: 'We left Scapa Flow this morning with the battle cruisers *Hood* and *Renown*, the cruiser *Edinburgh* and a convoy of 4 destroyers. We are going on patrol.' The force consisted of the fastest capital ships and newest cruisers in the fleet. They were ordered to search off the Norwegian coast 'with the object of intercepting enemy vessels returning to Germany', especially the liner *Europa*. But no enemy ships were found, and on the 9th the *Belfast* was detached with her sister ship *Edinburgh* 'to search from the Eastward around Iceland North-about and through the Denmark Strait, for merchant shipping which might be using this Northern route in order to avoid the established contraband control patrols'. Visibility was perfect on the 10th, but only the neutral Norwegian fishing fleet was in sight. The *Belfast*'s catapult had still not been assembled, and the *Edinburgh* had no pilot for her Walrus amphibian – her captain lamented that air patrols could have been useful in checking that no ships were trying to sneak through by hugging the coast. Visibility began to deteriorate on the 11th, and Boy Crawford noted, 'We struck bad weather today. Talk about waves as big as houses. They are crashing over our bows. Even as I write this we are heaving and I can hear the waves smashing on the [forecastle]. We have sprung a leak but I don't think it is bad.' There was another storm on the 13th, and both ships were forced to heave to for a while as the *Belfast* rolled through 10 to 15 degrees. On the 15th the two ships arrived at Sullom Voe in Shetland, a 'bleak spot' with little opportunity for recreation according to Thring. The fjord was only lightly protected against submarine attack, but Crawford noted, 'Arrived here at 5 o'clock in the evening, we passed through a string of mines between one piece of an island to the other.' They refuelled from a tanker, and Read remembered the old days of coaling in which the whole crew was involved in the filthy work for many hours – but now only thirty men were needed to connect oil pipes. Mail arrived and Crawford got a letter from his mother. His own letters from the *Belfast* have not survived, but if they were anything like those he wrote from the *Hood* in the following year, he was deeply unhappy with sea life and constantly seeking a shore appointment.

Engine Room Artificer George E. Finch had joined the navy as an apprentice in 1930 and trained at HMS *Fisgard*, a shore base near Portsmouth. His early training was in craft skills, especially metalwork. 'The task – to carve a hexagon from a cylinder of steel without hammer and chisel, and then finish the piece with files to produce a true hexagon correct in all angles and dimensions … As the long days passed, the hands holding the hammers began to burn with open blisters which were later to spread into areas of raw, exquisite pain.' Over the next few years the boy would learn turning, milling, boring and grinding. One admiral commented, 'Many of the exercises especially in chipping are more in the nature of muscle builders than test of skill.' But that was only half of the artificer's training: he also studied marine engineering, engineering drawing, mechanics and electricity. He was also expected to understand the working of engines and eventually to take charge of a watch in the engine room. Now Finch was settling into the ERA's mess on the starboard side of the ship under the leadership of Chief ERA Tom King. He 'soon welded us into a happy department. He was never brusque in his approach and made a point of engaging the younger members of the Mess in quiet informative chats when time permitted'. The ERAs took over a small workshop in the boat deck to play darts in the evenings, but it was cramped and cold, and the lights went off every time the door was opened. Back in the mess they played 'uckers' or ludo as many seamen did.

On Monday the 18th the *Belfast* joined the cruisers *Sheffield* and *Aurora*, and the crew heard that the aircraft carrier *Courageous* had been sunk by a U-boat. On the way back into Scapa Flow, according to Crawford, 'a torpedo was seen to pass about 50 ft astern of us. When we passed through the entrance boom defence ships dropped the submarine net and we were told later that one submarine was caught in the net and half an hour later two more came to the top and surrendered. They had no food, no water and their batteries were needing charged.' But this was an optimistic rumour.

Soon afterwards Read took part in an antiquated ceremony as pay-day came round again:

The seamen 'mustered by the ledger' on Sunday the 24th that is the Captain took up his position in the quarter deck alongside a table where a Petty Officer Writer stood with the pay ledger and the seamen were marched on to the quarter deck in fours and halted at a line drawn on the starboard side about two paces further forward than the Captain. The Petty Officer Writer called out each man's name … upon which he turned right and marched into a circle in front of the Captain, turned left so as to face the Captain, saluted, told the Captain his rating, non-substantive ratings, number of good conduct badges he possessed and anything else for which he got paid, again saluted, turned right and marched off …

According to Read, the object was to give the captain the chance to see every man in the ship individually. In addition, it allowed the medical officer 'to spot anyone who looked "a bit seedy".' Read thought they seemed quite healthy with very few exceptions, although it was five weeks since they had had fresh vegetables apart from potatoes.

On the 25th the *Belfast* and the 18th Cruiser Squadron formed part of a fleet operation to rescue the submarine *Spearfish*, which had been damaged off Horns Reef and was unable to dive. They were subjected to high-level air attack, but this was easy to evade as Roderick Macdonald reported on a slightly later operation, when he and Terence Lewin were stationed aft with binoculars. '"Bomb doors open, sir." Then "Bombs away!" He then put the wheel hard over one way or another. It always worked, as the explosions and columns of water erupted where we would otherwise have been.'

Back in Scapa Flow, the *Belfast*'s Walrus flying-boat had finally arrived. It alighted beside her and was hoisted on board, then launched from the catapult. Read observed, 'Great interest was evinced by everybody in that operation, as it was the first time we had performed it.' Four more launches were carried out that day. On Sunday 1 October the captain addressed the crew as usual and raised hopes of a trip to Rosyth and leave – at least a visit to 'the Noo', or Edinburgh, if not home leave. But hopes were dashed during the afternoon when it was learned that the programme had been altered and on Monday they were to sail to join the Northern Patrol once more. 'Such is war,' wrote Read.

By 2 October, the *Belfast* was on duty between the Faeroes and Iceland. Captain Scott made sure that two officers were always on watch on the bridge, and he came up himself occasionally to 'yarn with one or the other'. He discussed the war situation with Thring. 'We agreed that it would probably be a short war, that after a few months, reason would triumph; Germany would realise that the British Empire and France were being firm at last; she would then call off her conquest and become a normal nation with different rulers … the Captain then went on to say that if we did not have peace in a few months, total war would set in, and that would be too ghastly to contemplate.'

No vessels were sighted on the 3rd and 4th, while a strong south-westerly wind forced a reduction in speed from 16 knots to 13½. At last on the 5th they sighted a Norwegian factory ship with her six accompanying whalers. The sea was 'confused and ugly', and boarding had to be carried out by one of the ship's cutters, but Captain Scott was aware that these ships had 'already caused misapprehension as to their character', so he decided to take the risk. Thring was in charge of the duty boarding party, and the boat was lowered into the water using new-fangled electric hoists, which were distrusted at first but soon proved themselves. 'There was a heavy swell running; it was not without some anxiety that we started off. The Crew were very young, but very keen, and one had a couple of seasoned hands at bow and stern. We got away easily in the lee of the ship, no time wasted. It seemed a very long climb up the side of the heaving Neutral with her enormous free board. We accomplished this with greater ease than we expected, though burdened with the most awkward weapons of war.' The Norwegian captain was friendly and showed Thring around the vast oil holds of the ship. Her papers were in order, and the cutter returned carrying a gift of two bottles of whisky, with which the boarding party toasted the Norwegian captain.

There was another blank day on the 6th, then the *Belfast* moved west to take up another patrol line vacated by the *Newcastle*. On the 8th the chaplain delivered a very depressing sermon in which he 'urged us all to prepare to meet our maker and he did it in such a manner as to make [us] imagine we were all about to lose our lives'. They sighted the Swedish ship *C. P. Lilljevalch* carrying iron ore to Baltimore. They might have searched her, but Scott decided that a heavy sea from the south-east would have rendered boarding an extremely dangerous operation, particularly as 'the *Lilljevalch*, when stopped, rolled so heavily that no boat could have approached with safety'. Since she was outward bound and not acting suspiciously, he allowed her to proceed. Next day the weather was a little better when they boarded the Norwegian *Tai Yin*, also bound for Baltimore. This one was on the Admiralty list of suspicious ships, so a prize crew was put on board and she was sent to Kirkwall for further examination. The cutter returned to the *Belfast* and was hoisted on board.

ERA George Finch had worked almost entirely in repairs since 1933 and had little seagoing experience. As the most junior of the ERAs with a full watch-keeping certificate he was considered the least necessary, which is why he had been chosen as the senior engineering member of No. 1 boarding party. He was resting that afternoon when another ship was seen on the horizon. Course was altered to intercept her, and she was seen to be flying the Swedish flag with the name 'Ancona' painted on her bows. The reference books showed no Swedish ship of that name, and at close range it became clear that it had been painted recently on top of another name that was embossed on the hull. Action stations was sounded again, and No. 1 boarding party was ordered to its station. The cutter was launched with Lieutenant Commander Seale in charge of the boarding party and the young Terence Lewin commanding the boat, whose crew included three boys. Finch and the other members were dressed in standard uniform with gaiters to give a more military appearance, but he had no boots to wear with them and they rode over his shoes. The voyage across was rough: 'It was soon obvious that boarding would be a hazardous exercise. She was rolling slowly and our cutter was rising and falling in the swell. A rope ladder provided with narrow wooden rungs had been thrown over the side and swung slowly with the movement of the ship. Our helmsman brought us into the ladder and the struggle began ... the climb seemed endless, the ladder twisting and turning with every step. The sailors and marines were badly hampered by the rifles slung over their shoulders and frequently trod on the fingers of the men below them.'

On the bridge of the merchant ship the captain offered the bearded Seale a razor but soon admitted that she was a German ship called the *Cap Norte*, eighteen days out from Pernambuco carrying 164 men and seven women, either the wives of crew members or stewardesses. Finch was anxious to get below to check for flooding, but he had to wait until his assistant, Stoker Sheridan, was released from his work handing up stores from the cutter. They found that the ship had no provision for scuttling, but checked all valves, inlets and so on for tightness. He was pleased to find that the engine room layout was very similar to the repair ship *Cyclops* in which he had served for some years. The cutter was sent back to bring more men, and eventually a prize crew of Seale, Torpedo Gunner Wright and 20 ratings was established on board before the ship was sent on her way to Kirkwall. Finch and Sheridan were joined by Stoker Barrett and two more, but the five of them could not cope with the strange engines without the assistance of the prisoners, who were sullen at first. Second Engineer Plüschau was contemptuous and told Finch, 'The war will be very short. You British are very obstinate. Together with our friends the Russians, you have no chance to survive if you do not make peace and end this stupidity. We have so many U-boats in this area that you will never get our ship to England.' Indeed, the prize crew was dismayed as the *Belfast* turned east to resume her patrol rather than escorting them to Orkney. Gradually some of the Germans became more friendly, for merchant seamen were 'men of the world' who had not necessarily been infected by Nazi propaganda. A German greaser (the merchant equivalent of a stoker) who spoke in 'twangy American-English' approached Finch and told him there was a plot to scuttle the ship as soon as she was close enough to land for rescue. Some of the men would create a diversion by blowing off steam in the engine room while the others would break open the sea cocks. Finch told Seale, and extra guards were stationed in the engine rooms. Eventually the second engineer offered his word of honour that there would be no sabotage. Off Kirkwall the guard was reinforced by 30 men who arrived in a drifter. The exhausted Finch was glad to get some sleep in 'the softest bunk I can remember', but on awakening he was shocked that the new guards slashed kitbags and rifled private property, undoing the friendly relations. The ship arrived safely in Kirkwall next morning. The Northern Patrol intercepted 172 ships up to 12 October, but this was only the second one found to be German.

The *Cap Norte* and her cargo were eventually valued at £77,000. In an earlier age this prize money would have been divided among the officers and crew; the captain, with a quarter share to himself, would have become quite wealthy. But the issue was already under discussion in government circles. Despite Churchill's wish to maintain tradition, it was accepted that prize money was a lottery, no longer appropriate in the days when ships were mostly sunk rather than captured, while aircraft or intelligence services might play a part in the capture, and the whole issue was very divisive. Eventually the money went into a general fund, which was distributed throughout the navy at the end of the war.

The crew of the *Belfast* were also disappointed not to be sent back to Orkney with the prize. She was back on her patrol line, and in the afternoon of the 12th they sighted the Swedish *Uddeholm* heading for Savannah. She too was on the list of ships to be sent in, so another armed guard was needed to take her to Kirkwall. With her crew now depleted, the *Belfast* was ordered back to Scapa. The great anchorage was strangely empty when the cruiser arrived on Friday 13th. Intelligence suggested that the Germans had a force of 800 bombers ready to attack the ships, and the air defences were very weak, so Admiral Forbes had decided to use Loch Ewe on the west coast of Scotland as a temporary base. The only large ship still in the Flow was the battleship *Royal Oak* of 1914, left behind because she was too slow to keep up with the fleet. Read went ashore after 'a very successful and satisfactory patrol', and in the canteen they were treated as heroes by men from other ships. During the night of the 13th/14th Ordnance Artificer Harrison heard some thuds, but paid no attention as strange noises were quite common. Midshipman Syms was on watch at six in the morning, but he, 'and presumably the rest of the fleet, had no inkling of what had been going on.' Thring was woken by a signalman bearing the message that the *Royal Oak* had been sunk and that all ships were to put to sea as soon as possible. She had been torpedoed by *U-47*, entering the Flow through the gap noticed by Roderick Macdonald. That night 786 men were killed, and ERA Finch lost two friends: he suffered a shock that 'bit deep and numbed my senses for many days afterwards'. The remaining ships left 'precipitously' for Loch Ewe that morning, the *Belfast* weighing anchor at 0741.

* * * * *

Ships' boats were very important to the Royal Navy, and not just as lifeboats. It was said that 'a ship is known by her boats', for warships spent much of their time at anchor or in protected corners of dockyards. The boats took the officers ashore and to other ships on business or for leisure, they landed crewmen for 'liberty', and the public saw them at close quarters far more than the ship herself. They also provided training in seamanship and responsibility for the midshipmen who might take command of them, and 'pulling' (i.e., rowing) or sailing boats were often used in regattas between ships or departments – a practice that survived in wartime when *Belfast* held regattas off Iceland in 1943. They were, of course, essential for boarding a suspected ship.

Until recently all boats had been propelled by sail, oars or steam, but a new generation of power boats had arrived with internal combustion engines. In a steamboat the reaction was always slow, as the coxswain had to ring to the stoker to change the revolutions or the direction of the engine. In the new powerboats this was done by simple levers. 'The coxswain stands at the wheel in the ordinary way, but instead of ringing gongs to the engine room, or working with an engine room telegraph, he will move the reverse lever forwards or backwards, as the case may be.' Moreover some of them, especially those made by Vosper of Southampton, were designed for high speed by 'planing' or using hydrodynamic forces to lift most of the hull above the water. This naturally appealed to young midshipmen, and Syms reported, 'A sought-after harbour duty was as coxswain of one of the ship's power boats, one's first command, one might say' – though he regretted that in wartime midshipmen would no longer carry ceremonial dirks. The speed and fragility of the boats worried many officers, however. Captain Scott repeated the orders issued by O'Conor: 'In these planing boats it is … necessary not to try to run too slow except when approaching, as when the boat is only half planing it is neither efficient as a planing boat nor yet as a displacement boat.' It might be difficult in rough seas, but in that case 'it is advisable to ease up a bit or else alter the course so as to take the waves as they come at an angle to the bow one side or the other.'

Boats became even more important in Loch Ewe, where there was no regular base and the ships were largely left to their own devices. Syms got his wish to take charge of a high-speed boat, but had trouble on anti-submarine patrol. 'While I was conscientiously motoring backwards and forwards in my motor boat at the entrance, there was a general alarm and exodus, with the fleet departing rapidly and unexpectedly so far as I was concerned. It was only very late in the day with the *Belfast* already under way that I made it back to the ship to be hoisted rather unceremoniously aboard like a seaboat.'

* * * * *

The *Belfast*, with her catapult fitted and her aircraft finally operational, was going to sea in the company of the powerful but ugly battleships *Rodney* and *Nelson*, the beautiful but flawed battlecruiser *Hood*, the eccentric aircraft carrier *Furious*, the small cruiser *Aurora* and nine destroyers. They were ordered to reinforce the Northern Patrol after a report that a large number of German merchant ships was about to pass through the area to get home. On the way, according to Boy Campbell, 'It was about 3 o'clock this afternoon when the order came through to load the after guns and stand by for a submarine attack. We dropped 6 depth charges but she got away.' Thring reported that the only result was to kill fish – 'herrings, and more herrings! How one wished to lower a boat, and collect all that wasted food.' The regular warships encountered no enemy vessels and endured some rough weather, but armed merchant cruisers in the area captured one enemy ship and caused another to scuttle herself. They returned to Loch Ewe on 22 October, where Commander Roper called the master-at-arms and chief boatswain's mate into the cabin to tell them in confidence that the ship would soon sail for Glasgow, and long leave would be granted. As soon as she sailed, this was announced over the loudspeakers. She was to go to Harland & Wolff's other shipyard at Govan on the south side of the Clyde, where outstanding items such as a second gyro compass were to be fitted, and she was to be docked and repaired. They sailed down through the Minches between the Outer and Inner Hebrides in company with other ships on a very dark night when rain squalls often reduced the visibility to nothing. They were ordered to zig-zag according to a prescribed pattern, and there was a bad moment when the watch that timed the procedure stopped. Thring wondered if it was worth the danger, since there were only a few U-boats at sea.

As they sailed up the narrow upper Clyde, Thring noticed that nearly all the building slips were now occupied, a contrast to the days of the Great Depression and 'signs at least that we were getting down to it'. To Read it was 'a very interesting trip'. One man counted 78 ships including the great liner *Queen Elizabeth* building at Clydebank and the new battleship *Beatty*, later renamed *Howe*. Both watches were given long leave of four days each, but there was anxiety as it took a long time to manoeuvre into the dry dock, the men worrying about catching the last train of the day. But they did, and Thring went home to his family. 'That four days leave probably meant more than any leave we have had before or since.' He 'counted the hours, determined not to waste a moment'. In the second party awaiting long leave, Read and his comrades went into Glasgow, where 'it seemed quite strange to be amongst traffic again and we also had our first experience of a blackout on shore'. Then he went home to Banbury in Oxfordshire, where his wife and daughter had moved from Portsmouth. Arriving there, 'my beard was the biggest sensation'. ERA Finch was able to have his much-delayed visit to his worried mother. The hands on duty worked clearing the ship for the dock, cleaning and then repainting her. A cartridge that had been dropped under 'A' turret was removed and made safe – Captain Scott insisted that it had been left there by the shipyard, not by his own men. Then, as Read noted with professional concern, 'Unfortunately there were quite a lot of men overstaying their leave that night and as they were not taken before the officer of the watch they thought they were getting away with it.' The ship sailed, and 'nobody on the lower deck knew (officially) where we were going but as the anti-aircraft guns' crews were told that they must be more than usually alert it was surmised that we were on our way to Rosyth'. This was correct: the ship was to join the *Edinburgh* as part of the 2nd Cruiser Squadron, a striking force for the North Sea. Thring thought it was 'a position of honour', rather like the Harwich Force, which had distinguished itself in the last war. They sailed north about, and on the 9th they anchored near the Forth Bridge. Read and his comrades went ashore the next day and 'discovered quite a roomy, comfortable canteen'. There were plenty of men from other ships in port and 'lots of yarns were exchanged'.

They sailed again on the 11th amid the usual rumours about the destination, in company with the *Southampton*, *Glasgow*, *Edinburgh*, *Aurora* and a destroyer flotilla. They went south along the tortuous channel that was swept clear of mines off the east coast of England and arrived at Immingham in the Humber estuary. No shore leave was given, but in any case the prospect did not look very inviting to Thring. He found his brother-in-law serving in the destroyer flotilla, and both were pleased to hear that Mrs Thring had given birth to her second daughter – the telegram arrived during a false alarm of an air raid. Thring got permission for the *Belfast*'s artisans to repair a motor boat belonging to his brother-in-law's destroyer, in the tradition that 'big ships should help the littler ones in all such matters'. Read managed to get leave to look up his cousin, the town clerk of Grimsby, but he only got as far as the pier head before there was a general recall of all libertymen. The ship was raising steam and went to sea soon afterwards. The squadron got separated in fog, but *Belfast* arrived off Rosyth on 17 November to be greeted by the captain of the *Edinburgh* waving his cap from his bridge.

On the 19th the admiral came on board and explained his reasons for not giving more leave. He offered advice on dealing with an air raid, having experienced one recently in the *Southampton*. The officers amused themselves by visiting the Hawes Inn in Queensferry, made famous in Robert Louis Stevenson's *Kidnapped*. They discussed the recent air raids, which had slightly damaged the *Southampton*, and Thring made a bet that the Forth Bridge would not be standing by the end of the war. When he wrote his memoirs in 1943, the issue was still unresolved.

They also discussed rumours of magnetic mines, but chief engineer Lister and his assistant Ferguson were apparently not fully aware of them yet. They were encouraging the men to think about some of the hazards of a new and unknown war. They could see that 'all sorts of new and unusual problems' might arise from attacks by shells, bombs, mines, torpedoes and even 'bombs designed to be dropped ahead of the ship and to rise again so as to explode beneath the ship's bottom'. They recognised it was useless to set hard and fast rules, but suggested, 'A lot of serious mistakes might be avoided, however, if each responsible individual concerned has given thought to the various problems of the type which might arise due to damage.' They proposed, 'Each officer and rating is to think out for himself what he considers to be the best action to be taken to cope with the damage in each case and is to write down the answer ... and return it to me ...' Engine Room Artificer Finch found that 'These proved to be very valuable in that most of us, particularly those who had joined only recently, began to take a more serious interest in the ship – more personal in that we needed no reminder that our lives could well depend upon it.' The paper is undated but there are no replies to be found with it, so it seems likely that it was written not long before the 21st of November. The men were being encouraged to 'expect the unexpected', and soon it would come to test them.

4

REPAIR

CAPTAIN SCOTT DID WELL IN KEEPING THE *BELFAST* AFLOAT
when she was mined, but it was Commander Roper who gained the
credit, with the award of an OBE in March 1940 for 'exemplary
conduct and cheerfulness in adversity after an explosion had
occurred in his ship'. Joiner 1st Class Samuel Davies was awarded
the British Empire Medal for rescuing comrades. Meanwhile it was
discovered that Scott had leaked photographs to *The Times* – in
November 1939 it published a shot of the *Belfast*'s anti-aircraft guns
firing and another of the cutter going out to the *Cap Norte*. Neither
could be said to compromise security or discredit the service in any
way, but Scott incurred the 'severe displeasure' of their Lordships of
the Admiralty. He moved between various staff posts in London, but
was found to be 'highly strung'. He took command of a destroyer
depot ship but felt the strain when left in temporary charge of the
flotilla. His health had always been indifferent, and the commander-
in-chief of the Home Fleet considered him 'most unsuitable for
command of a training establishment'. In July 1941 he was invalided
from the service with the rank of rear admiral.

On 24 November 1939, Winston Churchill told the War Cabinet
that he expected the repair of the *Belfast* to take five or six months.
Constructor Hill took charge of the work at Rosyth. The ship was
placed in a dry dock in the middle of January, and the water was

pumped out to let her rest on blocks. Divers monitored the progress, but it soon became clear that 'as the weight of the ship came on the blocks there were signs of excessive wearing' – the keel was 'hogged' (bent) to be up to three feet out of line at station 80, about a third of the way from the bow and under the rear of the bridge. The operation was abandoned, the ship was taken out of the dock and her gun turrets removed to reduce weight. She was docked again, on blocks fitted with soft caps that would give way to allow for the irregularity.

The Admiralty was generally satisfied with the *Belfast/Edinburgh* design, and early in 1940 there was talk of ordering more ships. There would be one major change: the beam would be increased by 2 feet 8 inches, as the treaty limits were no longer in place. The after gun turrets would be fitted a deck lower to increase stability, and extra armour would be added to increase the tonnage by 316. In fact, the navy was already committed to building the 'Colony' class, which was slightly shorter than the *Belfast* but retained the 12-gun armament with the after turrets a deck lower. However, the engine arrangement was far more conventional, with the forward funnel just aft of the bridge structure. After the *Edinburgh* was lost in May 1942, *Belfast* was unique with the great gap in the centre of the ship. Cruiser design also moved in a different direction towards the smaller ships of the *Dido* class with 5.25-inch guns mainly for anti-aircraft purposes. However, a great deal of shipbuilding effort was needed urgently for escort vessels and aircraft carriers, so the new ships were never ordered. It was too late to change the turret and armour arrangements of the *Belfast*, but in February 1940 it was ordered that her beam should be increased by 2 feet 6 inches. This would be done by adding bulges to her sides and fitting the armour outside them. As well as increasing stability, it would increase buoyancy, allow the ship to carry more equipment and would strengthen the damaged hull.

The war became more serious in April when the Germans defied British sea power to invade Denmark and Norway. Winston Churchill left the Admiralty to become Prime Minister just as the Germans launched their devastating invasion of France by way of Belgium, the Netherlands and Luxembourg. By 3 June the navy, assisted by the famous 'little ships', had completed the evacuation of a third of a million British, French and Belgian troops from Dunkirk. France surrendered on 22 June despite Churchill's entreaties to fight on. This was now the total war that Captain Scott had feared.

* * * * *

It had been decided to transfer the *Belfast* to Plymouth for more extensive repair. The hull was strengthened temporarily by fitting longitudinal bulkheads and girders over the fractured area, along with reinforcements to the bent parts of the decks and patches in the damaged plating. ERA Finch was still with the ship when she left on 28 June and headed north. She had only a skeleton crew on board, and there was a great fear of air attack, so the men off watch had to keep a look out. However, a general 'chumminess' developed according to Finch. She arrived at Devonport on the 30th after passing round the north of Scotland, and Finch was pleased when Chief ERA Tom King asked him to be one of six ERAs who would stay with the ship during her long-term repair, together with an ordnance and an electrical artificer and three officers.

In Plymouth, stores were taken out and the machinery was removed from the forward engine room and both boiler rooms. She was to rest on blocks of varying height with soft fir caps. Special watch was kept as the dock was drained, but no further strain could be seen. Careful measurements were taken of every part and compared with the ship's plans. There was good news in that the decks forward and aft of the break still followed the line of the keel, and the structure was not distorted there. 'After some consideration' it was decided to remove the temporary structure fitted in Rosyth and allow the ship to settle slowly into its true shape by easing out wedges in side blocks. After sixteen days of this, the keel was touching the blocks from the bow to frame 66 and from frame 93 to the stern, but it was still hogged around frame 80. The constructors tried to rectify this by filling tanks with water to force it into shape, but that had no effect. By February 1941, well over a year after the mining, it was decided to remove all the structure in the fractured area and rebuild it. Constructor Nicholls, the Manager of the Constructive Department, saw himself as 'surgeon-in-chief' for a major operation and describes how 'all the members destroyed in the vicinity of the fracture were cut away, and the ship gradually brought together to a compact whole'. In June 1941 he was succeeded by Constructor Payne from Singapore Dockyard, who was horrified that the ship had taken up a dry dock for so long – the navy had only fifty of its own and they were urgently needed for shorter-term repair work. He sent some jobs out to contractors to find more men to finish the *Belfast*.

It is not hard to see why Plymouth had been considered more suitable for the repair early in 1940. It had a very experienced workforce well used to naval work, whereas Rosyth had been placed on 'care and maintenance' since 1923 and had only recently re-opened. Much of the early German air effort was directed at the Scottish naval bases, and the Firth of Forth had been raided several times. Britain's radar chain was perfected so that any raid making the long voyage over the North Sea could be detected in time for fighters to take their positions. A raid on the north of England on 15 August was beaten off with heavy losses, and after that the principal German effort was made to the south. Plymouth had seemed much safer until the Germans stormed through France, bringing them to within a little over a hundred miles of the base. Plymouth became the most heavily bombed town in Britain, raided 21 times by the end of October, before the Luftwaffe switched its main efforts to London. The attacks built up again by March 1941, and on the 21st Finch was at the Palace Theatre watching the entertainer Billy Cotton when bombs began to fall outside. The audience stayed put and the star was 'irrepressible', but at 11 p.m. there was an enormous detonation from behind the stage and panic began to spread. The band played the *Trumpet Voluntary* to calm nerves. Out in the street, 'A wave of burning hot air hit us like a tidal wave, choking, full of the stench of burning buildings, rubber, oil – indescribable in its foulness. On both sides of the street looking towards what had been the city centre, every building was burning.'

The men of the *Belfast* had to carry out fire-watching duties in the dockyard and chose to stay in the ship because it provided some cover from splinters. On the 23rd a bomb fell at the dockside and displaced the high-angle director, which they used as a base. After another raid a month later it was reported, 'Most buildings in the South Dockyard destroyed by [high explosives] or fires, which are not yet under control. Serious damage also in the North Dockyard, [Royal Naval Engineering] College, R.N. Hospital, Royal Marine Barracks, Army Gunwharf and Army Raglan Barracks.' The cruiser *Kent* and the destroyer *Lewes* were damaged that night, and later the cruiser *Trinidad*. The ordeal only ended in the middle of the year, when the Luftwaffe turned its attention to the Soviet Union. The

Belfast was barely damaged in these raids, but services were disrupted, workers lost sleep, and there were numerous delays. Early in 1942, ERA Finch was disappointed to be drafted elsewhere – he had hoped to see the repairs through to their completion and had 'formed a warm regard for this ship above all others in which I had served ...'

* * * * *

By August 1942 the ship was reconstructed and afloat, though only in an enclosed wet dock where more work was to be carried out. A strict programme of daily activity and tests was set: for example, on the week beginning 7 September the anchors and cables were to be embarked, followed by echo sounding trials, preliminary aircraft inspection, tests of navigation lights, then trials of forward and after capstan gear. The ship was put back in dry dock on the 21st for final inspection while tests continued on the galley, gunsights, aircraft cranes and anti-submarine gear. She went back into the dry dock again on 5 October for two weeks, and finally on 7 November she was 'unbasined', or taken out of the wet dock.

As with her original building, the ship had a growing band of naval personnel to 'stand by' her during the repair – though less extensive than in Belfast, because this time she was in a Royal Dockyard rather than a private shipyard. The first to arrive was the gunnery officer, Lieutenant Mountifield who had entered as a Special Entry cadet and was commissioned as a sub-lieutenant in June 1934. After service in the destroyer *Escort*, he attended the gunnery school at *Excellent* in 1938 and was on the staff there when the war started. As usual, the engineering team were among the first, with three lieutenants in June and July to be followed by Commander (E) James H. B. Dathan in August. He had started as a Special Entry cadet at the age of eighteen, just three weeks before the First World War ended. His career had not been promising at first – he was described as 'rather dull and requires a lot of keeping up to the mark', while another report claimed that he was good natured but lacking tact. He was gravitating towards engineering by 1921, and perhaps that was the only way of maintaining his career. However, his position improved: he was promoted to commander in 1935, and at the beginning of the war he was executive officer of the Mechanical Training Establishment at Chatham. He was familiar with the engine-room layout of the *Belfast*, for he had served as chief of her sister ship, the *Edinburgh*. He was familiar with Arctic waters too, in the very literal sense that he had been rescued from them when the ship was sunk by a torpedo in May 1942. He was awarded the Distinguished Service Cross for 'coolness and determination' that were 'a great inspiration to all' and because 'his department was well organised and answered every call that was made on it'. The new executive officer of the *Belfast* was Commander Philip Herbert Welby-Everard, a 40-year-old gunnery officer and member of an aristocratic family that claimed descent from William the Conqueror.

Then, at the end of November the new captain, Frederick Robertson Parham, arrived to take charge. By coincidence, he was a native of Bath like his predecessor Scott. He had entered Dartmouth in 1913 and excelled in seamanship, navigation and gunnery. By 1919, after service in the battleship *Malaya*, he was found to be a very good all-rounder: 'He has carried out his executive duties in a very capable, zealous manner, as officer of the watch at sea. He is very reliable, has displayed [excellent] judgement and sufficient knowledge of how to handle a ship at sea.'

Parham became a gunnery officer, one of a group who tended to regard themselves as the élite of the navy. An ambitious seaman officer would be well advised to specialise rather than remain a 'salt-horse'. Of the options open to him, navigation would call for much time in pouring over charts with no chance to develop leadership. 'Torpedo' actually involved a great deal of electricity, and an officer studying it was likely to be sidelined like the engineers. Physical training was too far from the main function of the navy, but gunnery very close to it. The gunnery officer of a ship was in charge of the main armament, with a large team under him. Parham's career was very much tied up with the gunnery branch in the 1920s and 1930s. He was selected for the course at HMS *Excellent* on Whale Island, near Portsmouth, and within that for the 'long course' for the truly expert gunner. One sceptical officer complained that this course was far too technical: 'If Whale Island's methods were followed in other walks of life, applicants for motor driving licences would be examined in thermodynamics, and the manufacture of motor-car steel, whilst medical students would undergo a course of cutlery before being allowed to handle surgical instruments.' Parham won the Egerton Prize for the best student, then served as gunnery officer of the cruiser *Canterbury* and the battleship *Nelson* followed by a period as commander of the Experimental Department in *Excellent*. By this time, it was reported, 'Should be very valuable in higher ranks, able loyal, level headed and clever. Tactful.' He had his first command with the destroyer *Shikari* in 1937 then went on to become executive officer of the cruiser *Southampton*. He commanded the crack 'Tribal'-class destroyer *Gurkha* in the Mediterranean at the beginning of the war but saw no action before he was promoted captain and went to staff duties in the Naval Ordnance Department early in 1940, where he gained valuable experience in developing gunnery radar. Naval staff officers were usually moved on to gain sea experience after about two years, and Parham was selected to command the

Belfast in the autumn of 1942 as the ship neared the end of her long repair. He was a 'very gentle sort of gentleman' according to Able Seaman Burridge. To Signalman Tyler he was 'the sort of man who would always take an interest in other people'.

The gunnery, torpedo and navigation officers were all regular Royal Navy but were mostly lieutenants rather than lieutenant commanders, for experienced officers had to be spread thinly in the wartime navy. The torpedo officer, Lieutenant Edward Palmer was a rare example of a regular officer who had risen from the lower deck. The son of a shoemaker in Northamptonshire, he began his boy training at HMS *Ganges* in 1932, where he gained the nickname of 'Handy Andy' because of his various skills. In 1936 he was one of twelve men selected for a year's officer training before being commissioned as a sub-lieutenant. He had already won the Distinguished Service Cross for helping sink a U-boat.

The senior officers in a cruiser like the *Belfast* were all regular naval personnel at this stage, though in the rest of the navy reserve officers were beginning to take command of new escort vessels, landing craft and torpedoboats. However, even the *Belfast* saw an increasing number of officers from the Royal Naval Volunteer Reserve. A few had trained before the war, like Lieutenant A. E. Bugler, the only permanent RNVR officer in the ship, who had achieved his current rank in the Sussex Division in 1937. Early in the war it became necessary for the navy to find officers from well outside its normal sources. A few were yachtsmen, but none of these served in the *Belfast* at this time. The most prolific source was what became known as the CW scheme, after the Commissioned and Warrant Branch at the Admiralty. Potential officers were identified among the ratings at the training bases, often men with a far higher standard of education than normal recruits, and after basic training they were sent to sea for at least three months as ordinary seamen. Richard Wilson describes the draft sent to the *Belfast* late in 1943: 'Our nine who came to the ship are rather an odd mixture. An [old Etonian] and a Wykehamist [from Winchester School], both fairly true to type, neither very distinctive, one serious and slightly naïve Yorkshireman who reads HG Wells *Outline of History* with pencil notes, one humourist, one strong silent man, one fool, two miscellaneous and me. Odd how people vary, isn't it.'

If they passed that test and a subsequent interview they were sent to HMS *King Alfred*, a set of training bases on the south coast near Brighton, still wearing the lower deck 'square rig' uniform, distinguished by a white cap-band and the title of 'cadet rating'. There they underwent an intensive course in navigation and in the duties of an officer. Up to 30 per cent might fail and be sent ignominiously back to the lower deck, but if successful they donned the uniform of a naval officer, which Alec Guinness (later Sir Alec, the actor) considered to be 'gorgeous'. They were known as 'Temporary sub-lieutenant RNVR' – the use of the RNVR being largely a device by the navy to distinguish wartime officers from regulars; some of the pre-war RNVR resented the use of the term for men who were not volunteers in any real sense. *Belfast* had two temporary lieutenants and four sub-lieutenants from the RNVR. The senior one, Peter Brooke Smith had already served in the cruiser *Glasgow* and the destroyer *Opportune*. RNVR officers were to be found in other branches. They dominated the medical staff of the *Belfast* with a surgeon commander, two surgeon lieutenants and a dentist, A. D. McIntyre – Richard Wilson commended his ability as he 'thought nothing of extracting wisdom teeth while the ship was doing a 30 degree roll'. The most junior engineering officer was also temporary RNVR, along with an instructor lieutenant and a paymaster lieutenant and sub-lieutenant. Despite a certain amount of variety, Captain J. G. B. Powell of the Royal Marines was disappointed with the wardroom when he joined the ship late in 1942. He found the younger officers were either married or very juvenile; 'shop' was talked all the time, and he feared it was the only thing Commander Welby-Everard could talk about.

Cruisers and battleships were the last to be manned mainly by regular navy personnel, but even they were beginning to see changes by 1942. As Captain Oram put it of the cruiser *Hawkins*,

In effect the ship was steamed and defended by a cross-section of British provincial life with a handful of South Africans thrown in as leaven. The Jolly Jack of peacetime was a rare bird indeed, so rare that one was tempted to pipe a tear of affection for the breed, now a practically extinct prototype. The wartime sailor, faithfully modelling himself upon his glamorous predecessor, was conscious of the ready-made aura which attached to his own interpretation of the part. He was often dismayed to find that the dazzling mythology surrounding this sea business did not quite come up to expectation. There was much to be said for the 'new boys', though. The model set for them to follow was good and by his exacting standards we were able to run our complicated machines on a very weak mixture of RN spirit!

Most of the wartime entrants were conscripts, though there was an element of choice – each man could choose the navy or air force in preference to the army. The navy was popular, as a Mass Observation report of September 1941 showed. The army was discredited after its defeat in France and by memories of the Western Front in the last war. The popularity of the Royal Air Force was declining due to its perceived failure to stop night bombing raids.

But the men of the navy, it was felt, were 'as always doing their job magnificently' – every seaman was 'worth six British soldiers, and three British airmen'. This created a favourable atmosphere, and for most of the war the navy only took about a third of the men who applied, so it had quite a high quality of entrant.

Men were recruited for 'hostilities only', or the duration of the war, and were sent to training bases around the country, sometimes purpose-built, sometimes converted holiday camps. Each class was a very mixed bag according to Alec Guinness, who was at HMS *Raleigh* in 1941:

> We came from every sort of background, numbering among us butcher's assistants, a housepainter, a maker of pianos, a couple of schoolmasters (whom I thought rather intolerable, with their condescending airs), an aggressive, foul-mouthed Post Office clerk from Manchester, who could have served Hitler well, a Scottish Laird of great distinction and a dozen or so drifters from all over. Most were great swillers of beer. When in small, intimate groups, they chatted quietly of their mothers and sisters; once they were gathered in larger groups, however, the conversation, loud and hyphenated with four-letter words, was of football and the crudest sex. Nearly all wished to be taken for old salts within days of joining up.

The issue of the rather strange naval uniform was a defining moment as described by John Davis: 'Getting into the jumper was an all-in struggle, no holds barred, a wild waving of arms followed finally by a condition of complete helplessness.' Future prime minster James Callaghan wrote, 'We were taught how to tie knots and we discovered how to launder our new, dark-blue collars so that they appeared as faded and washed out as those of any veteran seaman ... All these matters were important to us.' Potential seamen learned seamanship such as knots and splices, and rowing a cutter. They learned gunnery, which in the tradition of the navy was largely about foot drill, or 'gravel grinding' as they called it. They also learned naval tradition and vocabulary – official terms such as 'port' and 'starboard' and more specialised ones like 'boot-topping', 'broaching-to', 'ground tackle' and 'mousing a hook'. There were unofficial lower-deck terms such as 'the owner' for the captain, 'Jimmy the one' for the first lieutenant, and 'the sky-pilot' for the chaplain. The senior chief petty officer of the seamen branch was the 'Chief Buffer', and the master-at-arms, responsible for discipline on the lower deck, was 'the jaunty'. 'Winger' or 'Oppo' was a friend, a 'party' was a girlfriend, and the navy was known as 'the Andrew'. Men also had nicknames according to their surnames or other features.

> 'Shiner' Wright, 'Dusty' Miller, 'Pincher' Martin, 'Nellie' Wallace, 'Topsy' Turner, 'Pusser' Combe, 'Hookey' Walker, 'Smouge' Smith, 'Paddy' Walsh, 'Nobby' Clark, 'Bungy' Williams, 'Jack' Hilton. All Thomases are 'Tommo', and all members of the Day clan are 'Happy'. Tall men are alluded to as 'Lofty', short men as 'Stumps', 'Sawn-Off' or 'Shorty'.

The trainees left the bases as Ordinary Seamen or the equivalent in other branches, described officially as 'Men not fully trained, but generally employed at sea'. As one officer of a training base wrote, 'F[robisher] 88, fashioned and welded together in five weeks, was returning to its individual components, but each man was taking away with him more than he brought in. Each could look after himself and his kit; whatever his category, each could swim, and pull and sail a lifeboat; each knew enough about fighting a ship not to be a nuisance at sea. And, above all, they had a sense of belonging, a rock-bottom foundation for living together, in preparation for the time when they would be locked together for months on end in a steel box far from land.'

The nautical language of the training bases – 'decks' for floors and 'going ashore' for leaving the base – began to make sense to Richard Wilson when he arrived on the *Belfast*. 'To come suddenly to a great ship afloat, where these terms had real meaning, and where the whole routine was the daily life of men who were engaged in the serious business of war, was like entering a new world.' Stoker Arthur 'Larry' Fursland of Bridgewater in Somerset was drafted to the ship in October, from Stamshaw Camp, a temporary barracks and training base near Portsmouth. He had already served in the cruiser *Newcastle*, where he had to take part in the 'bloody awful' task of boiler cleaning. Then he was drafted to one of the notoriously unstable four-funnelled ex-American destroyers. After that a big ship like the *Belfast* seemed 'formidable', and he soon settled in to No. 26 Mess. The usual career path for a stoker was with the boilers, then in the engine-room proper and then with the auxiliary machinery. Fursland had reached that stage, and he was ordered to look after a diesel generator down a seven-rung ladder in the bowels of the ship. It was very noisy and he attributed his later deafness to it. Stokers were trained separately, in two parts: Part I, lasting five weeks in 1943 and four weeks in 1945, was in naval discipline and was similar to that for the seaman; Part II lasted six or seven weeks and taught the men about work in the boiler and engine rooms.

✳ ✳ ✳ ✳ ✳

The single most important development in naval technology in the three years since the *Belfast*'s mining was radar. From having none in 1939, she now had the latest equipment, with no less than sixteen sets of ten different types. Essentially there were two main functions, to search and to control gunnery, and two main areas, the sea and the sky. Developed from Type 271, which essentially won the Battle of the Atlantic with its ability to detect a surfaced U-boat, Type 273 was used for surface warning. It had a parabolic aerial rather than the cheese-shaped erection of the Type 271, which gave greater depth and range, and would prove its value in action. The operator had to be close to the aerial and sat in a characteristic Perspex 'parrot's cage' above the rear of the bridge. Type 281 had its transmitter at the top of the foremast and its receiver at the head of the mainmast. It was used for long-range air warning. Type 284 was fitted on top of the main armament directors to give ranges for firing – direction was measured more accurately by sight. Four Type 283 sets were used to control 'barrage' fire by the 6-inch guns, making a wall of exploding shells in the path of enemy aircraft. Type 282 controlled the 'pom-pom' guns on either side, and there were three Type 285 sets for high-angle radar-controlled fire, one on each side of the bridge and one aft. In addition there was a jammer for enemy radar and three different types of IFF (Identification Friend or Foe) to give the ship's identity to friendly radar or interrogate approaching ships or aircraft.

George Burridge of Haslemere in Surrey was one of the young men who would operate the sets. He was selected after an aptitude test in the training base HMS *Glendower* in North Wales and sent to HMS *Valkyrie* at Douglas Head on the Isle of Man where various sets could be operated over relatively safe seas. One seaman described his experience there:

First impressions were that it appeared to be of bewildering complexity with a mass of coloured knobs, dials, meters, switches, co-axial cables, handles and cathode ray tubes. It was the size of a bulky wardrobe and the transmitter, buried in the basement, the size of a small room. The Instructor gave details of how the instrument was switched on and gave a practical demonstration with the CRT [cathode ray tube] lit up with a vivid emerald green tinge, on the left side a large blip caused by the ground returns and the top of the trace, an 'A' trace, looking like grass, which was the term for it, this was the equivalent of noise in a radio set plus odd returns from mountains and the like. Turning a large wheel in the front of the set rotated the aerial so that it was pointing at the mountains of the Lake District some 60 miles away and on the CRT appeared a large blip on the 60 mile range; our first echoes.

Burridge arrived at the *Belfast* late in 1942 to find the ship in 'a real mess' with dockyard workers all over it.

It was not just the navy that had changed in the nearly three years since the *Belfast* was almost sunk. The great battlecruiser *Hood*, including many of the *Belfast*'s former crew, was sunk by the *Bismarck* in May 1941 before being sunk herself by the combined forces of the Home Fleet and Force H from Gibraltar. Carrier-borne aircraft delivered the most crippling blow, and battleships were needed to complete the task, but the cruisers *Norfolk* and *Suffolk* distinguished themselves in shadowing her, and the *Dorsetshire* finished her off with torpedoes.

Britain was no longer alone in Europe after the Germans invaded the Soviet Union in June 1941. Churchill, despite his hatred of communism, immediately told the British people, 'The Russian Danger is ... our danger', and vowed to offer as much help as possible. This involved sending convoys of supplies to Russia – through great discomfort and danger, as the men of the *Belfast* would find out. The Soviets fought back far better than expected, and by November 1942 they were beginning to break the siege of Stalingrad. The United States entered the war after the Japanese attack on Pearl Harbor in December 1941, which brought American troops, aircraft and a few ships to Britain. Meanwhile they defeated the Japanese decisively at the Battle of Midway in June 1942, and by September they were deeply engaged in their first offensive operation, to take the island of Guadalcanal. The British fought a separate war in the Mediterranean. The heavier ships of the Italian navy were defeated quite easily, but their light forces were more dangerous, including human torpedoes that severely damaged two battleships in Alexandria Harbour and caused ships to be diverted from the Home Fleet. The land war in North Africa moved backwards and forwards until November 1942 when General Rommel was forced to retreat from El Alamein with his Afrika Korps, just as Allied forces landed at the other end of North Africa. In home waters, the navy was humiliated in February 1942 when the powerful battlecruisers *Scharnhorst* and *Gneisenau* were able to sail through the Strait of Dover without serious damage. The Battle of the Atlantic was still raging as U-boats had a good deal of success in stopping vital supplies to Britain. Allied forces were in the ascendant in Russia, the Pacific and the Mediterranean by the end of 1942, but the issue was still in the balance in the Atlantic.

* * * * *

Thus the Second World War was close to its climax as the *Belfast* commissioned formally at 0900 on 3 November 1942. An hour later a large draft of men from the naval barracks came on board to make up the bulk of the ship's company – though individuals and small groups would continue to arrive over the next few weeks. The total number was now raised to 800 plus 17 for the Fleet Air Arm flight.

The engines of the ship were unchanged, and the engineer complement was exactly the same. The marines gained a few men, with their non-commissioned ranks raised from 82 to 89. Captain Powell was quite happy with his detachment at the end of the year: defaulters were rare, the men were 'extremely proficient' at gunnery, and their turrets were 'simply streaks ahead' of those manned by the seamen. He wrote, 'I am very lucky in this show with having an efficient sergeant major and gunnery instructors. Even the corporal of servants is excellent so that I haven't had to go to battle stations over my "hotel" interests.' The seaman numbers rose most, from 332 to 371, including 47 in the new anti-aircraft 'non-substantive' rating. Thirty-eight radar plotters were also allowed for, including some who might be trained on board. The accommodation below decks had been rearranged, with the different branches changing places in some cases, but the principles were still the same, with ratings forward of the engines and marines, stokers and seamen separated.

That day the crew were issued with a provisional watch bill and were probably pleased to find that they were in three watches – red, white and blue – instead of the more traditional two. This would allow more free time and leave when on normal duties, though it would make little difference in combat zones where constant alertness was needed. Stoker James McCarthy was No. 364 on the ship's books; he was in No. 29 mess, his kit locker was numbered 449 and his bathroom locker was 628. He was allocated to the second part of White Watch and was stationed in the after engine room for normal steaming, and also for general quarters or action stations, fire quarters and collision quarters. If the order to abandon ship were given he was to fall in at the port waist, near the centre of the ship. This must have seemed a real possibility to McCarthy, who kept a four-page pamphlet called *If You Have to Abandon Ship ...* It contained advice such as 'Never give up hope, however tough the going may be ... Sleep dressed or [in] an emergency with your lifebelt always available, if not actually worn ... If you have to swim through oil, keep head and eyes high and mouth closed ... Remember that men have been picked up off bare rafts after four days without sleep, food or water.'

While in the dock in Plymouth, overnight leave was normally granted to two of the three watches. There was plenty more to do as stores and ammunition were loaded, compasses were calibrated and gunnery parties went ashore daily to train on the range at Wembury. Basin trials were carried out by tilting the ship, and on the 25th she steamed out of the dockyard to secure to a buoy in Plymouth Sound. The dockyard workmen left the ship by boat, though not for the last time as their help would be needed over the next few days. One task relevant to the *Belfast*'s own experience was to 'degauss' her, to reduce her magnetic field so that she was less vulnerable to mining. This was done in a range just outside the Sound. In one respect her appearance had changed radically since the mining in 1939, for now she was painted in a camouflage pattern using dark and light grey and two shades of light blue. The pattern for individual ships was probably drawn up by the Directorate of Camouflage. It was intended to break up the outline of the ship by using a disruptive pattern, and also to have at least one of the colours difficult to see in any possible light conditions.

The crew and most of the officers probably had no idea where the ship was going to fight, though according to Leslie Coleman they were issued with tropical clothing, which caused much speculation. The special sea duty men were called at 0820 on 10 December, and an hour later they slipped the cable attaching them to the buoy to head out into the English Channel. They soon turned to starboard and headed west, which opened up all sorts of possibilities of exotic foreign service, but then they were told they were heading for Scapa Flow and the Home Fleet. At 1222 they were three miles south of the Lizard promontory in Cornwall when the course was altered from 244 degrees to 281 degrees, west-south-west to just north of west and following the coast. The ship altered course again to 022 degrees at Wolf Rock, then steered across the Bristol Channel.

The ship's log does not record particularly strong winds for the crossing, only Force 6, but the swell was coming directly from an Atlantic storm and 45-foot waves were hitting the ship beam on. The new crew had not got its sea legs yet. Some of them had never been to sea before and George Burridge records seeing 'the whole ship strewn with bodies being seasick, all the gangways, all the passageways'. Water and vomit made the messdecks uninhabitable. Even hardened seamen were affected, and the captain told them

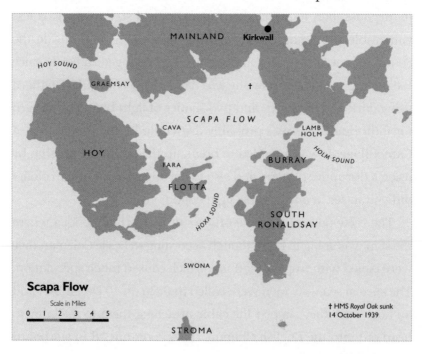

MAINLAND Kirkwall

HOY SOUND

GRAEMSAY

†

SCAPA FLOW

CAVA

LAMB
HOLM

HOY

HOLM SOUND

FARA

BURRAY

FLOTTA

SOUTH
RONALDSAY

HOXA SOUND

SWONA

Scapa Flow

Scale in Miles

0 1 2 3 4 5

† HMS *Royal Oak* sunk
14 October 1939

STROMA

'not to be ashamed of what has happened, we're all seasick, even the professionals'. Experienced hands like Stoker Fursland might be influenced as men started to vomit around them; he was seasick for the only time in his life, but it was even more uncomfortable as he could bring nothing up. One officer told them that the best thing about these conditions was that submarines could not operate. The sea swell moderated as the ship steamed into the Irish Sea, but it took longer for the men to recover. They passed the Mull of Kintyre at 0400 on the 11th with the swell down to 22 feet, though it went up again to 32 feet as they went out into the Atlantic. They exercised dawn action stations at 0815, but it is not clear how many men were fit. The sea was much flatter after they rounded Cape Wrath to turn east, and at five to four that afternoon they completed the 792-mile journey to enter Scapa Flow and drop anchor half an hour later.

The geography of Scapa Flow was the same as it had always been. The anchorage was a roughly square area measuring about ten miles on each side, enclosed by the Orkney Islands. The hills were low-lying except for the island of Hoy to the south-west. There was good anchorage within the Flow, with a suitable depth of water, slight currents and shelter from the worst effects of the wind. The passages to the east where *U-47* had entered to sink the *Royal Oak* were being blocked by the permanent 'Churchill Barriers', but friendly ships could enter the harbour through lines of mines and anti-submarine booms by way of Hoy Sound to the west and Hoxa Sound to the south. The islands abounded with bird life and archaeology, but that did not usually tempt the young men of ships like the *Belfast*. The small towns of Kirkwall and Stromness offered little to the visiting sailor, while the new naval base at Lyness on Hoy had some maintenance and leisure facilities, which had improved over the years, as D. A. Rayner of the destroyer *Shikari* observed when he visited in August 1943 after a three-year gap: 'Where there had been miles of muddy roads and open fields there were now hard roads and serried ranks of good huts. There were canteens for the men and there was also a giant mess for the officers. A busy town had sprung up in the salty wilderness, and there were even Wrens about on roads where before only the male of the species had ever been seen.' But there was nothing to get excited about, and one sailor recounted, 'Harbour routine at Scapa was the same day after day: clean guns; clean ship; watch-keeping; divisions; evening quarters; store parties and sometimes a day on the Island of Flotta doing military training and fraternizing with the local crofters and A.-A. gunsite crews based on the island.' This would be *Belfast*'s main home for more than a year. The crew already knew who would lead them in battle.

5

RUSSIAN CONVOY

BELFAST HAD AN INTENSIVE and thorough programme of working up based at Scapa and with much emphasis on gunnery. The 6-inch guns were controlled from the director tower above the bridge, with another aft in case of damage or action from astern. The forward director was now fitted with radar to assist in ranging a target, with the bedstead-like aerial of the Type 284 across the top. After the target was selected by the captain, the director turned towards it. At action stations it contained seven men. The gunnery officer was in overall charge and seated in front of a window to the ship's gyro compass, with a view outside through slits in the armour. To his left was the rate officer (who might be a petty officer). His job was to follow the target, noting any change of course. On the other side was the spotting officer who would observe the fall of shot, whether 'over, 'short' or 'straddling'. At a slightly lower level within the tower, the director layer sat at his sight. He was invariably an experienced gunnery petty officer – his responsibilities were great as he kept the director trained on the target. 'On the Director Layer, more than any other individual in the ship, except perhaps the Control Officer, depends the success of a gunnery action … He must practice in all weathers and especially at night, because he is the eyes of the guns … If his opponent in the enemy ship is quicker and steadier than he … his ship will be sunk instead of the enemy's.' The director trainer sat on the other side of the tower, with only slightly less responsibility, and the two had to work as a team. There was a cross level operator whose main duty was to 'hunt the roll', making sure that the guns were fired at the right point in the ship's movement. His success depended on 'intimate knowledge of the behaviour of the ship under all conditions of roll, and an enormous amount of practice'. The party in the tower was completed by a telephone man to pass on messages.

Pointing the gun at the target was not nearly enough. The shells might have to travel up to fourteen miles to their target and the enemy could move by perhaps half a mile during their journey. Numerous corrections had to be applied, including own speed, range, wind direction and speed, and enemy speed, inclination and predicted movement. Data was fed to the fire-control table in the transmitting station deep in the ship. This was a kind of manual computer, in which members of the Royal Marines band turned numerous handles to input the data. The result was transmitted electrically to the trainer and layer in each turret, who followed a dial to set the bearing and elevation of the gun. Once it was loaded and on target, a signal was sent back to the gunnery officer, who pressed the firing button. All the guns in the salvo fired at the same moment, making it easier for the spotting officer to assess the aim; a buzzer rang when they were due to hit. Midshipman Garnons-Williams operated the spotting plot at one end of the fire-control table – his job was to mark the fall of each shot from a light signal sent by spotters around the ship, telling whether it was GG (over), SS (short) or KK (straddling and therefore on target). Corrections were applied as necessary before the next salvo was fired.

Sub-calibre firing was used inside the Flow as in 1939, with the lighter gun attached to one gun in each turret in turn, but this time there was much more opportunity for full-calibre firing, using several methods all of which had their advantages and faults. A battle practice target might be towed some way astern of a tug, as was done on 14 January, but it tended to move very slowly. It was faster if pulled by a launch, which was done to exercise the 4-inch armament on 30 December. A radio-controlled target ship might be used, and this was perhaps the best method, but none was available to the *Belfast*. Other possibilities included 'throw off' firing in which the ship set her guns about six degrees off the true aim on another ship. On 6 January the *Belfast* was paired with the *Glasgow* for such an exercise, and it went well until the last shot, which was 1,000 yards short because the fuse cap had been left on. With 'throw short', the dummy shells were arranged literally to fall short, giving practice in finding the line of the target. It came in different forms. On 3 February this was done with the *Uganda*, when the sub-calibre guns were fitted but the range was set as for full calibre so that the shells aimed at 10,000 yards range fell at 5,000 yards. The next day they used a different form, firing full calibre with reduced charge – when the *Uganda* was at 18,500 range, the shells fell at 15,000 yards. 'Throw off' and 'throw short' both allowed a certain amount of realism in dealing with enemy manoeuvres, but it was impossible to assess the fall of shot accurately. In the end that could only be done in an actual battle when all the elements came together.

The anti-aircraft guns were exercised by firing at a sleeve target towed by an obsolete aircraft, such as the Blackburn Roc used on 18 December. The ship practised manoeuvring against torpedo attack in which various different aircraft, including Swordfish biplanes and the more modern Beaufighters, dropped smoke flares and the ship twisted and turned to avoid them. The ship's own torpedoes were tested on several occasions, not without problems. On 26 December one went round in circles and sank before it could be recovered. On the 30th one torpedo ran well but the other doubled back and ran across the *Belfast*'s bows, but at least both were recovered this time. Finally on 4 January Midshipman Garnons-Williams recorded, 'Both torpedoes were recovered after doing a successful run (a change)'. Other anti-aircraft practice included barrage fire, in which the 6-inch and 4-inch guns were controlled by Type 283 radar to set up a 'wall of fire' at a fixed range, usually 2,000 yards, from the ship. A pedal was pressed in the 'auto barrage unit' to fire the guns at the correct moment.

Various problems were encountered on the way. On 17 December the capstan engine failed to work, not for the first or last time. During full-calibre firing on 23 December, the table was set incorrectly so that three salvoes could not be observed. During a night-encounter exercise a shot went off by mistake and hit the cruiser *Carlisle*, apparently without doing any damage. Then it was found that there was not enough electric power to run the *Belfast*'s searchlights and all four gun turrets at the same time. Just after midnight, to complete a disastrous day, the starboard paravane got 'caught in a wiggle' and delayed the re-entry to the Flow until 0100.

Working up was interrupted by the traditional naval *saturnalia* on Christmas Day. Only the midshipmen of the gunroom decorated their mess, but after morning church the newly joined Midshipman Herbert Smith attended the captain's Christmas Day rounds party. 'The youngest boy in the ship was dressed as the master-at-arms. The commander and first lieutenant were impersonated by two seamen and a marine was dressed as the captain of marines. All the ships officers followed the captain, who was preceded by the sergeant major of marines making hideous noises on a bugle, around the messdecks.' Then the midshipmen were invited to the wardroom, which was so crowded that it was difficult to open the door. Many of the officers had dressed up – Smith did not notice Captain Powell of the marines as a bigoted, eccentric Home Guard colonel, but he commended the first lieutenant as a dockyard workman and the warrant shipwright, who was almost naked. They slept in the afternoon, and in the evening the usual class barriers were ignored as the chief stoker was invited to the gunroom for drinks with the midshipmen.

Work resumed, and on 4 January 1943 they exercised refuelling a destroyer at sea. Midshipman Smith noticed that the crew of the smaller ship was more efficient: 'The destroyer with fewer hands carried out the job with less shouting and fuss than the *Belfast* with her large numbers of men congregated on the forecastle and flight deck. However except for the parting of the heaving line when the hurricane hawser was being passed across the evolution seemed to go quite smoothly.' The *Belfast* herself was refuelled by the tanker *Blue Ranger* on 22 January, and the midshipmen described these exercises in some detail in their journals, for this kind of old-fashioned seamanship was much appreciated by the examiners.

All this was done in the worst of the winter weather. Sometimes it was difficult to see the bow of the ship from the bridge because of the snow. Midshipman Garnons-Williams was at the sharp end in more senses than one:

> We let go the port anchor, I had to lean over the guard rail and hold a torch which shone onto the cable, and also shout out how the cable was growing. We went to 10 shackles, and then let go the starboard anchor under foot. I had to do the same on that side. By the time we had cleared the forecastle I was hoarse, wet through and bitterly cold.

The situation improved when the first lieutenant stood him a whisky and three beers in the wardroom, and he began to warm up. Sometimes whole days were lost due to bad weather, giving the crew an occasional rest.

There was a damage-control exercise on 21 January when compartments were flooded to list the ship by ten degrees and the crew went to action stations. Announcements were made that certain areas were flooded, and the men had to simulate pumping them out. There were night-encounter exercises with other ships, while the midshipmen practised signalling with flags and buzzers. One of the last exercises was shore bombardment, conducted on the tiny but much-battered island of Stack Skerry, 40 miles west of Scapa, and disturbing the thousands of gannets that nested there. The programme was completed during February, and *Belfast* was now ready to face the enemy again.

* * * * *

On 12 January 1943 the crew paraded as Rear Admiral Robert Burnett came on board to the shrill sound of the boatswain's whistles and his flag was hoisted at the masthead. He had started as a *Britannia* cadet forty years earlier, just before Captain Scott, but he had a far less complex personality. Academically he was undistinguished, but he was a keen sportsman, having qualified as a physical training instructor in 1910. He commanded torpedoboats and destroyers during the First World War – according to the great Admiral Andrew Cunningham, 'The best officers to be found in big ships have come from submarines and destroyers.' Like Scott, Burnett had his problems with groundings and collisions, but in later life he was as proud of that as he was of his alleged lack of 'brains'. He displayed a photograph of the grounded *Torpedo Boat No. 26* in his cabin with the caption, 'Alone I did it.' Despite this, as early as 1920 he was considered 'in all respects fitted for promotion to the highest ranks in the service'. He spent much of the inter-war years organising sports and physical training across the navy but was appointed executive officer of the new battleship *Rodney* in 1928 under the future Admiral Cunningham – the outgoing captain was not flattering when he asserted that 'the ship had already as many brains as it needed and that was why he was selected'. But Cunningham considered him to be 'a man with a good hold and an excellent way with his men'. This earned him promotion to captain and he spent much of the 1930s on overseas stations and in staff jobs. He was promoted to rear admiral in November 1940 and posted to take charge of the minelaying operations of the Home Fleet at Scapa and then to command the destroyer flotillas and finally a cruiser squadron. Unlike Captain Parham, he had much recent war experience, and in the right theatre of operations, where he was well-known as a daring and resourceful tactical commander.

As a long-course gunnery officer, Captain Parham might be said to represent the kind of 'brains' that Burnett claimed not to have, but the two worked well together. The captain did not mind the admiral's great popularity with the lower deck as 'I loved him so much myself' – Burnett was 'a tremendous personality' and 'a fighting admiral'. According to Ordinary Seaman K. J. Melvin, 'Lower deck opinion was that our much admired "Nutty" Burnett was game enough for anything – a view reinforced by his own admission that that he kept his brains in the seat of his trousers.' Signalman Lance Tyler was in the admiral's boat's crew and often took him ashore in Scapa to play golf where the admiral saw that he was entertained to a 'most magnificent meal' in the kitchen of the officers' mess.

When Richard Wilson missed his boat back to the ship at Scapa one night, a 'large burly figure' offered him a lift and turned out to be the Admiral: 'By small gestures of this sort he had acquired considerable popularity with the lower deck.' He was 'not at all remote or superior, but genial and forthcoming'.

The hoisting of the rear admiral's flag was an honour to the *Belfast*, but it had its down side as he moved into the stern cabin and his staff took up precious space – though the cabin was quite small compared with some admirals. The staff included Lieutenant Commander William Hawkins, a Special Entry cadet of 1925 who had already distinguished himself in command of destroyers and won the DSC at Dunkirk. He was about to be awarded the DSO for his part in Operation 'Harpoon', a convoy to Malta. Hawkins was the Staff Officer (Operations), and Burnett also brought a paymaster lieutenant commander as his secretary, a signals officer as Flag Lieutenant and a junior paymaster as Assistant Secretary. Cabins were now in short supply, and there was less space in the wardroom. Moreover, some of the ship's senior officers had to take on extra duties with the squadron staff – Parham was designated Chief Staff Officer, and the senior gunnery, torpedo, navigation, medical, accountant and marine officers had extra duties on squadron work. The admiral brought ten more ratings with him, including his personal coxswain, two 'writers' or clerks and seven domestic staff. For the lower deck, according to Able Seaman Burridge, it involved more work because the flagship was expected to be better than the other ships, and officers and petty officers were under more pressure. Burnett had strong views on how a ship should look even in wartime. One of his first orders was that the grey camouflage paint on the decks should be scraped off to reveal the bare wood.

This created extra work for the crew, but there was a feeling that they too liked their ship to look well.

* * * * *

The control of the ship's movements was exercised from the upper bridge, or 'compass platform' as it was often known. It might be done by the officer of the watch in normal day-to-day sailing, and by the captain during difficult manoeuvres or in action. The upper bridge was at the top of the forward deckhouse, five decks above the forecastle deck. The *Belfast*'s layout was regarded as advanced when she was built, for the Admiralty had ordered the magnetic compass moved to the upper bridge, while the wheelhouse below was to be fitted with a pelorus (a tool for maintaining bearing) to take bearings, sliding windows and a 'Kent clear view pane' for the helmsman. These modifications were to be applied to other ships in due course. The upper bridge had a view that was cut off 32 yards ahead of the bow and 35 yards aft of the stern. Its area narrowed towards the bow, and it was rounded at its forward end, which reduced wind resistance. It had stanchions for a sun awning above, which was not often needed in northern waters, and glass screens all around, but otherwise it was open to the weather – officers believed they had to feel the wind in their faces. The after part had the tower for the Type 273 radar, with searchlight sights and air-defence positions on either side. Forward of that was the circular support for the main armament director tower, with a shelter for the captain inside it. On either side were torpedo control positions. The foremost part, from where the ship was controlled, had a platform in the centre with wooden decks so that they would not interfere with the magnetic compass, which was positioned in the middle. Behind that was a hooded chart table, with a wooden seat for the captain or the officer of the watch on the port side. There was a captain's sight on each side of the bridge, so that he could point it at whatever target the main guns were to aim at, and the bearing was transmitted automatically to the gunnery officer.

There were several means of communication within the ship. The bugle was still regarded as useful, and as late as 1945 the 61 authorised calls included modern ones such as 'Flying Stations' as well as the more traditional 'Officers dress for dinner'. Another long-established method was the boatswain's whistle, which could be used to direct deck operations with calls such as 'Heave round the capstan' or 'Hoist away', or for ceremonial functions such as piping an officer on board. The ship's bell also had a certain amount of ceremonial value and was used to mark the passage of time, being rung every half hour of a watch until it finished with eight bells. General announcements, such as calling groups or individuals or reporting events, could be made by the loudspeaker system or Tannoy. Orders to the engine room were transmitted by means of a telegraph in the wheelhouse below the bridge; a bell would ring in the engine room as the dial was pushed to 'ahead' or 'astern'. Speed could be 'slow' or 'full', in which case the engineers produced a number of revolutions as pre-arranged between the captain and the chief engineer. The normal setting, however, was 'half speed', in which case attention was turned to the revolution indicator, which was wound to the number of revolutions per minute the bridge wanted to maintain to give a particular speed. Specific actions, such as the dropping of depth-charges, could be ordered by buzzer. The ship also had a telephone system. Calls routed through the telephone exchange were mostly for administrative purposes between different departments. Direct telephones were set up between the different parts of the engine and boiler rooms, installed in sound-proof cabinets so that they could be heard and with lights that would flash when a call was made. There was another system between the different parts of the signal organisation: the wireless telegraphy office, with coders, signal distributing office and transmitting station.

These modern methods were not fully trusted in action. The old-fashioned voice pipe was the preferred means of communication for sending rather peremptory orders to the different departments. The voice pipe was the main way of sending helm and engine-room orders to the wheelhouse in normal sailing or in action. As refitted in 1942, the *Belfast*'s bridge had voice pipes leading to the wheelhouse, the various radar plotting rooms, the chart room, signal house, plotting office, meteorological office and the captain's and admiral's sea cabins.

The admiral, captain and navigating officer all had sea cabins in the bridge structure where they could live in simple conditions without having to be called from their more spacious quarters aft. The admiral had a separate bridge in the enclosed deck under the upper bridge, but that seems to have been shared with the wheelhouse, so it was probably not ideal. He also had his own plotting room just aft of that for his staff to calculate the position of friendly and enemy ships and aircraft. Burnett usually worked from there, according to Captain Parham, and he rarely came on the upper bridge. The ship had its own plotting office aft of that. It was centred on the Admiralty Research Laboratory plotting table, which had not changed much since Midshipman Syms had operated it in 1939:

At sea in Belfast my watch-keeping station at defence and action stations was the plot, a small compartment in the bridge structure under the compass platform where we kept track of our own movements and those of other friendly and unfriendly forces so far as we knew them. There were three of us to share the watches in the plot, the young school master lieutenant and two midshipmen. It was up to 'schoolie' to teach us how to manage the [Admiralty Research Laboratory] table on which our ship's movements were automatically recorded by a moving spot of light. Most of the operational signals came into the plot and were accumulated in their appropriate logs; we were well aware of the local and general situation and it was up to us to display on the plot anything that might affect the ship.

Aft of that was the remote-control office from where the radio equipment was operated. Then there was the aircraft plotting office where contacts, both friendly and enemy, had to be marked at great

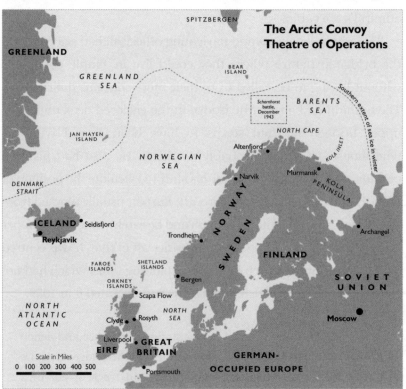

speed. Finally on that deck, the signal house was a base for the visual signallers, who used lamps and flags to communicate with ships in sight. On the deck below were the 'offices' for the different types of radar – Type 281 for long-range air warning, 284 to direct the main guns and 285 to control the anti-aircraft guns. Type 273, for sea warning, was situated in the 'parrot's cage' above the upper bridge. With information coming in from so many different sources and orders going out, the communication system might be under great strain during an action. Burnett was clearly not satisfied with the bridge arrangements, and early in December 1943 he had them altered at Lyness in Scapa Flow, 'in anticipation of the approval of my Lords'. It is not clear what changes were made, but they may have improved the facilities for the admiral.

* * * * *

The first convoy to carry guns, tanks and aircraft to the hard-pressed Soviet Union had set off from Liverpool in August 1941, but after that they usually assembled in Iceland or western Scotland. They were routed to Archangel in the autumn and Murmansk in the depths of winter. According to Winston Churchill it was 'the worst journey in the world'. Weather was often bad in the North Atlantic where the bulk of the U-boat war was fought, but it could be far worse around the north of Norway. Like the Mediterranean convoys, the ships for Russia were subject to many kinds of attack – by dive-bombers, torpedo-bombers, U-boats and destroyers – while there was also the threat of the great battleship *Tirpitz*, sister ship of the *Bismarck*. In the summer the ships could be routed far to the north but were vulnerable in the long hours of daylight. In winter they were protected by almost constant darkness but had to go much further south to keep out of the ice-pack. Nevertheless, losses were slight for the first few months, until PQ 16 lost seven merchant ships out of 36 in May 1942. After that came the disaster of PQ 17, which had to be scattered because it was believed the *Tirpitz* was out, with the loss of 23 merchant ships out of 36. The convoys were suspended as soon as the last one, PQ 18, had reached safety.

It was decided to resume the convoys towards the end of 1942, using the darkness to protect against air attack – though larger numbers of U-boats were concentrated in the area, and there were several major surface ships in Norwegian waters. The first convoys of the new series, coded JW 51A and B, sailed on 15 and 22 December and managed to avoid enemy action, though two ships went missing. The return convoy, RA 51, had to fight its way through attacks by the German cruisers *Hipper* and *Lützow*. Admiral Burnett, then flying his flag in the *Sheffield*, had exchanged fire with the *Hipper*, but it is doubtful if anyone was around to remember the *Belfast*'s successful impersonation of that very ship in 1939. The next convoy, JW 52, was a success: one ship out of fourteen had to turn back, but none were lost on the outward trip and only one on the way home.

The third one was delayed by bad weather but assembled in Loch Ewe early in February. The object of the operation, according to Admiral Tovey, the Commander-in-Chief, was 'the safe arrival of JW 53 at Kola Inlet and RA 53 in the United Kingdom'. The role of the 10th Cruiser Squadron, known as 'Force R' for the purpose of the operation, was to provide cover for the convoy rather than to give close escort, which was done by a force of destroyers. Stoker Fursland used a football analogy – the cruisers were the half-backs in defence, the much larger battleships were the full-backs guarding the goal – which assumed that the convoy and its destroyers were the forwards or strikers. The *Belfast* was ordered to go to Loch Ewe in north-western Scotland so that Burnett could attend the convoy conference.

Belfast sailed from Scapa Flow at 0900 on the 14th but soon hit bad weather so that her capstan engine forward on the forecastle deck was flooded; but that did not stop the ship dropping anchor when she arrived in the Loch on the 15th. A strong north-westerly was blowing and ships' boats could not be used, so Admiral Burnett went to the convoy conference in a fishing drifter. By the time he got back at 1300 the capstan engine had dried out, but it was expected that repairs would take another 24 hours. Burnett believed the capstan would be essential in the rough and primitive anchorages of Seidesfjord in Iceland and the Kola Inlet near Murmansk, so he decided to delay sailing. Work was completed a little ahead of schedule at 1030 next morning and the raising of the anchor began, but the capstan broke down before the anchor was fully up, and the seamen had to get out long bars to insert in the holes and raise it by hand as in the days of Nelson. 'How antiquated can it be?' asked the radar operator George Burridge. It was not possible to delay any longer, and the *Belfast* steamed out of the Loch to head for Iceland. That evening they met the 8th Destroyer Flotilla and accepted an offer to screen for submarines, but the weather got worse and the destroyers could not keep up. *Belfast* steamed at seventeen knots, rolling heavily in 40-foot waves. Most of the crew had got over their seasickness by that time, though according to Denis Watkinson she was 'a terrible ship for rolling'. Ordinary Seaman Melvin wrote, '*Belfast* rode the gale well and suffered only superficial damage to boats, rafts and other upper deck fixtures, but a 50-foot wave smashed over *Sheffield*'s forecastle and carried away the roof of a turret forcing him to return to harbour.' Burnett ordered a change of course to ride the storm out.

They arrived off Seidesfjord in eastern Iceland in the afternoon of the 18th, expecting to refuel and assemble the cruiser squadron. It was a narrow, steep fjord with a population of 90, dependent on the herring fishery. The approach was reasonably easy in daylight, but it was known for strong winds, up to 90 miles per hour, which funnelled down between the hills. As the *Belfast* arrived they met a destroyer coming out to tell them it was impossible to get the tanker alongside in these weather conditions. Burnett eventually decided to send in the small cruiser *Scylla* and five destroyers, which were in danger of running out of fuel, and stayed outside in company with the 8-inch-gunned cruiser *Cumberland*. Eventually at midnight the destroyers reported that conditions had improved, but it was six next morning before visibility allowed the two cruisers to anchor off the Fish Factory Jetty and let the tanker *Scottish American* come alongside. Midshipman Smith thought it was a 'beautiful place with high mountains on either side and a quaint little red roofed village strung out along the foreshore'. He went ashore to find 'a very pleasant town and the inhabitants were friendly', though goods in the shops were few and very expensive. Admiral Burnett, however, was in a 'constant state of anxiety' while in the anchorage, as the 8-inch gunned cruiser *Norfolk* dragged her anchors and other ships were seen to be in difficulty. He did not feel he could wait for the arrival of the *Glasgow* – convoy JW 53 was already at sea. Instead he was allowed to take the *Norfolk* under his wing. This began a 'day of ill-omen' for the *Belfast*. The capstan engine failed again, and the whole cable had to be raised by hand. Then the cable of the port anchor got tangled around one of the flukes, presenting 'an interesting seamanship problem'. Worse still, the engine room reported that it could not raise steam because of water in the fuel oil. Fortunately the anchor held while the problem was solved. The

Glasgow arrived just as they were leaving, but there was no time to wait for her to refuel. The *Belfast, Norfolk* and *Cumberland* sailed together at 1600 on the 21st.

Soon the crews were experiencing the full horror of the Arctic winter. Stoker Fursland and his mates did not mind too much: they had no real need to go on deck, and the engineering spaces and messdecks were warm enough. But even radar operators like George Burridge had to go on deck when not needed for watch-keeping on the sets. It was 'very, very cold. It was made quite clear that if you went on the upper deck ... unless you had gloves on, if you touched any part of metal with your bare hands ... your hands would just stick to them.' It was considered 'very routine' to chip ice off the guns and fixtures on the upper deck. Ordinary Seaman Melvin wrote,

> For this convoy the worst and most feared enemy was ice – it formed everywhere – on deck, on masts and superstructures and on the turrets and torpedo tubes – creating top weight and threatening to roll ships over on the heavy seas. During daylight hours all available hands were employed on chipping away at the ice and blasting it with steam hoses. But it was a losing battle – as soon as the brief arctic daylight faded into dark, the ice returned.

The radar operators were kept on the alert. Immediately after sailing, an aircraft was identified on the radar and then sighted, but it was not clear if it was an enemy Focke-Wulf or a friendly Catalina. Soon afterwards, a Focke-Wulf was definitely seen, and Burnett's force was considered to have been 'sighted' by the enemy. By the afternoon of the 24th the convoy was about 25 miles ahead and steaming at 9½ knots when the signal 'strike' was heard from the 3rd Destroyer Flotilla. This meant that enemy surface ships had been found on the radar. Burnett formed his three ships into line ahead in traditional fashion, to use his guns to maximum effect if the enemy were found. At the same moment there was a report of a surfaced submarine from the Type 273 radar, but it soon proved to be false. Burnett had grave doubts about whether the enemy was really out as he felt sure they must be aware of the powerful covering forces: 'I could not believe that even Admiral Doenitz could throw heavy surface ships in the dark on such a force.' Nevertheless he took up a position to cut the enemy off from his bases if the report turned out to be true. It was not, and soon the destroyers sent the signal 'negative strike'. However, the message to resume the protective screen was not fully received and Burnett had to break radio silence to check it.

Burnett positioned his cruisers 30 miles off the main German base at Altenfiord. 'Whether the admiral's plan was to keep the enemy ships penned in their base or whether he hoped to draw them out … was never revealed to the ship's company.' According to Ordinary Seaman Melvin, the commander's messenger,

> All through this somewhat dubious exercise the ship was closed up at action stations. We were however, permitted to doze off – indeed some of the 'inside' men even managed to get a little sleep – not the commander and his messenger. Our action station was at the After Control Position on the searchlight deck and it was from here that the commander would have fought the ship in the event of the Captain being killed and the wheelhouse destroyed.

They flaked large ropes round the inside of the control position to create a sheltered area called 'Welby's nest' where they 'crouched through those freezing hours, wrapped in sheepskin coats and helmets', and fortified at intervals by bully beef and gallons of 'pussers kye', or cocoa. They failed to flush out the enemy, and

Melvin for one said 'thank God' as they took up station again on the convoy's starboard quarter, between it and the coast.

There were numerous radar echoes that were identified as ice floes. In the morning of the 25th another small echo on the Type 273 was reported at 3,000 yards, but it was difficult to identify as snow was falling. Course was altered and Burnett arranged his two 8-inch cruisers in a separate group to starboard of the *Belfast* – their heavier guns would be more useful at long range if an action materialised. The snow stopped, and it became clear that the echo was just a shadow inside a squall. Another echo was obtained, but it was soon found to be a wooden raft. That afternoon the force swept back for an hour, while the convoy was found to be 30 miles astern. On the 26th they were driving through pack ice at 28 knots when the Aurora Borealis appeared. Melvin was not impressed: 'We were silhouetted against a magnificent background of multi-coloured lights made all the more intense by the reflection from the ice. We were a perfect target for a lurking U-boat ...' Early that morning Russian pilots were taken on board and the ships entered the Kola Inlet. By 0615 the *Belfast* was at anchor in Vaenga Bay. The convoy arrived next morning with no losses, though six ships out of 28 had turned back.

The Kola Inlet was in the middle of barren country and was further north than the major port of Archangel, but the North Atlantic Drift prevented it from freezing in winter. The inlet was a fjord, 31 miles long and 1¼ to 3¼ miles wide, leading to the rapidly expanding port of Murmansk, which was linked to the rest of the Soviet Union by a railway line. The inlet offered very little relief from either danger or discomfort. There was an air raid on the 28th in which a merchant ship was damaged and there were several hits on the docks. The Russian people were looked on as heroes in Britain and the United States, as the only forces directly engaged with the full might of the German army and suffering enormous losses as they did so. It looked rather different to the sailors in Kola Inlet. Vice Admiral Sir Lennon Goldsmith, the commodore in charge of the merchant ships, blamed the left-wing *Daily Herald* and *New Statesman* for the adulation of the Soviet Union and demands to open a 'second front' in Europe against Germany – though he did not mention that the conservative *Daily Express*, owned by Lord Beaverbrook, was strident in its support. Sir Lennon was shocked at reports of Soviet brutality against their own people and their obvious poverty – labourers unloading ships were seen to make holes in bags of flour and eat handfuls. He also noted a change in the Bolshevik message – the Red Army uniform had been replaced by one very similar to the older Tsarist one, with prominent shoulder boards indicating rank, and medals such as the orders of Suvorov and Kutusov commemorating Tsarist heroes – as Stalin fought the war on a patriotic rather than a communist programme. Meanwhile, the sailors of the lower deck had little contact with Russians, being confined to the area around the ship. The only pleasant moment was when a 30-strong Russian concert party performed on board the *Belfast*, and 'charmed everyone with their excellent singing', according to Burnett.

The conference for the return convoy, RA 53, was held on board the *Belfast* in the afternoon of the 28th, and Burnett addressed the masters of the merchant ships. He was pleased to see some 'old convoy mates' among them, for he had been in the theatre for some time. Next morning the convoy began to leave the harbour, and Burnett's group sailed at 1000 on 2 March. Passengers included 'nine Russians, two American seaman offenders, a British seaman suspected of murder and a mental defective'. Out at sea it was reported that various U-boats had been identified by their radio signals and were shadowing the convoy at 20 or 30 miles' distance. Burnett altered course to take account of this, as the weather got steadily worse. The convoy could make only 6.8 knots instead of the planned 8. Ice was breaking up and small floes interfered with navigation, while a block of solid ice was identified in a fog bank just north of the ship's course. There were reliable reports of two U-boats in the area, but Burnett hoped they were on the wrong side of the ice. He decided to cross to the stern of the convoy to provide cover. There were frequent snow squalls on the night of 2/3 March, and the ships were iced over by next morning. There was more ice on the 4th, though Burnett, who had already had Arctic experience, considered it was 'never really cold', the lowest temperature being 12 degrees Fahrenheit, or minus 11 Celsius. On the 5th an enemy aircraft shadowed Force R all day, and the 4-inch guns were fired at it to no effect – such firing was 'only a token' according to George Burridge.

On the 7th the force entered Seidesfjord to refuel, and conditions were not much better there. The pilot book claimed that it was easy to find because of the 'two remarkable mountain chains' around it, but that was no help in the pitch dark, and the lights were inadequate. The master of the tanker *Matincock* refused to manoeuvre his 30-year-old single-screw ship alongside the much larger cruisers. Instead Burnett ordered his three ships to go alongside the tanker in turn. The admiral commented, 'The handling of all these ships on going alongside a much smaller vessel than themselves in not too pleasant weather was admirable.' The operation was completed by 1530 on the 8th. By the 9th they were all in a good covering position 50 miles south of the convoy, though it was actually 35 miles from its planned route. It had hit heavy weather and many of the ships were scattered. Two of the stragglers were sunk by U-boat on the 9th. That night the *Belfast* warned an American merchant ship that she was heading straight for a minefield. She 'expressed her gratitude'; the British officers did not express their feelings about her neglect. Her signalling, however, was 'of a very high standard'. The squadron was now close to Orkney, but a Force 9 gale was blowing up from the south-west with heavy snow. Burnett took his ships to the east of Orkney to avoid it, and entered through the Hoxa Gate. Midshipman Smith wrote, 'I think most people were glad to see Scapa again, almost as glad as they were to leave it before.' Four merchant ships had been lost, one by the weather and three by U-boats. Burnett commented with his usual understatement, 'Altogether not one of the more pleasant northern trips, anxiety without the thrill of action and when the weather was not foul, ice.' But he agreed that it was a 'pleasure trip' compared with conditions on the destroyers. His chief, Admiral Tovey, informed the Admiralty that, 'The compete convoy cycle occupied 27 days of bitter winter weather at the height of the worst storm season recorded in 20 years.'

6

THE WAR IN THE NORTH

THE CREW OF THE *BELFAST* would probably not have been disappointed if they had known that the Russian convoys were now suspended. The destroyers that escorted them were needed urgently in the North Atlantic, where the U-boat war was approaching a climax with the sinking of 62 British ships of 385,000 tons in March 1943, while the lengthening spring nights made the passage to Russia all the more difficult. The cruisers were not much use against the U-boats. The *Belfast* was typical in that she had an Asdic mainly for defensive purposes, to detect a torpedo attack. She carried six depth-charges on racks and fifteen more in reserve. An anti-submarine ship such as a frigate would carry a much more powerful Asdic and could fire a single pattern of fourteen depth-charges, with 150 more in storage. Most of the cruisers stayed with the Home Fleet and now there was a little time for more formal activities. On 15 March the *Belfast* arrived at Scapa Flow with the *Glasgow* and, according to Ordinary Seaman Melvin, 'We learned that *Belfast* was shortly to have a Royal visit. That meant just one thing – "All officers and men to paint ship". It wasn't long before they were all at it – even the Padre was given a piece of the action – the port side of the after funnel.' However, Melvin, as commander's messenger, was one of the very few people excused. By the 19th, wrote Midshipman Smith, 'The ship was looking like a new pin, much better than she had looked at any time since her refit.' His Majesty came aboard, inspected the ship and had tea with the officers.

The *Belfast* and the other cruisers were now allocated to Patrol White, guarding the Denmark Strait between Iceland and Greenland, to intercept enemy blockade runners and raiders – for it was known that a strong German force including the battleship *Tirpitz*, the battlecruiser *Scharnhorst* and the cruiser *Lützow*, was stationed in northern Norway. Admiral Doenitz had taken over from Admiral Raeder as head of the German Navy, and it was believed that he would adopt a more aggressive strategy. And it was also believed that Germany's aircraft carrier, the *Graf Zeppelin*, was nearing completion.

Belfast's new base was Hvalfjord in Iceland, where she arrived on 21 March. This sixteen-mile-long fjord was just north of the capital Reykjavik. There was shallow water on both sides of the entrance but good anchorage inside. It was possible for the crew to have leave and travel about ten miles to Reykjavik. On the 25th Midshipman Smith was taken there by the destroyer *Brecon* and then a steam drifter, 'a very dirty affair'. The town had a population of 38,000, nearly a third of the inhabitants of Iceland. It had grown very fast in recent decades and many of the roads were unpaved, but it was surprisingly sophisticated. The crew liked the central heating, almost unknown in British houses at the time but powered by geysers in Iceland. However, the people were not friendly, as their country had been invaded by the British: the Naval Intelligence Division reported that the 'armed protection' from Britain and the United States was not welcomed. They accepted the situation with 'good sense and dignity', but 'their pride restrains them from public gestures of affection towards the occupying forces'. It also reported that, 'There is hardly any prostitution, but promiscuity is common in the towns' – which was not likely to benefit the transient and unpopular British sailors. One advantage was that the NAAFI manager could acquire nylon stockings to sell to the crew. These were unobtainable in Britain and made highly valued presents for wives, girlfriends and sisters. There was already friction between the crews of the *Belfast* and the *Glasgow*, which flared up in the canteen one day when the *Glasgow*'s liberty men arrived first and took up the best places. There was a fight and 'a considerable amount of damage done'.

The crew had to make their own entertainment between patrols. Football was the first love of the lower deck and rugby of the officers, but there were no facilities in such a remote spot. Rowing was another possibility. Rory O'Conor had written in 1937, 'Eleven men only can represent their ship at football, and in cross country running the largest team is thirty, but in a big-ship Regatta a team of nearly three hundred officers and men goes forth in the boats to do battle for their ship ...' Wartime regattas were not on that scale but still involved large numbers. The ship's 32-foot cutters and 27-foot whalers were lowered into the water and the different departments rowed them over a two-mile course. 'Larry' Fursland was in the winning crew for the starboard division of stokers, and it greatly increased his standing. His petty officer had been against him, but now he could do no wrong. However, the *Belfast* was not successful in an inter-ship competition, coming last in eight out of nine races because the whaler had a hole and had to be pumped out. It was cold in the fjord, and George Burridge found it difficult to climb back on board because his hands were frozen.

Patrol White involved a few days in the icy waters until relieved by another cruiser and a return to Hvalfjord. It was not very exciting, because the Germans made no attempt to break out, and often downright unpleasant – the area had almost constant low pressure as cyclonic storms came in from the Atlantic. On two typical days on the *Belfast*'s second patrol, 8 April began with the ship in 35-foot seas, zig-zagging continuously on a set pattern as usual, as a guard against torpedo attack. From 0400 her MLA, or 'mean line of advance', was due north. The crew was roused for the exercise of dawn action stations at 0600, then went back to the third degree of readiness, used when 'contact with the enemy surface forces is possible but not imminent'. She sighted the high-sided, three-funnelled outline of the *Cumberland* at 0715, and the two ships approached one another to exchange signals by flashing light. The *Belfast* went onto an MLA of 240 degrees, altering course occasionally to avoid ice, then to 40 degrees; for the rest of the afternoon it did an hour or so at 40 degrees followed by one at its exact opposite or reciprocal, of 220 degrees. It stayed on 220 degrees during the night and repeated dawn action stations next morning. The ship passed an object thought to be a mine at 0735, while the 040/220 courses were resumed, and the waves rose to more than 40 feet. More objects were sighted at 1645 but were not considered dangerous. With its combination of boredom, storms, mist, cold and ice, Captain Parham regarded Patrol White as 'one of the most arduous and unpleasant duties which the ship had to undertake'.

* * * * *

Thus life went on as the ship settled into a routine. The crew seems to have found its sea legs by this time apart from one chronic case of seasickness who had to be sent ashore. Besides lookouts, duty radar operators and gun crews standing by, the men spent their working hours washing and scrubbing decks when there was no ice to remove. The ship, like all cruisers and battleships, used 'general messing', in which the food was cooked centrally, rather than the older system by which each mess cooked its own food. The 'cook of the mess' was chosen in rotation but no longer had to prepare food, just be issued with the mess's meat, take it to the galley and then collect the food just before the mealtime, including perhaps a 'fanny' of soup. In rough weather he might struggle to take it to one of the lower messdecks. Stoker Fursland was one of those who enjoyed the food, saying 'the bigger the ship the better the grub' and 'I never had better grub.' Even Ordinary Seaman Richard Wilson, used to a higher standard of living as the son of a prosperous doctor, was pleased: 'The food, etc, here is very good.' Roast beef was Fursland's favourite, and he enjoyed duff for afters. According to reports from other cruisers in 1944, the seamen's least favourite was herring in tomato sauce.

'Pusser's' kye or cocoa was issued to men on watch, but the rum ration was far more popular. The 'tot' was issued ceremonially just before lunch, diluted with two parts water for ratings below petty officer. The 'rum bosun' of each mess was expected to collect it in turn and was entitled to 'sippers' for his trouble, a sip from each man's ration. George Burridge declined his rum and was 'teetotal' for naval purposes, getting a small cash allowance instead. He was not discriminated against in the tolerant atmosphere of the messdecks – Denis Watkinson said, 'You were taken for what you were on board ship.' A man was entitled to 'gulpers', or a larger draught from each of his messmates' tot, on his birthday. This got Leslie Coleman into trouble: he was put in a cell overnight with no proper bed for getting drunk but was not formally punished. A large favour might earn a man 'downers', the whole of another man's tot, but that was strictly illegal.

The messes were even more crowded than in peacetime, and Hostilities Only ratings had to get used to complete lack of privacy of any kind. They were in close contact with other people all the time – even the toilets did not have full sized bulkheads so that a man could sit with his arms on the sides. Wilson wrote that 'living in a ship is rather like living in the middle of a wireless set, there is so much machinery'. Each mess had a leading seaman in charge, but sometimes, especially in a new branch like radar, all the men were HOs. Coleman reported that there was no bad friction in his mess, just good comradeship, and that was a common experience. CWs were usually mixed with other ratings and Wilson wrote towards the end of 1943, 'Next to me at this mess table is an enormous hairy leading seaman with a great black beard making a woolly dog for his children's Christmas. It is frightfully good but it is laughable to see him doing it.' Like many CWs he noticed the large amount of swearing. 'They peppered every sentence with obscenities, which were used so often that they became meaningless. A seagull was invariably a 'fucking great shite "awk".' George Burridge found that his mess was very stuffy, but many seamen preferred it that way after having more cold air than they wanted while on watch and only a limited time to warm up again before the next duty.

Conventional naval uniform meant nothing in the north, and Coleman's tropical kit was thrown overboard to save space in his locker. After the first voyage in which they got very cold, the men were issued with quilted and bulky 'long-johns', or one piece underwear, but hardly ever wore them. They donned the more conventional boiler suits, naval duffel coats and any kind of fur or woollen gear they could find. When sheepskin coats were issued Signalman Tyler found them 'magnificent'. Among other advantages, it was possible to make a bed out of one during long hours at action stations, with boots under the head. Wilson wrote, 'It is cold up here, but not too bad really. I have a whacking great sheepskin coat and can sit by the hour on a damp deck and regard the Northern lights with slight disfavour. One keeps warm with cocoa and keeping quite still … Although some low specimen of humanity has collared my sheepskin gloves, I don't get any chilblains. Must be the salt.' Official issue leather seaboots, according to Coleman, were good and quite warm.

Faces were nearly always white on the messdecks, and racism was largely taken for granted in the navy. There were few people of ethnic minorities living in Britain at that time, and they were not encouraged to join the navy. In practice, as well as an Indian engineer officer, the ship carried an African known as 'Johnny', who came from Accra in what was then called the Gold Coast. He formed part of a boat's crew and was taught English and writing by Larry Fursland and his messmates.

Gambling was forbidden but flourished on some messdecks. Fursland won during a single game but gave half the money back and never played again. There was no real opportunity for exercise beyond walking the decks, despite Admiral Burnett's past as a physical training instructor. Some men conducted their own small businesses on board, following a long-standing naval tradition. Fursland charged 6d for a haircut, and his customers included the ship's chaplain. There were tailors to carry out modifications to uniforms, and some even had small sewing machines on board. Some men ran 'dhobying' businesses to do others' washing. Clothes had to be washed in salt water, and the special soap provided was unpopular and difficult to use. However, the drying room was considered to be very good.

Captain's rounds, the inspection of the messdecks and other spaces, took place at sea and in harbour at 2045 as often as possible.

Parham, it was said, was meticulous in looking at everything. At night the messdecks were more crowded with hammocks than ever. The men were always touching each other when all the hammocks were in use, though normally that was only in harbour. Wilson was optimistic as ever in his letters to his parents – 'we are pretty comfortable – hammocks are wonderful things', but he had found that 'the best and most convenient places were the perquisites of old sailors who had been long in the ship'.

With no room on the messdeck, he was forced to sleep in the capstan flat. It was bitterly cold there, and the ice banged on the hull outside, but 'a hammock is the warmest, as well as one of the most comfortable, of beds'; it 'swayed slowly with the movements of the ship along with hundreds of others slung between the decks'. Denis Watkinson sometimes slept on the seats with his gas mask as pillow, while some regarded the table as the best berth. But according to Wilson, 'At sea, sleep is erratic and one gets very dirty.' In the daytime the hammocks were bound up with seven lashes round each, strictly enforced by traditionalist petty officers. If a man found free time to sleep in the daytime, he would have to find a space on a bench, or 'get his head down' on the table.

* * * * *

The Engineering Department under Commander Dathan had its own organisation. He was responsible to the captain for the efficient running of the engines and other equipment, but he was expected to delegate much of the routine supervision to his deputy, 'the second', rather like the captain left the detailed running of the ship to the commander. In this case the second was Lieutenant Commander W. L. G. Porter. Engineer officers in cruisers were still largely regular navy, and only one of the four junior engineer officers was RNVR. In a surprising example of ethnic inclusiveness, they included G. K. Uttam Singh of the Royal Indian Navy. It was becoming common to send midshipmen from the engineering college at Manadon to sea to gain practical experience, and the *Belfast* had two of them. The chief and second kept no watch, but the others had various duties. Normally each was responsible for the upkeep of a department, such as boilers and funnels, engines, damage control, auxiliaries or administration. The officer should report any defects in his department in a book kept in the engineers' office. He was advised,

> If a defect is discovered in your dept. don't run for help to the Senior, (if its urgent send to tell him) but ask your C[hief] or E.R.A. his opinion, try to work out a solution yourself, then, armed with these proposals, go and see the Senior, tell him about the Defect and what you propose to do about it. He may or may not agree, but don't expect him to solve your difficulties for you every time without your taking any trouble.

At sea the junior officer would be in charge of a watch both day and night, and new officers were given advice on how to cope with this. 'Find out how long it takes you to wake up completely and adjust the time of your shake to make sure that you arrive at the [engine room] 5 to 10 minutes before the beginning of your watch, thoroughly awake.' An officer should not look 'sleep sodden' even at 4 a.m. and should put his head in a basin of cold water if necessary. He had probably slept in his clothes, but if not, he should not wear his pyjamas under his overalls, as 'they nearly always show at the wrong moment'. He should wear a good pair of shoes with leather soles. He should appear cheerful: 'A smile at the beginning of a morning Watch will set your Watch up much more than a frowsty growl.' He should aim to get a complete grasp of the situation before taking over and make notes of any special orders. He should look out for efficient combustion of oil fuel in the boilers, which was best seen by the appearance of the flame – 'bright, clear and compact, and free from smoke or sparks'.

A normal steaming watch had a chief ERA in charge of each of the boiler rooms with a stoker petty officer as water tender for each group of boilers – an important task because it was very dangerous to let the water level get too low. There was a stoker for each individual boiler and one to act as messenger, with an ERA to look after the auxiliary equipment in the boiler room. Another chief or senior ERA was in charge of each engine room with two or more ERAs to operate the throttles that controlled the speed on orders from the bridge via the engine room telegraph. There was a petty officer or leading stoker in charge of four stokers, who would monitor dials and deal with matters such as lubrication. Other stokers looked after the various items of auxiliary equipment under a senior stoker petty officer with a 'roving commission' to visit the men in charge of such machinery as generators, air compressors, evaporators, refrigerating plant, capstan machinery and steering gear. They were junior stokers with auxiliary watch-keeping certificates, and it was 'vital to build up a reserve of trained Watchkeepers in case of casualties'. Other members of the department were mostly on 'day work'. There was a regulating chief stoker in charge of discipline, plus storekeepers, messengers and a writer or clerk who had done a special course. Messmen looked after the needs of the chiefs and petty officers of the branch, and they should be elderly three-badge men – young men should be given as much experience with the machinery as possible.

* * * * *

The *Belfast* was back at Hvalfjord on 13 April, where she conducted height-finding exercises and harbour drills. On the 23rd she had gunnery exercises off Iceland. On 2 May there was another sailing race between the ships at anchor. After it had started, a strong gust of wind capsized the cutter belonging to the battleship *Anson*. Its crew managed to reach a small cluster of rocks while the boats of the *Belfast*, *Jamaica* and *Anson* went to the rescue. Meanwhile a whaler belonging to a minesweeper also capsized in much more serious circumstances. All the men were picked up, but one was unconscious and died on the way to the *Jamaica*. Despite that, there was another regatta on 9 May, but that had to be cancelled after four races as the weather turned nasty.

On the 11th the *Belfast* left Hvalfjord with the *Jamaica* for interception exercises with the destroyer *Middleton* in the Denmark Strait. These included throw-short firing by the *Jamaica* at the *Belfast*. She was back in Hvalfjord on the 13th, and on the 21st she set sail for Scapa, having been relieved on the station by the *Kent*. She sailed again on 25 May as an anti-aircraft escort for a minelaying operation codenamed SN 111B three miles off the south-east coast of Iceland, and on the 27th she was back at Scapa. She was visited by the new commander-in-chief, Admiral Bruce Fraser, on the 30th, and he explained his policy on leave – he would like to give it every six months but 'he reminded the ship's company that we were at war and the fleet in Scapa had to be maintained at a certain minimum strength …' Burnett, meanwhile, left the ship for a short spell as temporary second-in-command of the Home Fleet.

* * * * *

The *Belfast* still had her flight of two Walrus amphibians, which could alight on either sea or land, along with two hangars, servicing facilities and a launching catapult. The flight was headed by Lieutenant Commander Tom Sargent. There was also a sub-lieutenant pilot and two observers, a petty officer and one RAF airman left over from the days when the navy had to form its own air arm very rapidly on the eve of war. There were three skilled air fitters who specialised in airframe, engines or ordnance; they wore a simpler version of the officers' uniform, which one wearer claimed looked like 'a cross between a taxi driver and a workhouse inmate'. The flight was also allocated six less-skilled air mechanics in the 'square rig' dress of the seaman and two men of the seaman branch as aircraft handlers – one at least was a long-serving 'three-badge AB'.

Flights could be hazardous, and Midshipman Garnons-Williams described a hair-raising take-off in Scapa soon after he arrived in December 1942:

> In the forenoon the Walrus was catapulted off, to carry out an [anti-submarine] patrol. The wind was just abaft the port beam, and was fairly strong, so when it was shot off it was not properly airborne, consequently it dived towards the water and tried to turn up into the wind, so it hit the water three quarters on, and bounced off after being twisted round to starboard. It climbed a little only to turn back to port and in doing so it hit the water again with its wing tip, but by a miracle it recovered and succeeded in climbing out of danger at last to fly away under complete control.

The instructions for launching were rather complex, and it is not surprising that there were mistakes. In May 1943 one of the aircraft was damaged when a tripping lever was left engaged. Recovery could also be difficult. On 7 January both aircraft flew off smoothly and landed on the water but had their wing tips damaged against the ship's side during hoisting.

The days of the ship's flight were already numbered, however. A survey of operations for April 1940 to April 1942 showed that the average warship launched her aircraft on 19 percent of days at sea, and they flew for an average of 20 hours per month. Of course, the *Belfast* was in dock during this period, but her sister ship *Edinburgh* was above average with flights on 22.5 per cent of days, 6.5 launches per month and 22 hours flying before her loss in April 1942. At the Admiralty many officers were in favour of keeping the aircraft and argued that the main function was spotting the fall of shot for the ship's guns, so close integration with the gunnery organisation was desirable. It was suggested that the aircraft might be retained in cruisers but not capital ships, but the final decision was that they should be removed from both to save space and topweight, and to free air and servicing crews for other tasks in naval air stations and aircraft carriers. The *Belfast*'s aircraft were taken away on 6 June 1943, and the catapult was later removed. One hangar was converted into a church and cinema, and the other became a messdeck. Denis Watkinson was happy to move into comparatively spacious quarters.

* * * * *

On 9 June the ship left Scapa to cover another minelaying operation known as SN IIIC. She was back by the 12th when Burnett re-hoisted his flag. By now she was in need of some maintenance work and Parham suggested to the new commander-in-chief, Bruce Fraser, that the *Belfast* and the flagship *Duke of York* might travel to Rosyth together. The admiral replied, 'That would be very nice indeed, but I don't think that would be fair on the railway company, to expect them to lay on enough special trains for both ship's companies to go on leave at the same time.' The *Belfast* left Scapa to enter No. 1 dock at Rosyth on the 18th. Captain Parham had already told the crew that 'the usual system for cruisers when they give leave is to split the ship's company into two and divide the leave period between them'. In this case, he said, 'We are in the fortunate position of being divided into three watches.' Only one watch was needed on board at any given time, so he suggested a plan. 'One watch, to be drawn from a lot, will be given the whole leave and the other two watches will get half the leave each.' This was met with cheers. Since the ship was in dock at Rosyth from 18 to 30 June, two watches had six days' leave each and the other had twelve, so most of the men could briefly return to their families.

Back in Scapa, the ship took up her harbour routine. There was some attempt to keep up traditional naval discipline in port, and divisions were held each Sunday, when the crew mustered on the quarterdeck in their best uniforms and were inspected. Now there was no chaplain for the Roman Catholics, so they were taken ashore or to a depot ship for mass. Church attendance was not compulsory in theory, but to most men it was in practice. Fursland resented this. He obeyed the order 'Fall out the Roman Catholics', though he was not of that faith, then he spent his time hiding until the service was over. He claimed he was not against religion, just compulsion. Burridge recognised that it was 'close to compulsory' and attended a service that was rather like matins in the Church of England. According to Fursland, off duty the chaplain was 'down to earth' to the extent that he indulged in swearing and smoking, and he once had to take him back to his cabin drunk.

* * * * *

In harbour, each of the junior engineer officers had duty as officer of the day. He would take over from his predecessor just after divisions in the morning and go around the department to see what was happening. He had to know what 'notice for steam' the ship was at, how many hours were allowed to light boilers and heat up the water in case of sudden sailing. The engineer should take an interest in the food being prepared for his men in the galley, inspect them at evening quarters and take a tour around the department during the dog watches. He should have an early supper then report to the chief or second engineer. The engines would still have to provide certain essential domestic services such as heat, light, power and water. Auxiliary watchkeepers were needed for this and might be divided into four watches in harbour. Two watches were on board alternating on 'watch and watch' each day, then the other two watches the following day. This allowed reasonable shore leave, and 'if ratings come aboard after having a quantity to drink they do not have to go on watch until the next day at noon'. If major repairs had to be done, the engineer officer had to look after the welfare of the men doing them. Before entering ports he should pass round 'the buzz' that work was needed in order to 'prevent the disappointment of men who have organised "dates" ashore'. When work started he should make sure that their meals were ready and take an interest in the work without too much supervision – 'Ratings invariably resent being continually watched and petty interference is equally disturbing.' And a junior engine officer should 'on no account go ashore, except on urgent duty, when the ratings of his department are being employed effecting a repair of a major character'.

One of the least pleasant duties for the stokers in harbour was boiler cleaning, which, according to regulations, had to be done every 750 hours of steaming. The *Engineering Manual* gave some idea of the unpleasant labour involved:

All fittings inside the boiler are removed for cleaning, and the internal surfaces of a boiler are scrubbed clean with wire scrubbers, scrapers and light chipping hammers being used if necessary in cylindrical boilers. Special wire brushes are used for the tubes of water-tube boilers. Men working in water-tube boilers must not be allowed to take in with them anything which may fall into the tubes, and all articles used in the boiler should be mustered and accounted for before the boiler is closed.

Long leave, allowing the men to travel to their distant homes, was only given when the ship was undergoing major repair, as at Rosyth. Otherwise there was 'liberty' or short leave in port – in Scapa it was usually from 1315 to 1830 for one watch, with an hour extra for chiefs and petty officers. A drifter might take the men ashore to the improvised naval base at Lyness, where there was a canteen and a cinema, though many were pleased just to be in open space and get their feet on land. According to Wilson, 'We went ashore in a pinnace to amuse ourselves as best we could at the NAAFI restaurant, at the fleet cinema or at a third rate ENSA show.' The ship was expected to mount a shore patrol to maintain discipline. Each member was issued with gaiters and a belt, but according to Leslie Coleman some took them off and joined the others in a bar. There were films in a cinema constructed for the army and occasional shows by the Entertainments National Service Association, ENSA or 'every night something awful'. Despite the high quality of scriptwriter and cast, Larry Fursland was bored stiff by a production of *A Tale of Two Cities* starring John Mills. On 9 June there was a dance for Wrens on board the ship which Midshipman Smith regarded as a great success – but events like that were aimed at officers rather than ratings. Early in 1943, Captain Powell of the Royal Marines apologised for not writing to his parents enough. 'Such little to write about. Where we are it is pretty distant and bloody cold, it has started snowing. There is almost nothing to do ashore even when we get there.' He played rugby against another ship, though the ground was not level and both its sides were waterlogged. He took two baths afterwards but still did not get all the dirt off. Sailors spent a good deal of time writing to their families, as the only way to keep in touch during long years of war. Incoming mail was equally important to them, and in September at Hvalfjord, Burnett was furious that none had come due to alleged inefficiency at Scapa, until a minesweeper arrived with 87 bags. According to Scott's orders of 1939, the ship's postman was to be a Royal Marine Corporal who would go ashore when the ship arrived in harbour 'to collect mails and information as to the times of receipt and despatch of mails which he will promulgate by notices on letter boxes'.

* * * * *

The *Belfast* sailed again on 7 July. Burnett was to act as senior officer of Force Q, part of Operation 'Camera', which was intended to simulate an invasion of Norway. This was much feared by Hitler and was aimed at distracting enemy resources from the real invasion of Sicily that week, so the ships made every effort to make their presence known to the enemy. One Junkers 88 was sighted, but that was the only enemy activity seen. On 5 August the *Belfast* and the 10th Cruiser Squadron left Scapa for Operation 'Quadrant', escorting convoy TA 58 – actually the *Queen Mary* taking Winston Churchill and a staff of more than 200 to meet President Roosevelt in Quebec. They sighted the great liner only briefly on the 6th after she sailed from the Clyde. Smith noted that in a gale, 'The seas did not affect the *Queen Mary* at all but they knocked the cruisers about that were going at full speed.' They returned to Scapa Flow two days later after the *Queen Mary* had passed through the danger zone.

On 12 August the King visited Scapa again, and it was reported that he remarked on the smartness of the *Belfast* as he passed her. Next day he visited the Royal Navy theatre on the island of Flotta and was entertained by a concert. Midshipman Smith reported proudly, '*Belfast* provided several items and our band was especially praiseworthy.' On the 14th they exercised at sea with the King on board the *Duke of York*. Captain Parham told the crew the King had said, '"Your ship looks magnificent", which he said was good enough for us'.

There were more minor operations. On 15 August the *Belfast* left Scapa for Operation 'FN', to prevent a possible breakout by the cruiser *Lützow*. They stopped off at Skaalefiord in the Faeroe Islands, where Captain Powell of the Royal Marines was tragically killed in a cliff fall. On the 22nd they left Scapa for Iceland with the *Norfolk* and the destroyer *Impulsive* to take part in Operation 'Lorry', covering the passage of the destroyers *Musketeer* and *Mahratta* to Kola with mail and stores, and again there was no action. On 8 September they sailed from Hvalfjord with the *Impulsive* to rendezvous with the Home Fleet. It had been reported that enemy units were on the remote Norwegian island of Spitzbergen where the Allies had established a meteorological party. The enemy force included the mighty *Tirpitz* on a rare foray and the battlecruiser *Scharnhorst*, but it was too late to intercept them and the operation was cancelled. The *Belfast* returned to its familiar fjord. After a fruitless search for a blockade runner they were back in Scapa on 27 September after five weeks based in Iceland. As Smith wrote, 'We were very glad to return to Scapa as it offers more attractions ashore then Hvalfjord, especially in winter.'

On 2 October they left for Operation 'Leader' under the command of Admiral Fraser, and the crew had a glimpse of a new kind of warfare. A concentration of troopships, tankers and storeships supplying the isolated German garrisons had been reported in the Bodo area of Norway and was to be attacked by the American aircraft carrier *Ranger* supported by the battleships *Duke of York* and *Anson*, which formed a diamond round the carrier with the cruiser. The *Ranger* flew off 52 bombers and fighters, and the ships went to the second degree of readiness, but there was no counterattack by the Germans. The American aircraft began to arrive back at 1000; three of them were missing. Then *Ranger* provided fighter escort for the force and shot down two shadowing enemy aircraft. One fighter was lost attempting to land, but the pilot was picked up by a destroyer. The operation could claim a certain amount of success: intelligence reports showed that three ships had been beached and burned out and five more damaged.

On 13 October the *Belfast* sailed south through the Minches, which separated the Outer from the Inner Hebrides, to Greenock on the Clyde. The Firth was full of shipping, and they saw several of the new escort carriers or 'pocket aircraft carriers' as Smith called them. It was a 'very pleasant break', and leave was given for a watch and a part of a watch on Wednesday and Thursday from 1245 to 0930 next morning, with time for a night ashore in the city of Glasgow. Then they came to the main purpose of the visit, which was to carry out shore bombardment practice, a foretaste of the ship's future. On Friday they weighed anchor at 1000 and sailed for the range at Inchmarnock off the Isle of Bute. According to Smith it was 'a very important affair and was watched by a large number of high ranking army officers'. The ship made its first run with the fall of shot being spotted by an army forward observation officer ashore. The army officers came on board for the second run, which was carried out at much shorter range with the spotting done from the ship. Smith claimed that, 'both runs were a tremendous success and everybody seemed very pleased as we steamed away from the Clyde'.

The *Belfast* sailed with the *Kent* and the *Norfolk* on 29 October in support of convoy RA 54A, 'returning the empties' from Kola Inlet. Arriving at Seidesfjord in Iceland, Burnett was furious when he found that his arrival was not expected; and, though the weather was good, the captain of the duty tanker still refused to manoeuvre alongside the cruisers. Burnett countered by bringing his ships alongside both sides of the tanker and refuelling in record time, but he made it clear to his superiors that a better tanker was needed. The weather was surprisingly warm for five days after they went to sea, and the temperature did not fall below 34 degrees Fahrenheit or one degree Celsius, but the winds became strong and the convoy proceeded slowly. Burnett planned to station himself between it and any possible attack, but neither party could give an accurate position when clouds obscured the sky, so he had to second guess the speed of the convoy. He did not hesitate to disagree with the Admiralty, who estimated it at a maximum of 6½ knots – 'from weather conditions over the last 48 hours, I considered an average speed of 8 knots to be much more likely.' Fortunately the convoy was not detected by the Germans.

Back in Scapa, Captain Parham used faint praise and vague optimism when he assembled the crew on 13 November to review her first year in commission. He told them that, 'considering all things the ship had done well'. He was 'sorry that he couldn't let them know more about what was happening on our various operations … he made a forecast of what might happen in the near future – a month to six weeks in Hvalfjord, then a busy period and then he said he thought we might go into dock for a refit'.

Outbound Russian convoys resumed with the sailing of JW 54A from Loch Ewe on 15 November and JW 54 B a week later. The *Belfast* sailed from Seidesfjord with the *Kent* and the *Norfolk* to cover this, and by 20 November they were at anchor off the northern Icelandic port of Akureyri. Smith found it 'a beautiful spot especially with its background of mountains and the houses with their snow-capped roofs'. It was Iceland's second biggest town, but the shops were even more expensive than Reykjavik. Germans had built the town's magnificent cathedral, and anti-Allied sentiment was strong. It was now very cold and ice was seen in the fjord, with gales every day. Activities were organised to stave off boredom and despair. There was a 'brains trust' of ships' officers who led a discussion group every Tuesday. An arts and crafts exhibition was planned and, according to Midshipman Smith, 'the ship is full of woolly dogs and models of the ship'. On a more positive note, 'We have managed to secure several very good films and there have been many program-mes of entertainment on the sound reproducing equipment.' On 22 November they sailed to replace an American cruiser with the battle fleet for the second phase of the operation, the return passage of RA 54B between 26 and 16 degrees east. They went back to Scapa where the midshipmen left to do their exams, leaving a gap in certain areas such as the gunnery plot. It had been a cold, stormy and generally frustrating year – '12 months of chasing up and down the Arctic Circle', as Lieutenant Palmer put it.

7

THE SCHARNHORST

THE *BELFAST* ARRIVED AT LOCH EWE on 11 December 1943 so that Vice Admiral Burnett could attend another convoy conference. He addressed the merchant ship and escort captains and was pleased to find 'a grand old warrior of 73 who scorned my remarks about the last struggle', for he had taken part in the Spanish-American War of 1898. The *Belfast* sailed before the convoy at 1330 on the 12th to avoid interfering with it and headed towards Iceland for a refuelling stop. Richard Wilson, on his first voyage, was seasick continuously as the ship 'pitched and rolled and lurched through the great seas'. At Seidesfjord, it seemed at first that the refuelling arrangements had not improved because the two tankers could not come alongside even in a flat calm. The *Rapidol*, one of the twin-screw class of Royal Fleet Auxiliaries that Burnett had demanded in October, arrived and fuelling went on. The *Belfast* left at 2100 on the 15th with the *Sheffield* and the *Norfolk*, forming Force 1 to cover convoy JW 55A.

The great battleship *Tirpitz*, with her 15-inch guns and 14-inch armour, had been put out of action by a midget submarine attack on 22 September. She was not sunk, but British intelligence knew she would not be ready for battle for many months, if ever. The main threat now came from the battlecruiser *Scharnhorst*, with almost the same thickness of armour but only 11-inch guns.

These, however, were far more than a match for the 6-inch guns of the *Belfast*, or even the 8-inch guns of the *Norfolk*. The *Scharnhorst* was a great *bête noir* to the Royal Navy. In 1940 she and her sister *Gneisenau* sank the armed merchant cruiser *Rawalpindi* and then supported the invasion of Norway, sinking the carrier *Glorious* and two destroyers. The two ships raided British commerce in 1941 and sank a total of 22 merchant ships. They retired to Brest, then in February 1942 they made a risky voyage back to Germany through the English Channel, and the Royal Navy was humiliated by its failure to stop them. The *Gneisenau* was mined then bombed, but the *Scharnhorst* went north to Altenfjord in northern Norway as a permanent threat to the Russian convoys. The Admiralty made sure that the battleship *Duke of York*, with 14-inch guns, was covering convoy JW 55A in case the *Scharnhorst* came out. The battleship formed Force 2, along with the cruiser *Jamaica* and a destroyer escort, under the personal control of the commander-in-chief, Admiral Bruce Fraser. Intelligence suggested that a foray was highly likely. Burnett, like Fraser, was on the exclusive list of officers who were to be told about 'Ultra' decrypts, the radio signals from the German 'Enigma' system that were decoded at Bletchley Park. It was clear that the *Scharnhorst* was getting ready for action.

Burnett's self-confidence was high, and he was apparently given a good deal of leeway by his superiors. His reports are peppered with phrases like 'I had decided ...', 'I had intended ...' and 'I considered it unlikely ...' He made it clear to the crew that he was looking for a fight, as Richard Wilson recounted:

His speech was a remarkable one. He told us bluntly that he was going to seek an engagement with the enemy if he could possibly manage it. 'I am going' he said 'to trail my coat'. He told us with no beating about the bush his reasons for this attitude. 'Unless I can strike a blow against the enemy, this will be my last voyage. I shall be retired, I intend, therefore, to do my damnedest to bring about an action.' We were astonished – like a figure from another century – 'Fuck this for a lark' was the prevailing opinion on the messdecks.

The ships sailed at 2100 on the 15th for a covering position off the north coast of Norway. The weather was excellent, but Burnett would have preferred more cloud as the bright moonlight might give them away. He had decided to wait there for two hours then head eastward at high speed, but just as he got there he made radar contact with a group of ships 27,000 yards away. It was the convoy, 25 miles south of its planned route. Richard Wilson could see locomotives lashed side by side on the decks of merchant ships, giving a reason for their voyage into these cold and turbulent waters. Burnett headed away to open the range to 32,000 yards when contact was lost. Early on the 18th Burnett planned to head westward again to seek out the enemy, but several U-boats were located by radio direction finding, so he carried out a broad zig-zag to the north and north-east of the convoy route. They overheard the radio of the convoy escorts, making it clear that submarines were in contact. At 1710 that evening a radar echo caused the cruisers to make an emergency turn but eventually it was found that this and other echoes were just rain squalls.

Wilson and his shipmates made the best of the conditions:

We were well fed, we slept like tops in our hammocks, and on watch we were wrapped up in sweaters and oilskins and sheepskin coats and, with few responsibilities, could look at the endlessly beautiful spectacle of three cruisers cutting their way through the heavy sea, while overhead the northern lights played across the sky in darkness. At the end of our watch we would go aft where there was an enormous tub of boiling cocoa, made by directing a hose of steam from the engine room onto raw cakes of cocoa and slabs of sugar. This made a splendid and satisfying brew. My Glaswegian and Liverpudlian messmates, whose extreme ignorance of the world went with strong principles of share and share alike, would, moreover, never touch their food until portions had been put aside in the small mess heater for those up top on watch.

At 1745 Vice Admiral Burnett received a signal from the Senior British Naval Officer in North Russia suggesting that the *Scharnhorst* was out. He was sceptical about this because the convoy was not yet in its most vulnerable position; 'if an attack was contemplated it seemed certain that it would be made in daylight and if so, that the 'Scharnhorst' would not leave her base until dark the day before.' But he could not rule it out, and next day he took up position 40 miles east of the route. He did not go to the westward as he suspected Fraser might take up position there, 'hovering in wait for the *Scharnhorst'*. Nothing happened, and on the 19th Burnett increased speed to 24 knots and headed for Kola.

The three cruisers anchored in Vaenga Bay, where Wilson saw no improvements in the conditions since earlier in the year:

It was excessively grim and squalid. In the grey, leaden obscurity we tramped round among a succession of huts and barracks, surrounded on all sides by trodden snow, blackened with dirt. Dotted about were latrines in the form of little round huts, from all of which there came a strong and pervading smell. A small booth sold the curious Russian cigarettes and small, dingy, unintelligible newspapers ... The only presentable building in the place was the Red Army club, a gloomy establishment decorated with huge

photographs of Stalin and the other Soviet leaders. We returned
feeling that we had exhausted the possibilities of arctic Russia.

* * * * *

Burnett attended the conference for the return convoy, RA 55A, on
board his flagship. It took longer than expected because some of the
merchant ship masters arrived late, and it did not finish until eight
in the evening. That night the Soviets put on a concert on board the
Norfolk. Burnett was pleased to be invited to lunch next day with
the Soviet commander-in-chief, who was 'most cordial, though not
in the best of health'. A female reindeer called Olga had been
presented on an earlier trip, and Admiral Golovko wanted to give
her a 'playmate' – he might have given a 'husband', but male
reindeer were scarce. Petrushka arrived on board the next day to the
admiral's delight, and Wilson was one of the ratings ordered to look
after her.

The three cruisers sailed again at one in the morning of the 23rd,
into a Force 7 wind from the south-west. Soon there were two
convoys at sea, RA 55A on the way home and JW 55B heading out.
Burnett did not think an attack on the homeward convoy was likely
as it had apparently not been sighted, but JW 55B was being
shadowed and it would pass through the most vulnerable area on
26 December. He surmised that if an attack was indicated, Fraser
would head east to enter the Barents Sea. Therefore he decided that,
rather than heading west to cover JW 55A to the west of Bear Island,
he would stay to the north of the outbound convoy's route, hoping
to sandwich the enemy between the battleship and his cruisers. The
cruisers spent Christmas Eve in position, and Wilson wrote, 'We were
knocked about by enormous waves. The ship heaved and shuddered,
water slammed over the bows and broke against the bridge and we

lived with the low wrenching movements and creaks and groans of a ship under stress.' Meals of bully beef and biscuits were issued from time to time. The merriment of last Christmas was out of the question, but the crews at readiness did their best as the festival approached. Lieutenant Brooke Smith's men were high up in the 4-inch director where they were exposed to the full force of the wind and spray. They sang *Hark the Herald Angels Sing* and *The First Noel*, and men from other positions joined in. Brooke Smith managed to snatch a few hours' rest and optimistically hung up his seaboot stocking. At midnight an unauthorised humourist made a broadcast on the ship's loudspeaker – 'I wish you all a Happy Christmas – and many more like it – Ha, Ha, Ha!'

At four in the morning of Christmas Day, Burnett altered course to the west, following the expected movement of JW 55B. Brooke Smith was surprised to find that someone had put a bar of 'nutty', or chocolate, in his stocking. The weather was rougher than ever, and Wilson remained sceptical: 'None of us on the lower deck really expected to meet the *Scharnhorst* although the Captain had told us that Russian reconnaissance had reported she was out and we had a 50-50 chance of running into her. We had been at 2nd degree of readiness for a day or two, which meant that we never undressed, and had to stay near our posts.' Christmas dinner was served, consisting of bully beef and jacket potatoes. Brooke Smith's men tried calling the beef turkey but 'it tasted the same'. At three o'clock they listened to the King's Christmas broadcast over the noise of the wind and were moved to think that their loved ones at home were hearing the same words. That night Wilson slept on the deck in his sheepskin coat and woke up an hour later in two inches of water. Down in the shell room of 'A' turret, a young sailor made the best of it: 'After supper we get our heads down. This is a very complicated operation, as it takes at least a quarter of an hour to get in a reasonably comfortable position free from drips.' At 0217 that morning the Admiralty sent out the emergency signal based on 'Ultra' intelligence – 'SCHARNHORST PROBABLY SAILED AT 1800A/25 DECEMBER.'

* * * * *

With almost constant darkness and often very poor visibility, the *Belfast*'s only hope of finding the *Scharnhorst* was by radar, which was under the command of Temporary Acting Lieutenant Keith Day of the RNVR, later commended for 'his unremitting zeal and efficiency in training and maintenance'. For the moment the most important set was the Type 273, intended for long-range sea search. It was 'centimetric', that is it had a far shorter wavelength than the other sets for it had been designed to detect partly-submerged U-boats in mid-Atlantic. Most radar sets had the cathode ray tube situated well below deck in a special 'office', and there were several of these on the Belfast's wheelhouse flat under the bridge. With the Type 271 series, which included the *Belfast*'s 273, the cable between the aerials and the tube had to be as short as possible. The aerial was fitted in a cylindrical structure made of Perspex to avoid interference with the signal, with the operator in a small 'hut' underneath. The 'parrot's cage' had to be mounted high enough to get a good range, but not so high as to affect stability, and it had to be reasonably close to the bridge. In the *Belfast* it was the highest point in the ship except for the masts, allowing an all-round search. This contrasted with ships such as the *Norfolk* in which there was no spare space on the bridge so the set was mounted amidships and blocked by the bridge and funnels.

It took 21 operations to switch the set on, and it might take 20 minutes to warm up from cold. It was rotated by hand at about 180 degrees per minute, or 90 degrees in rough weather. It could only turn for 400 degrees before the wires became twisted, so it had to return in the opposite direction when sweeping. Operators were warned about different types of interference including tramlines, criss-cross pattern, double echoes, telegraph poles and railings. The set could carry out an all-round sweep or search a particular sector as instructed by the officer of the watch. The operator was given any information that might be useful in interpreting contacts – 'the position and movements of ships in company (or the bearing limits of the convoy), whether any ships or land are likely to be met with, and details of the zig-zag if in force.' The operator was usually told to report all echoes except those from ships in company, other identified echoes and any he might be told to 'disregard'. Operators changed every 20 minutes or half hour to aid concentration, with the new one climbing a fifteen-foot ladder up the side of the tower as the ship pitched and rolled.

At this stage very few ships had the 'plan position indicator', which translated the radar echoes into a map of the area. Fraser's flagship, the *Duke of York*, did have the PPI, and the admiral commented that it gave 'a clear picture of the situation throughout the engagement'. Despite Fraser's requests, the other ships still used the 'A system' to indicate a target. The range was shown by a blip on a straight line running across the cathode ray tube. The bearing of the target was found by the position of the aerial, and only one object could be kept in view at a time, while its position relative to other objects was not obvious without plotting on paper. Therefore the operator reported the distance and bearing of each to the plotting office as well as the officer of the watch, and echoes were marked on the table. Acting Lieutenant Day was in constant telephonic communication with the operators and 'quietly and coolly sifted and passed to the Plot the vital information which it required'.

* * * * *

At 0840 in the morning of 26 December, Acting Leading Seaman Dennis Lloyd was duty operator below the parrot's cage when he detected a signal. If he followed the correct procedure he reported, 'Echo bearing two nine five, distance thirty-five' – there was something at 295 degrees or a little north of west, at 35,000 yards' or nearly 20 miles' distance. The range closed rapidly, and it soon became clear that they were in contact with the *Scharnhorst*, to Burnett's delight. The crew went to full action stations at 0855. To George Burridge there was the usual chaos of 'people flying about in all directions' before the ship returned to perfect order. Down in the shell room of 'A' turret an ordinary seaman who used the pen name of 'Banderillo' noted the preparations: 'Everybody gets up, deflates and puts on their lifebelts which they have been using as pillows, the shell room's crew start unshipping the bars which hold the shells in place in the trays. The magazine and handling room men go down to their respective stations and the hatches are closed on top of them. Everyone is tensed for us to open fire ...'

Captain Parham was on the exposed upper bridge for most of the action, even though 'there was nothing to be *seen* from the bridge, it was pitch dark all the time'. Admiral Burnett was down below in the plotting room, where he was assisted by his staff officer William Hawkins, now promoted to commander. The actual plotting was done by Temporary Instructor Lieutenant Donald MacPhee, but the rest of the staff were 'inexperienced battle novices' according to Burnett. George Burridge was in the radar plot under the bridge and had a good idea of what was going on as he used coloured pencils to mark up radar and visual contacts on a rectangular table against the movement of the ship. He even had a certain amount of view outside after a blast removed the door. Richard Wilson was stationed in the Air Defence Position – 'I sat in front of a machine looking like the instrument panel of a car, and put on range, deflection and so on with knobs, which communicated with the gun, also passing orders to it on the telephone.' He told his father, 'I had a marvellous view … as my action station is right up at the top of the superstructure.'

At action stations in the engineering department, the usual policy was for the duty watch to remain at its posts, while the watch that had been longest off duty would go to provide extra support in the boiler and engine rooms, and the one that was last off would take up stations for damage control including flooding and repair parties, and standing by key pieces of equipment such as steering engines. This had

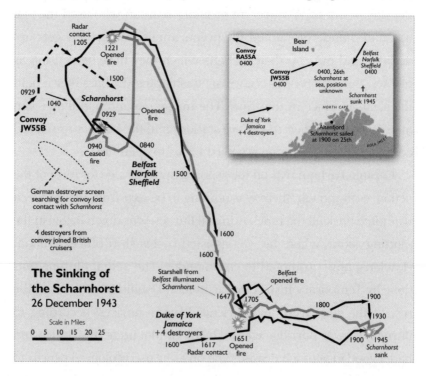

The Sinking of
the Scharnhorst
26 December 1943

Scale in Miles
0 5 10 15 20 25

the snag that a stoker woken up from a deep sleep would not always be clear whether his watch was 'longest off' or not, but it was apparently operated in the *Belfast*. Stoker Fursland would see nothing at all of the action after he went down to his noisy generator deep in the ship. He could not hear the announcements and could only follow the action by the vibration of the engines and the shock of the broadsides. The other members of the team in boiler and engine rooms under Commander Dathan would have to maintain machinery that had not been fully serviced since Plymouth fourteen months ago. They would sometimes have to operate at more than their nominal full power and change speed suddenly as the circumstances dictated.

Burnett informed the crew that they were in contact with the great battlecruiser, and up in the secondary armament director Brooke Smith's men commented, 'So the bastard's turned up at last.' At 0904 Burnett formed his three ships on a line of bearing at 180 degrees, that is to say they were 180 degrees to one another while they steered a course of 070 degrees, which would allow all the ships to engage when they formed a line of battle. At 0915 he changed it to 160 degrees so that it was at right angles to the line of approach. At 0921 the *Sheffield* signalled, 'Enemy in sight, bearing 222 degrees.' Three minutes later the *Belfast* fired starshell to illuminate the target, and soon the bright flares were descending by parachute – but still it could not be seen. At 0929 Burnett signalled his cruisers, 'Engage with main armament.' The *Norfolk* opened up with her 8-inch guns at a range of 9,800 yards, but she obscured the *Belfast*'s line of fire because Burnett had failed to alter the line of bearing after a change of course. Moreover, the *Belfast*'s fire-control radar was not fully fitted with the latest equipment and it was considered ineffective to fire 'blind' on a radar bearing. Nevertheless, Burnett personally saw two hits from the *Norfolk*'s guns. One shell failed to explode but may have told the enemy they were up against an 8-inch cruiser. Another knocked down her forward radar at the masthead. The battlecruiser was faster than the cruisers in rough weather and began to sail away to the northeast. Firing ceased at 0940 after eleven minutes. The crew in the shell room were anxious to know what had happened until Welby-Everard announced, 'After a few broadsides from the *Norfolk* the enemy, whoever she may be, has turned away and we are now chasing her.' Burnett came to believe that it had been fortunate that only the *Norfolk* had fired – the officers of the *Scharnhorst* would assume that there was only one cruiser against them. He believed the enemy ship was trying to manoeuvre to the northward and then launch an attack on the convoy.

Radar contact was lost at 1019 but soon four British destroyers were sighted, having been detached from the convoy escort force. They had not worked with the 10th Cruiser Squadron before, and their leader, Commander R. L. Fisher, was unsure of his status. He signalled to Burnett, 'Intend to await your orders before leading destroyers to attack.' This puzzled both Burnett and Parham, who signalled back, 'Attack what?' Fisher replied 'Anything that turns up.' The *Belfast* had also contact with the convoy, 28,000 yards away. Burnett seemed uncharacteristically cautious as he reported later to Fraser.

Considering my chief object was the safe and timely arrival of the convoy, and being convinced I should shortly make contact again, it would not have been correct tactics to have left the merchant ships during daylight to search for the enemy, nor to have split my force by detaching one or more ships to search, in view of the enemy's high speed and the weather conditions which still limited a cruiser to 24 knots.

In fact, Burnett believed that the enemy would return to try to attack the convoy from the north or north-east, though he was not as confident as he sounded and called Parham down to his plot to ask him, 'Freddie, have I done the right thing?' Parham answered that he was 'absolutely *certain*' that he had. The cruisers began a broad zig-zag ten miles ahead of the convoy, with the destroyers forming an anti-submarine screen. Admiral Fraser was doubtful, for he had much wider responsibilities and had to consider the possibility that the *Scharnhorst* might be trying to evade them altogether and break out into the Atlantic. He signalled to Burnett, 'Appreciate that Force 2 [the *Duke of York* and her consorts] will have little chance of finding the enemy unless some unit regains touch with him and shadows.' Though it did not include a direct order, the use of the term 'some unit' hinted that it might be better for Burnett to split his force. Burnett was far more sensitive than his bluff and hearty manner suggested, and Parham saw how he reacted to Fraser questioning his judgement, 'It was a terrible thing. Poor old Bob, he was a terribly emotional chap, he was jolly near in tears about it.'

From 0920 onwards Burnett's signals were also being relayed to the Admiralty in London, where his old captain Andrew Cunningham was now in charge as First Sea Lord. In addition, Bletchley Park was working so fast that the Admiralty received the German radio signals almost before their intended recipients. The movements of the ships were plotted on a large chart in the War Room. 'At the Admiralty we listened, watched and waited with what patience we could muster. There was nothing we could do to help. There were dismal faces.' But Cunningham knew how to delegate, unlike his predecessor Admiral Pound, who had intervened disastrously to scatter convoy PQ 17 in these waters. The decision-making was left to Burnett on the spot.

Back in the *Belfast*, Commander Welby-Everard considered it was time for food, so he put the ship's action messing organisation into force. He gave the hands 'action dinner' or 'mystery pie' as the lower deck called it – hot soup, meat pies and a jam tart. Chief Petty Officer Cook Albert Coombes and his depleted staff, according to Admiral Burnett, 'did excellent work in preparing and providing food and drink to the Ship's Company under trying conditions. … he put in long hours and it was through his efforts and devotion to his duties that the Ship's Company were provided with essential meals during the whole period of the action.' From the director control tower Lieutenant Commander Mountifield broadcast to his men, 'There will now be a lull in the action while the gunnery officer eats his lunch.' After half an hour a voice was heard on the multiphone from the Royal Marines turret aft, 'Ain't it about time the Gunnery Officer finished his dinner and we got on with the action?' By now it was about 1100 and 'dawn' in the Arctic. The sun never rose above the horizon at these latitudes in the depth of winter, but for about two hours there was twilight that was 'just sufficient to read a newspaper by', as Brooke Smith put it.

* * * * *

At 1137 *Sheffield* picked up a radar echo but soon lost it. At 1205 there was an echo at 30,500 yards, and this time it was held – Burnett's judgement seemed to be correct. He ordered an alteration of course towards it, with the destroyers on his starboard bow. At 1221 the *Sheffield* reported 'enemy in sight'. Burnett had been absolutely right. There was relief in London: 'Our suspense at the Admiralty lifted. We knew, and Admiral Fraser knew, that there was now every chance of the *Scharnhorst* being brought to action by the *Duke of York*.' The *Belfast* fired her starshell to confirm the sighting, and in his open bridge Captain Parham saw the outline of his opponent, looking '*extremely* large and *extremely* formidable'. Under 'A' turret 'Banderillero' heard the order 'Stand by' again, just before the gunnery officer pressed the button to fire her full twelve-gun broadside for the first time in anger. The whole ship shook violently. Down below the generator room, Stoker Fursland found that a ball race had collapsed and seized up, knocking two circulating pumps out of action and causing a risk of overheating and eventual seizure. The loss of the generator would reduce the *Belfast*'s electric power by a quarter, and it was barely adequate at the best of times. It would have put at least one of the gun turrets out of action. Fursland used a kind of initiative that was not always encouraged in the navy. He found a fire hose on the deck above and used it to circulate cooling water to keep the engine cool. 'This operation was not at all simple as it entailed the rigging of a canvas hose and the operation of several valves at a time when speed and calmness were essential in order to keep the machine in operation.' Blast also disrupted the even more vital Type 273 radar at some point, and Acting Petty Officer Radio Mechanic Ronald Colton had to act quickly to restore it.

In the shell room,

There is the most awful crash as our guns go off. I start taking shells from the trays and putting them on the shell ring round the three shell hoists. I repeat this operation every time the guns go off. Conversation starts again. 'This is the first time the ship has fired her guns in anger.' 'I wish they would tell us what we are firing at; anyway, I hope it is nothing larger than a destroyer.' 'It's pretty feeble enemy, it's not even firing back.' From the gunhouse comes a message, 'Well done, A and B turrets; now give X and Y a chance.' So we are one up on the Marines.

There was indeed a problem in 'Y' turret when the right-hand gun misfired and Marine David Eason had to act quickly to prevent a disaster.

The action continued with all three cruisers firing. Reginald Mountifield spent long hours that day in the director tower keeping alert, needing his 'quiet and able appreciation of the opportunities' and 'foresight to visualise beforehand' when they might have the next fleeting contact with the enemy. He was assisted by Chief Petty Officer Arnold Baldwin, who often had to shift from blind radar firing to visual aiming. Deep in the ship, Gunner Frederick Northam was in charge of the transmitting station and had to keep up his men's attention and interest during the lulls in the action, which might be resumed at any moment. He was hampered by the loss of the midshipmen who had gone off to do their exams but assisted by Royal Marine Bandmaster Douglas Colls, who supervised the very inexperienced clock operator and spotting plot operator at the fire-control table.

The *Norfolk* had eight-inch guns, which might just penetrate the *Scharnhorst*'s armour, so she set the fuses to delayed action: thus they would pass into the hull before exploding. The six-inch guns of the *Belfast* and *Sheffield* would not penetrate such armour in any circumstances, so they were set to explode on impact. That would only do superficial damage to the *Scharnhorst*, but they would be very effective against unarmoured destroyers, which might appear at any minute. In fact, the *Scharnhorst* had lost contact with her escort, but there was no way of knowing that. The two 6-inch cruisers both used 'flashless' cordite for the charges that sent the shells on their way; the *Norfolk* only had 'non-blinding' cordite, which did not live up to its name – the gun-control personnel of the ship did not sight the enemy at all during this phase of the action, while those of the *Belfast* and *Sheffield* did. Even worse, the *Norfolk*'s flashes seemed to give her position away, and most of the enemy fire was directed at her. At 1233 she was hit and 'X' turret was put out of action, while the *Sheffield* was 'straddled' with the shells of one salvo hitting the water on both sides, showing that the enemy had found their aim.

The British cruisers gave as good as they got. The *Norfolk* scored a certain hit as early as 1224, and it was seen from the *Belfast*. Others might have penetrated the armour and were not spotted. The *Sheffield* scored at least one hit, and at 1239 four shells from the *Belfast* were seen to explode just as the 'fall of shot' hooter sounded. Over a period of twenty minutes the *Belfast* fired nine twelve-gun broadsides and sixteen more from 'A' and 'B' turrets alone, as 'X' and 'Y' could not be brought to bear because of the ship's course. The early salvoes were fired using the radar for range and visual sighting for direction. The last eight were 'blind' using radar alone as range increased and visibility deteriorated. Despite his excellent view, Wilson was an ordinary seaman with no great knowledge of naval warfare, and to him this skirmish was 'just an appalling racket, and I saw a shower of sparks ahead when the *Norfolk* hit her, splashes round the Sheffield, a few round us, and later a black column of smoke from *Norfolk* when she was hit'.

Burnett was beginning to see that the enemy was being 'most obliging' as he retreated – if he continued with his present course he would eventually run into the 14-inch, 1,590-pound shells of the *Duke of York*. Burnett ordered firing to be 'checked', or stopped, at 1241, letting the enemy think he had damaged or shaken off the cruisers. Visibility was about seven miles. Burnett followed the *Scharnhorst* at seven and a half miles but kept in touch by radar. The *Scharnhorst* still had her after radar aerial but may not have used it because

Admiral Bey was obsessed with the possibility of their signals giving them away – in any case, the British operators could detect no signals from German radar during the operation. Two of the cruisers had trouble with their own equipment. *Sheffield*'s Type 284 gunnery set 'suffered in bearing accuracy', while the *Belfast*'s was out of action for much of the time due to interference from the radio. The well-established Type 273 would have to direct the fire of the guns while still searching for more enemy forces. Down in the transmitting station, Leading Seaman (Radar) Ronald Lomax had to deploy 'his own ingenuity of improvisation when the practised method of operation was failing to give results'. The *Belfast*'s forward turrets had used up all their flashless cordite by this time, but more was stored in the former aircraft bomb room. A hundred and eighty men of the turret crews and damage-control parties were organised in a chain to pass it forward to the magazines. They made sure that no more than three charges were exposed at any given moment, so it took over an hour. The rears of 'A' and 'B' turrets had become clogged up with empty cordite containers and these were removed. 'A' turret was almost flooded with water entering the cabinet during heavy seas, but the trainer, Able Seaman William Saunders, was commended for coping with it. 'B' turret was above that, but Chief Petty Officer John Yeo had to keep up morale and drill under a very inexperienced officer who had only just joined the ship and acknowledged his debt to the chief. But there was no mechanical defect during the long hours, partly due to Ordnance Mechanic Gerald Turvey for 'paying continual attention to the working of the machinery under his care'. Further up in the air defence position, Wilson reported, 'Then we shadowed for seemingly hours and hours.'

* * * * *

In fact, there were more than two hours of relatively uneventful sailing during which good navigation was required if the position relative to the *Duke of York* was to be calculated. Lieutenant Commander John Meares took star sightings during fleeting glimpses of the sky.

The shadowers' problems began during the afternoon. The destroyers were already falling behind because they could not cope with the weather, and at 1603 the *Norfolk* reported a fire and had to drop back and get the ship in a more stable position to fight it. Seven minutes later the *Sheffield* was seen to be losing speed and Burnett signalled impatiently 'Come on.' But one of her propeller shafts was damaged, and she had to slow down to ten knots to deal with it. Burnett signalled to Fraser, 'Am all alone'. If the *Scharnhorst* decided to double back the *Belfast* would be annihilated. Parham thought, 'She'd only got to turn round for ten minutes and she could have blown us *clean* out of the water,' but Welby-Everard decided not to tell the crew about that. After 40 minutes of this the two main British groups were in radar contact as Leading Seaman (Radar) Walter Fulcher found the *Duke of York* on the Type 273 at extreme radar range of 40,000 yards to the south. The *Scharnhorst* was now 19,300 yards from the *Belfast*, and the fleet flagship signalled *Belfast* to 'prepare to illuminate the target'.

Humorous signals were a tradition among naval officers, and Burnett drafted one to his admiral saying 'Dinner is now served' but thought better of it as Fraser would be too busy to appreciate it. The *Belfast* went up to more than full speed, her engines achieving 86,000 revolutions instead of their nominal 80,000. She fired starshell at 1647, aiming it ten degrees to the left of the radar echo so that it would burst right behind the *Scharnhorst* as seen from the *Duke of York*. On the *Jamaica*, Lieutenant Bryce Ramsden of the Royal

Marines saw a 'black silhouette against the flickering candle glow. Even at that distance the sheer of her bows was perfectly noticeable and she stood out clearly for an instant as if removed bodily from her page in *Jane's Fighting Ships*.' Even more striking, her main turrets were still trained fore and aft – she had not expected this moment and was not ready for battle.

Four minutes later the *Duke of York* opened fire, and her gunnery was excellent, straddling the target with the first and third salvoes and knocking an eighteen-inch hole in her hull. It was a terrifying moment for the Germans, a glorious one for Burnett and his crews. Up in the secondary armament director, Brooke Smith's range-taker called out, 'Whoa Neddy!' – he imagined a carthorse being reined back hard at this sudden and shocking development. Others cheered loudly, while Wilson wrote, 'There was a wonderful firework display on the horizon. The commander over the loudspeakers told us the bearings of the *Scharnhorst* and the *Duke of York* and we watched the battle. You could see a great red flash, and then the great salvos of tracer shells going slowly over in a great arc. It was extraordinary. You can see the shells right the way over.' He provided a running commentary for the crews below, while Brooke Smith did a more informed one for his men, which was taken down in shorthand by one of them at the gunnery plot and typed out afterwards. Further below, Stoker Fursland was still alone in his generator room with only the occasional visit of a petty officer to relieve his loneliness. He still he did not know if he had done the right thing in connecting up the fire hose.

The *Belfast* fired one salvo at 1657, but the target was lost. She began firing again at 1705 and in seven minutes she got off five salvoes from 'A' and 'B' turrets and two twelve-gun broadsides, all on 'radar bearing blind' but partly guided by the enemy's gun flashes. The *Scharnhorst* altered course to the eastward, and the *Belfast* and *Norfolk* conformed. Brooke Smith and his men were comforted by the thought that capital ships like the *Scharnhorst* rarely fired on mere cruisers. But 'suddenly my layer called out, "Look at that, Sir!" and I saw great columns of water rising in our wake, a cable length away. My crew's reaction was comical: "The ROTTEN swine! They're firing at us!" they said with great indignation.' The salvo might well have hit the *Belfast* if she had not altered course. Seconds later another was on the way and Brooke Smith's petty officer was not comforting when he took out his watch and counted the seconds since the *Scharnhorst*'s flash was seen. 'If she's made the right correction, the next salvo should hit – now'. The shells splashed in the water astern and the *Belfast* was safe. According to Brooke Smith, 'for the next hour or so the two heavyweights pounded away at each other' while he watched the 'ding-dong' battle from the tower. But even that could pall in the extreme cold, and after a while he trained the director aft to get more shelter from the wind. 'I'm ashamed to say that we professed to be bored in the middle of one of the most decisive actions of the war!' The engines were severely tested during the day, and Commander Dathan's care of them paid dividends. They were normally rated at 80,000 for full power, which was only used in exceptional circumstances. During the pursuit they achieved 82,000 for 1½ hours, and 86,000 for twelve minutes.

* * * * *

The battleships of the *King George V* class, which included the *Duke of York*, had two serious design flaws. Firstly, the Admiralty had insisted that the guns should have an uninterrupted fire forward, so the bow was low and tended to bury itself in the waves. The *Duke of York* had carried Churchill and his entourage across the Atlantic to meet President Roosevelt in December 1941, and at times her speed had been reduced to less than ten knots by the heavy seas. Lord Beaverbrook refused to return in her, proclaiming, 'Wild horses won't drag me aboard that submarine the *Duke of York*.' The *Scharnhorst* in contrast had a high forecastle, a flared bow and a higher top speed, 32 knots compared with 28, so she was pulling away from the pursuers.

Secondly, the ship's 14-inch guns and their mechanisms had been designed to an over-ambitious specification. During the fight with the *Bismarck* in May 1941, the *Prince of Wales* had to break off after the loss of the *Hood*, because two of her three turrets were out of action. Even in the relatively peaceful waters off Iceland in August 1941, the *Prince of Wales*'s 'Y' turret broke down in the presence of the Prime Minister. Now it was the individual guns that were failing. Four of the ten were giving trouble, so that the *Duke of York* only fired 446 rounds against the *Scharnhorst* rather than the 800 she should have.

Soon there were fears that the battlecruiser might still escape as she kept up a speedy retreat while firing on the pursuers from her after turrets. At 1702 Fraser asked Burnett, 'Any more news', but there was none. A chance for a torpedo attack was missed, and the range opened to nine miles by 1800. The *Duke of York*'s gunnery radar failed and the range was too great for visual aiming. At 1840 Fraser signalled to Burnett in despair, 'I see little hope of catching *Scharnhorst* and am proceeding to support convoy.' Burnett was reported to be furious. But already the range was decreasing as the battlecruiser lost speed – her forward boiler room had been put out of action by one of the *Duke of York*'s long-range shells, and she was down to 22 knots. The destroyers caught up, and Wilson saw what happened next:

The destroyer attack was a glorious muddle of starshells, pom-pom tracer, great deep and red flashes and what not, then there was another long pause, with occasionally a sudden flash from somewhere. Then suddenly everything happened at once. Everybody started shooting, the whole scene was lit up by starshell and there was the *Scharnhorst* steaming down our starboard side with smoke pouring out amidships. She fired a single starshell which landed right overhead, and there we were, lit up like Piccadilly and waiting for it. Then the shells came, but the big salvo fell aft and the tracer ones went overhead like cricket balls. I expect their gunnery control was all to bits.

The *Saumarez* went within nine cables or 1,800 yards of the target to release her torpedoes. For the crew of the Norwegian *Stord* it was more personal, so close to their occupied country, and they went within six cables, arousing fears that they might try to ram. Twenty-eight torpedoes were fired and four hits were claimed.

So far the torpedo crew of the *Belfast* under Lieutenant 'Andy' Palmer had been spectators.'Only once, early in the afternoon, did we get into a good torpedo firing position and the *Norfolk* fouled the range! So that we sat back hopefully right through the long action. We had a grandstand view of the gunfire and the very gallant attack by the destroyers in to Oerlikon gun range!' Perhaps they remembered the humiliating day, exactly a year ago, when one of the practice torpedoes went round in circles and then sank. At 1919 Fraser signalled the *Jamaica* to 'sink her with torpedoes'. Palmer and his torpedomen were 'a bit sick. We felt the prerogative of the cruiser flagship to do that ...' But a minute later Fraser issued the same order to the *Belfast*, and Palmer was delighted. 'We had to fire from just outside 6,000 yards and that's rather long to be certain of hitting.' The depths of the torpedoes were set at 22 and 18 feet to match the *Scharnhorst*'s estimated draught of 26 feet. All three of the 21-inch

Mark IX** torpedoes on the starboard side were fired on a bearing of 170 degrees against a target that was regarded as practically stationary. They waited four minutes and heard a single explosion. Palmer was convinced it was their torpedo: 'The tube's crews had a better view of her than I, being low down they saw the *Scharnhorst* silhouetted against the clear sky and both saw and felt the explosion when the torpedo hit.' He wrote to Petty Officer Moule who had left the ship, 'One of your torpedoes finally sank her'. But the authorities disagreed, ruling that 'The claim by *Belfast* cannot be upheld as the settings used should have precluded any possibility of hitting.'

In any case, they had to make sure. The *Belfast* had been the first to find the *Scharnhorst* on her radar, her admiral had predicted the enemy's movements, and she had shadowed her alone for nearly an hour, doing a superb job in the cruiser's main role of guiding the guns of capital ships on to the enemy. It would be fitting if she was able to administer the *coup de grâce*, like the *Dorsetshire* had done against the *Bismarck* in 1941. She turned around and got ready to fire her port tubes, but five more destroyers were going in to launch nineteen more torpedoes. As Burnett put it, 'At 1935 there appeared to be such a mêlée of ships and fire round the target, and you [Fraser] appeared to be approaching me, that I considered it prudent to withhold torpedo fire for a more favourable opportunity.' He headed to the south to find a different line of approach. At 1946 there was a heavy underwater explosion and the *Belfast* fired starshell to locate the target. Nothing could be seen, and at first the men on the 4-inch director thought 'Damn – they've managed to put the fires out.' In fact, the *Scharnhorst* had sunk beneath the waves unobserved by any other ship, leaving behind a pool of oil and a few survivors on rafts. Burnett noticed the 'chagrin of the torpedomen' at being denied a clear victory.

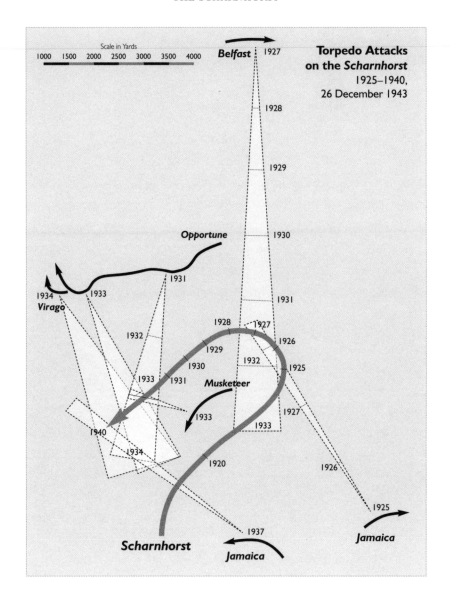

Torpedo Attacks on the *Scharnhorst*
1925–1940,
26 December 1943

Scale in Yards
1000 1500 2000 2500 3000 3500 4000

Belfast : 1927

1928

1929

1930

Opportune

1931

1934   1933
Virago

1932

1928   1927
1929   1926
1930   1932
1933   1931   1925
Musketeer

1933   1931

1940

1927

1934

1933

1920

1926

1925

1937

Jamaica

Scharnhorst

Jamaica

8

TO NORMANDY

AS THEY LOOKED THROUGH THE ICY DARKNESS at the patch of oil left by the *Scharnhorst*, the crew of the *Belfast* felt sympathy rather than triumph. Richard Wilson was sorry for 'those poor devils swimming round in the ice-cold water, with oil all over them and sleet beating down on them'. Marine Bill Withers came out of his turret to get his injured finger dressed.

> I stood on the upper deck looking at the destroyers picking up survivors and it was sheeting down. I thought how lucky we were as it might have been us and the other ships played our searchlights on the water and I could see Jerrys on rafts and some were swimming about … I was shivering with cold and I was dry.
>
> I've got to hand it to Jerry, he went down fighting and her forward turret was still firing when she went down so the gunners must have been drowned, they were either damn good sailors or they were locked in and couldn't get out.

The senior engineer, W. L. G. Porter, let one of the stokers go on deck to see what was happening, but he returned unimpressed. 'He said it was completely dark, snowing hard, and the sea smelt of fuel oil. I think he was glad to return to the heat and light of the Engine Room.' Stoker Fursland emerged from the generator room to find that he had done the right thing with his emergency repair – indeed when Burnett submitted the names of men he considered deserving of honours in order of merit, he was the first rating on the list. That night in the wardroom, according to Brooke Smith, 'a solemn toast was proposed, "To the *Scharnhorst*," and we gravely drank to our enemies who, though misled, had put up a gallant fight and had gone down with their guns firing, as we knew we would have done had the fate of the battle been otherwise.' There was only one fatal casualty on *Belfast* in the action. The reindeer Petrushka, locked up in the hangar, had been driven mad by the blast and gunfire and had to be shot. The hands went to supper at 2250 that night, and at 0045 on the 27th they resumed normal cruising stations and carried on escorting the convoy to its destination. After thirteen hours at action stations, Richard Wilson was as anxious for sleep as anyone else, but he had the middle watch and could not turn in until it finished at 4 a.m.

Burnett addressed the crew over the Tannoy and referred to the honours that were likely to follow: 'I shall get a great deal out of this and you will get nothing. But I want you to know that, in reality, anything given to me is given to the ship and to the squadron. Thank you all for your help.' According to Wilson, 'We felt drawn to the admiral. His complete absence of cant was refreshing. We realised, too, that we had none of us done anything, but each of us twiddle his particular knob and hope for the best.'

This was the Royal Navy's last major action between surface ships, before the submarine, aircraft and eventually the guided missile came to dominate sea warfare. Aircraft had played little part, largely due to bad weather. German aircraft had reported the convoy and found what seemed to be Burnett's Force 1 through gaps in the clouds, but mistrust between the German navy and the Luftwaffe was so great that it was not taken seriously, and signal intelligence was no more successful. Submarines were not in the area and did not intervene in the action, so the surface ships were left to fight it out. The most significant modern feature was radar, especially the *Belfast*'s well-tried Type 273.

At Kola, the ship loaded up nineteen tons of Soviet silver to pay for the deliveries of weapons. She sailed on the 30th and, with no convoy to cover, made good speed to arrive back at Scapa Flow on New Year's Day 1944, passing the Hoxa Gate at 2304 and dropping the anchor in thirteen fathoms of water twenty minutes later. Back in the familiar harbour, the seaman began to reflect on the action. Able Seaman Eddie Gould wrote to his aunt on 4 January, 'It was certainly a great thing to be in, but at the time one wishes he was a hundred miles away, but anyway aunty we can say that's another Jerry off the list.' He enclosed a *Belfast* Christmas card showing the ship steaming at high speed, and he was looking forward to the next day when they would finally celebrate Christmas, perhaps with turkey. The ship's log duly recorded that a 'special "Christmas Day" routine' was in force. Next day the ship set sail for Rosyth, where shore leave was granted, but not the much-awaited long leave that would have allowed the sailors to visit their homes.

There was a general feeling that the role of the *Belfast* had been underplayed in the press, cinema newsreels and radio, as the *Duke of York* and the destroyers were given credit for the sinking. Even within the 10th Cruiser Squadron, Captain Bain of the *Norfolk* was filmed stating: 'We were the first to sight the enemy, we were the first to open fire, we were the first to hit and we were the first to be hit.' The crucial role of the *Belfast* in shadowing, and the high performance of her radar and engines when others were breaking down, was largely ignored. Then there was the question of whose torpedo had finished the job. Bill Withers wrote, 'It was said in the news that the cruiser *Jamaica* gave the 'coup-de-grace' but there's a feeling on here that it was us because after the *Jamaica* had fired her torpedoes we went in and fired three and we wouldn't have fired if she'd gone down ... I ain't worrying much, we were all there and we did our bit and I came out of it with my life so I'm thankful ...' It rankled more with torpedo officer Andy Palmer, who wrote to his former petty officer, 'Naturally, everyone here is cocking a chest and indeed it is a proud victory ... I know and appreciate the work and the enthusiasm you put in on those torpedoes ... We're painting a swastika on X turret, from which the hitting torpedo came! A bit of a line shoot, but a justified one, I think.' It was still there in 1946. Admiral Tovey, former commander-in-chief of the Home Fleet, was appreciative in a letter to Parham: 'I knew that you and your fine ship flying Bob Burnett's flag would never let go of the brute unless the weather made it absolutely impossible for you to keep up.'

As a result of the action, Admiral Fraser became a Knight Grand Cross of the British Empire, and eventually he would be raised to the peerage, incorporating the name of the battle in his title as 'Baron Fraser of North Cape'. Burnett became a Knight Commander of the British Empire for 'great determination and skill throughout the action and in twice driving off the enemy and thus saving the convoy'. All the battleship and cruiser captains including Parham were awarded the Distinguished Service Order, while Dathan, Mountifield and Meares, the navigating officer, were given the Distinguished Service Cross. Only two ratings were decorated in the first announcement of awards on 5 January, neither from the *Belfast*, but at the end of February the King approved the award of the Distinguished Service Medal to eight more. Larry Fursland knew nothing about it until March, when it was posted in the *London*

Gazette. Captain Parham cleared lower deck to announce the awards, and Fursland was sent to St. James's Palace in London to receive it.

* * * * *

The *Belfast* sailed back to Scapa on 24 January and settled down to a slightly quieter life. With the *Scharnhorst* sunk and the *Tirpitz* out of action, there was less need for cruisers to protect the Russian convoys and she spent more time at anchor in the Flow, leaving for occasional exercises. On 3 February she practised anti-aircraft fire against a glider target and on the 10th she sailed on Operation 'Posthorn', escorting the old aircraft carrier *Furious* as she flew off Barracuda torpedo bombers and Seafire fighters to attack shipping off Norway. Not much was found in the low cloud, and only a ship that was already badly damaged was attacked. There was a squadron practice on the 17th when the captain and navigating officer were assumed to be out of action for the purpose of the exercise, and the ships manoeuvred in cooperation with Seafires and Barracudas before carrying out throw-off shootings and firing at battle practice targets.

On 1 March they sailed for Greenock and moored at buoy C4 in the Firth of Clyde. Burnett's time in command of the squadron was finally coming to an end, and at 1830 on 3 March his successor arrived on board. No admiral was better connected than Frederick Hew George Dalrymple-Hamilton. Though born in London, he was proud to be considered part of the Scottish aristocracy. His father had been aide-de-camp to Queen Victoria's third son, the Duke of Connaught, and when young Frederick entered the Royal Naval College in 1905 he was personally sponsored by Prince George, later King George V. He did moderately well at the college but soon found his metier in destroyers in the First World War. He proved to be a well-rounded officer, considerate to his men, tactful and skilful: 'Excellent in every detail, is especially suitable for destroyer service, his initiative, quickness of decision and sound judgement being most creditable.' In 1922 he accompanied the Prince of Wales on a round-the-world trip in the battlecruiser *Renown*, after which he was appointed to the Royal Yacht for the second time. As he rose through the ranks he had a good balance of seagoing, staff and administrative jobs. Just before the war he was in command of the Royal Naval College at Dartmouth when it was visited by his old friend King George VI, whose thirteen-year-old daughter Elizabeth met her cousin Prince Philip of Greece for the first time. It seems that neither the King nor Dalrymple-Hamilton noticed the impression the midshipman made on the young princess. Dalrymple-Hamilton was appointed to command the battleship *Rodney* in November 1939, and during the chase of the *Bismarck* in 1941 he cut through confused orders and made key decisions that led to the sinking, largely by the *Rodney*'s guns. Promoted to rear admiral, he took charge of the naval interests in Iceland then went back to Whitehall to the influential post of naval secretary to the First Lord of the Admiralty, where he was at the centre of the naval administration and advising the political head of the service.

Burnett's flag was lowered less than half an hour after Dalrymple-Hamilton arrived, and the two admirals spent the night on board. At 0900 next morning the new flag was hoisted and Burnett was taken ashore. He went on to become commander-in-chief in the South Atlantic, in a very different climate. According to Parham, Darlymple-Hamilton was 'a really, really charming man'.

* * * * *

190

The Russian convoys had gone well since the *Scharnhorst* was sunk. Escort carriers, the 'pocket aircraft carriers' seen by Midshipman Smith in the Clyde in October 1943, were used to provide air defence and hunt surfaced U-boats. The tide had already turned in the Battle of the Atlantic, so increasing numbers of destroyers, frigates and corvettes were available for close escort, including the famous group commanded by Captain F. J. Walker. The U-boats sank one merchant ship and one destroyer during January and February but lost five of their number, while air attacks on the convoys were beaten off. The only 'fly in the ointment' was that the mighty *Tirpitz* had at last emerged from the repair yard and posed a threat again. The *Belfast* was to take part in Operation 'Tungsten' with the dual purpose of covering convoy JW 58 to Russia, and sinking the *Tirpitz* with an air strike launched from carriers. Dalrymple-Hamilton left the *Belfast* temporarily on 26 March for the small cruiser *Diadem*, to lead the escort for convoy RA 58, leaving *Belfast* a 'private ship' without an admiral on board.

On 30 March she sailed from Scapa as part of Force 1, a fleet under Admiral Fraser that included the *Duke of York*, her sister ship *Anson*, the fleet aircraft carrier *Victorious*, which had already distinguished herself in the *Bismarck* affair, and five destroyers. Another force led by Admiral Bisset included the carrier *Furious* and four escort carriers. Fraser's ships exercised on the way out, the *Belfast* fired her 4-inch and close-range weapons at a glider target, and on the 31st she had to turn into wind several times to escort the *Victorious* as she flew off aircraft for exercise – very necessary, as she had only recently come out of the dockyard. By 1 April it was clear that the returning convoy JW 58 was making good progress despite being shadowed from the air. The Germans had made no attempt to seek out any surface covering force, so Fraser concluded that the *Tirpitz* was not likely to come out. He decided to advance the next phase of the 'Tungsten' plan by one day. The two carrier groups were united 120 miles north of Norway in the afternoon of the 2nd. The *Belfast* was now part of Force 7, which included the *Anson, Victorious, Furious* and her old rival *Jamaica*. Her crew stood by early in the morning of the 3rd as the first aircraft took off from the *Victorious* at 0415 and formed up for the attack. The second striking force took off an hour later, and they could only watch as one Barracuda crashed into the sea killing its three-man crew. The 40 bombers, escorted by 80 fighters, scored fourteen hits on the great battleship despite difficult conditions in the narrow fjord where she lay, and at 0615 the men of the *Belfast* watched as the first aircraft began to land on the decks of the *Victorious* and *Furious*. By 0830 they were able to resume their usual zig-zag course, and at 1050 they reverted to normal cruising stations as they left the danger zone. They stayed at sea for a few days while the carriers flew off aircraft for air defence, and returned to Scapa in the afternoon of the 6th. The *Tirpitz*, it emerged, had been damaged but not sunk. British estimates, which turned out to be optimistic, suggested she would be out of action for six months – but at the very least she would not be able to intervene in the next operation, the greatest of all, which was set for June that year.

On 16 April the *Belfast* sailed to the Clyde where a constructor commander came on board to assess her condition after months of hard service. On the 20th she anchored and carried out gunnery practice against shore targets in the Firth. One anticipated problem was that it would be difficult to spot the fall of shot, even from an aircraft, if they aimed in an area such as a wood. The answer was to include one smoke shell in each salvo, but that raised a new difficulty: a smoke shell had a different weight from a high-explosive

The launch of the *Belfast*, showing the 'knuckle' of the bow.

Above far left: A typical seaman's messdeck. This is on board the cruiser *Shropshire* in 1942, during the evening meal. (Imperial War Museum A 7596)

Above left: Captain Scott on the quarterdeck of the *Belfast*. (Imperial War Museum HU 4644)

Left: The *Belfast* at anchor in Loch Ewe in October 1939, with the battleship *Rodney* in the background. (Imperial War Museum HU1025)

Above right: The marine artist Harold Wyllie's interpretation of the capture of the *Cap Norte* in heavy seas in October 1939. (Imperial War Museum ART 16801)

Above: The *Cap Norte* under way. (Imperial War Museum HU 10272)

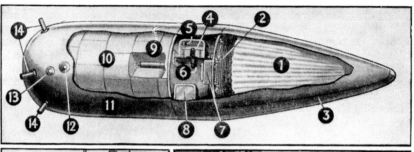

Left: A contemporary explanation of the workings of magnetic mines.

Below: The damage to the hull of the *Belfast*, in dock in Rosyth. (Imperial War Museum MH29235)

WEAK ELECTRICAL IMPULSES CAUSED BY METAL HULL OF VESSEL PASSING CLOSE TO MINE. THESE IMPULSES ARE MAGNIFIED INSIDE THE MINE UNTIL ENERGY GREAT ENOUGH TO FIRE THE CHARGE IS OBTAINED.

DETAILS OF THE GERMAN PARACHUTE MAGNETIC MINE

Fig. 14. *Top, section of magnetic mine. 1, Parachute. 2, Parachute ropes. 3, Parachute case. 4, Magnetic needle. 5, Contact. 6, Counter weight. 7, Relay. 8, Battery. 9, Detonator. 10, Explosive (650 lb.). 11, Metal case. 12, Impact detonator. 13, Hydrostatic valve. 14, Horns to prevent rolling. Lower left, what happens when a ship passes over a magnetic mine. Lower right, equipping a vessel with "de Gaussing" device*

Above: King George VI inspects the Royal Marine detachment on the *Belfast*'s quarterdeck. Captain Powell, commander of the detachment, is to the right. (Imperial War Museum A 18690)

Below: Captain Parham.

Right: Rear Admiral Burnett in his cabin in the *Belfast*, showing some of the irregular shape caused by the cruiser stern. (Imperial War Museum A 21758)

Above: Ice on the superstructure and being cleared from the *Belfast*'s forecastle during Arctic service in November 1943. (Imperial War Museum HU 8795 and A 20686)

Below: The *Belfast* under way off Scapa Flow, showing the camouflage pattern. (Imperial War Museum A 18642)

Above: The officers of the *Belfast* in 1943. Lieutenant Brooke Smith is second from the right on the front row
(Imperial War Museum A 21370)

One of *Belfast*'s Walrus aircraft is paddled towards the ship to be hoisted by crane.
(Imperial War Museum A 20690)

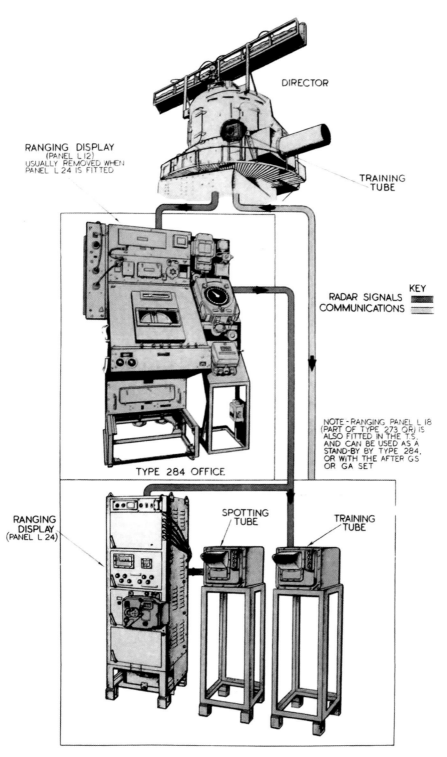

DIRECTOR

RANGING DISPLAY
(PANEL L 12)
USUALLY REMOVED WHEN
PANEL L 24 IS FITTED

TRAINING
TUBE

RADAR SIGNALS
COMMUNICATIONS

KEY

NOTE - RANGING PANEL L 18
(PART OF TYPE 273 QR) IS
ALSO FITTED IN THE T.S.
AND CAN BE USED AS A
STAND-BY BY TYPE 284,
OR WITH THE AFTER GS
OR GA SET

TYPE 284 OFFICE.

RANGING
DISPLAY
(PANEL L 24)

SPOTTING
TUBE

TRAINING
TUBE

The layout of the Type 284 radar system, which was used to direct
the *Belfast*'s main armament. (*Radar Manual,* 1945)

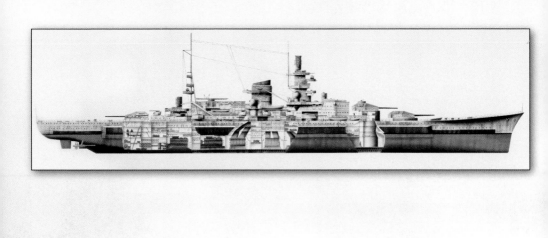

Left: A cutaway of the *Scharnhorst* showing the raised bow, which improved her sailing in rough seas. (Getty Images)

Below: The *Scharnhorst* photographed during the 'Channel Dash' of January 1942. (Getty Images)

Right: A 4-inch starshell, showing the parachute that would cause it to descend slowly.

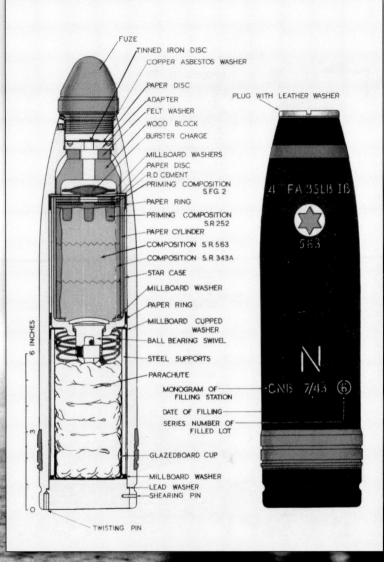

FUZE

TINNED IRON DISC

COPPER ASBESTOS WASHER

PAPER DISC

ADAPTER

FELT WASHER

WOOD BLOCK

BURSTER CHARGE

MILLBOARD WASHERS

PAPER DISC

R.D CEMENT

PRIMING COMPOSITION S.F.G.2

PAPER RING

PRIMING COMPOSITION S.R.252

PAPER CYLINDER

COMPOSITION S.R.563

COMPOSITION S.R.343A

STAR CASE

MILLBOARD WASHER

PAPER RING

MILLBOARD CUPPED WASHER

BALL BEARING SWIVEL

STEEL SUPPORTS

PARACHUTE

MONOGRAM OF FILLING STATION

DATE OF FILLING

SERIES NUMBER OF FILLED LOT

GLAZEDBOARD CUP

MILLBOARD WASHER

LEAD WASHER

SHEARING PIN

TWISTING PIN

PLUG WITH LEATHER WASHER

6 INCHES

4" FA 35LB IB

563

N

C.NB 7/43 (6)

Above: Shells in the *Belfast*'s magazine as they are displayed today. (John Lee)

Below: The *Belfast* at anchor firing on to the Normandy beaches. (Imperial War Museum FLM 4015)

Opposite page: The *Belfast*'s starboard 4-inch guns firing on Ver-sur-Mer on the night of June 27 and highlighting the ship's superstructure and gun turrets. (Imperial War Museum A 24325)

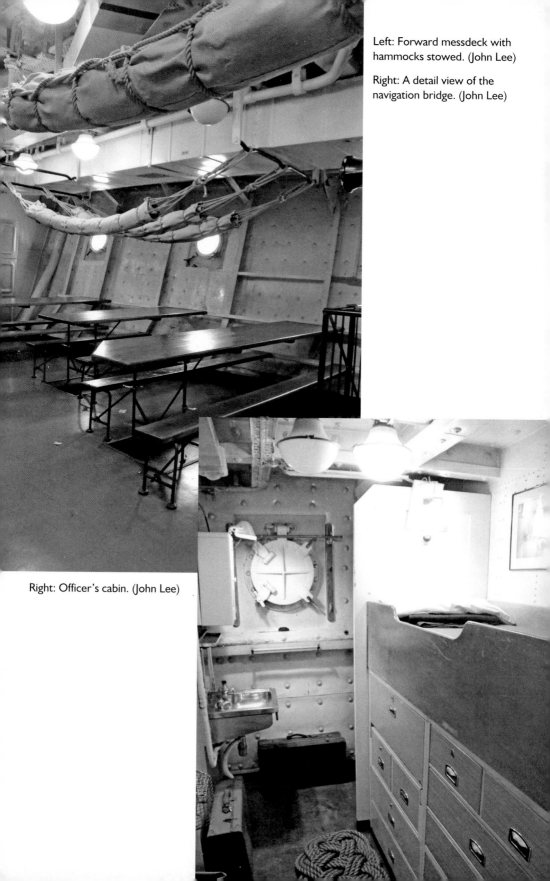

Left: Forward messdeck with hammocks stowed. (John Lee)

Right: A detail view of the navigation bridge. (John Lee)

Right: Officer's cabin. (John Lee)

Above: The compass on the Admiral's bridge. (John Lee)

Right: Overhead view of one of the port Bofors guns. (John Lee)

Left The ship's bell, presented in October 1947 by the City of Belfast. (John Lee)

Below: The *Belfast* firing a salvo from her 6-inch guns off the west coast of Korea. (Imperial War Museum A 31890)

Left: A three-quarter bow view showing the ship after the 1956–9 refit. (Imperial War Museum HU 4649)

Above: The ship's new superstructure and lattice foremast. (Imperial War Museum MH 28915)

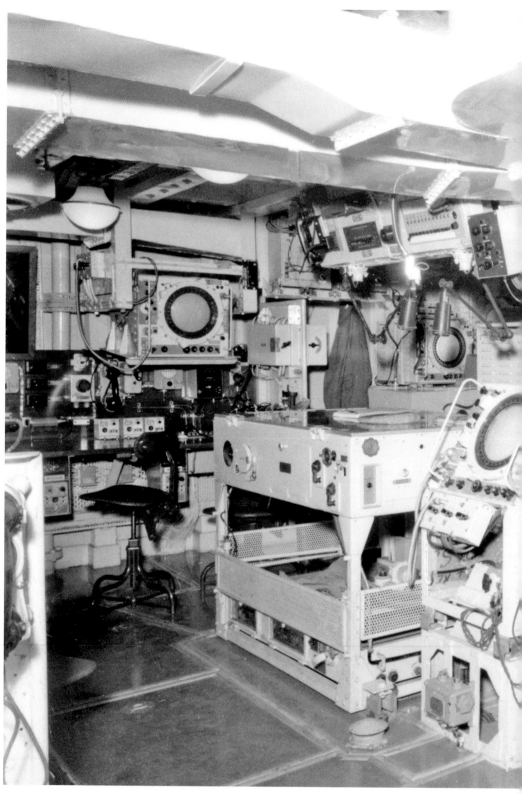

The new operations room as fitted in 1956–9. (Imperial War Museum MH 28959)

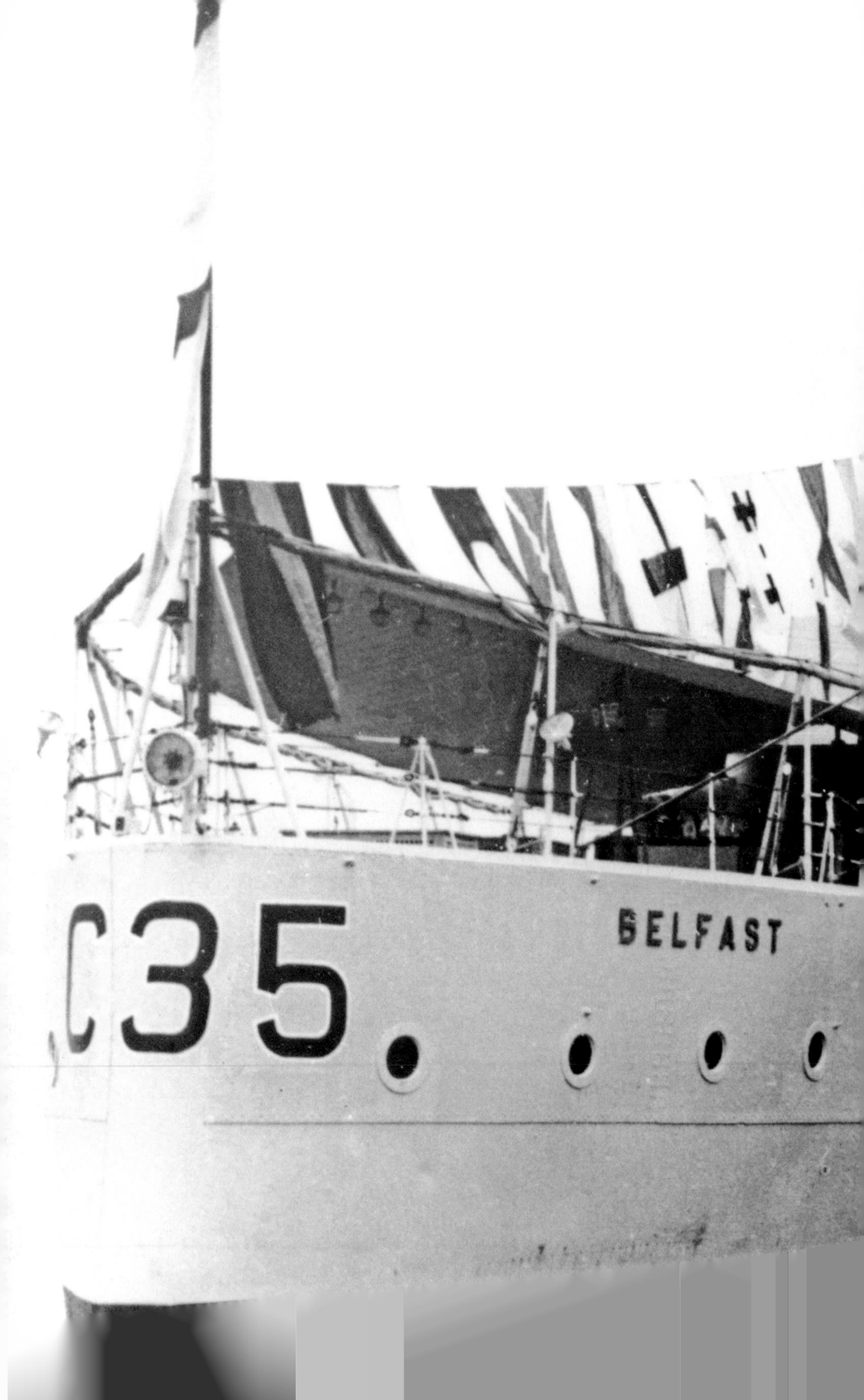
C35
BELFAST

The *Belfast* alongside a pier in Tokyo in June 1961, dressed overall to celebrate Queen Elizabeth II's official birthday. (Getty Images)

Above: The *Belfast* passing through Tower Bridge on her arrival in the Pool of London in 1971. (Imperial War Museum MH 15062)

Right: The *Belfast* as she is today, wearing her 1942 camouflage. (John Lee)

shell so that the trajectory was likely to be different. Parham therefore tested a system codenamed 'Battleaxe' on the *Belfast*. The pointer of one gun in each turret was fitted with an engraved brass strip that corrected for range and was to be used when this kind of firing was ordered. Though only four salvoes could be fired due to bad weather, Parham reported, 'mixed salvo firing should definitely NOT be regarded as impracticable'.

Commander Welby-Everard was transferred, and the new executive officer was Richard Tosswil, who had been the ship's navigator in the early days of the war. In the meantime he had served as navigation officer of the carrier *Illustrious* when her aircraft carried out a devastating attack on the Italian fleet at Taranto, in the Trade Division of the Naval Staff at the Admiralty and as staff officer to the Flag Officer in charge on the heavily bombed island of Malta. Denis Watkinson thought he was 'a great character', a real gentleman and a real sailor, constantly with his telescope under his arm and with a commanding voice 'in a nice way'.

The first task was to take the ship round to Rosyth, where she entered No. 1 dry dock on the 23rd for a more substantial refit. At last the crew were given long leave by their watches. They returned by 8 May and sailed to Scapa Flow. On the 13th they hosted the King on his fifth visit to Scapa. He boarded at 1130, to be welcomed by his old friend Rear Admiral Dalrymple-Hamilton, and down below he shyly asked Parham if he would like to have a signed photograph. The ship weighed anchor and proceeded out through the familiar Hoxa Gate with His Majesty on the bridge to sail around the fleet. He was cheered by the crew as he left by drifter at 1345 to go on board the *Victorious*. There was a more serious purpose on the 29th when the captains of five cruisers, the captain of the 25th Destroyer Flotilla and three destroyer captains came on board for a conference in *Belfast*'s vacant starboard hangar. The crew were, of course, told nothing, but there was little doubt that they were planning the forthcoming invasion of France.

* * * * *

With hardly any major German surface ships still operational, it was clear that the main role of the *Belfast* would be in shore bombardment. This had been one of the tasks of the navy for centuries, and it had left a mark on its personnel. In the days of smooth-bore guns the specialised mortar vessel was the main weapon, and in 1808 the Admiralty formed the Royal Marine Artillery to man them, replacing the army gunners who often had no interest in the running of the ship. They were merged with the Royal Marine Infantry in 1923, but marines still trained as gunners and operated *Belfast*'s 'X' and 'Y' turrets. In 1812 General Sir Howard Douglas watched the bombardment of northern Spain with more conventional guns, and the inaccuracy made him 'tremble for the laurels of the navy' – beginning a movement that led to the establishment of HMS *Excellent* as a gunnery school, where Parham, Mountifield and thousands of others trained. There were many shore bombardments to expand British imperial power throughout the world during the nineteenth century, notably of Alexandria in 1882 and Zanzibar in 1896. The rifled, shell-firing gun greatly increased the possibilities, but at the same time ships coming close inshore faced a growing danger from mines and torpedoes, while an enemy equipped with modern artillery could make a devastating reply. The Royal Navy's attempt to force the Dardanelles in 1915 failed dismally. Instead they began to develop monitors to operate in the shallow waters off Belgium against the flank of the German trenches on the Western

Front. Each had a hull fitted with the largest guns possible, bulge protection against torpedoes, but far less mobility than most warships. A late example was the *Roberts*, launched in 1941 and fitted with two 15-inch guns, which would soon fire them in action alongside the *Belfast*.

Now that sea superiority had been achieved, it was acceptable to take battleships and cruisers off their ocean-going tasks and face the risks of inshore warfare. The gun-power of a ship like the *Belfast*, not to mention that of the battleships which were also to take part in the invasion, was immense in the scale of land warfare and would be even more effective in the early stages of an invasion before the army artillery could be landed. In some ways it seemed easier than gunnery at sea: it was usually directed against static targets such as strongpoints on shore, and in this case the ships expected to be anchored while they fired. Perhaps this is why the gunnery department of the navy took little interest in it – it was barely covered in HMS *Excellent* and the other gunnery schools and was not mentioned in standard gunnery textbooks. Like all aspects of amphibious operations, it was neglected between the wars. Shore bombardment had its difficulties, in that the target could often not be seen from the ship, which was to be corrected by air spotting or by army officers on the ground known as 'forward observers, bombardment', or 'FOBs'. In addition, naval guns did not have the precise accuracy associated with land weapons, and even that tended to decline through long use. Their shells were designed to penetrate naval armour or explode on deck, and they were far less effective against concrete bunkers. Even at long range their trajectory was low compared with army howitzers, which could safely lob shells over friendly forces. Trainee officers were told,

Naval guns are normally High Velocity/Low Trajectory Guns. Problem of 'crest clearance' therefore arises. Special reduced charges, known as 'bombardment charges', are used to produce a howitzer effect. Accuracy is slightly affected and maximum range of guns, is, of course, decreased. Wear of guns also decreases their accuracy.

The *Belfast* was to be part of Force J for the initial part of the assault on 'Juno' Beach, under the command of Commodore G. N. Oliver, whose operation orders were issued on 19 May. They were to be 'kept locked up when not in use … They must on no account be allowed to fall into the hands of the enemy.' While the destroyers went close inshore to engage the enemy near the beaches, the cruisers were to carry out counter-battery fire in support of the landings. The *Belfast* was to anchor on the boundary between 'Juno' and 'Gold' beaches. As soon as air spotting became available she was to bombard a battery of 105mm guns at Ver-sur-Mer a mile inland near Fleury, initially under the orders of the commander of Force G attacking 'Gold' Beach. Once the battery had been destroyed or captured she was to transfer to the control of Force J and support the 3rd Canadian Division on 'Juno' Beach and 'to await calls for fire from impromptu targets'. Dalrymple-Hamilton, with his flag still in the *Belfast*, was to cause his ships to lay Dan buoys to mark their positions, and 'to order any necessary action in the event of air or submarine attack'.

The battleships, cruisers, destroyers and monitors were not the only ships to be engaged. Even closer inshore than the destroyers would be several types of landing craft equipped with guns, notably the 'landing craft gun (medium)', which could fire its army-type 25-pounder while at sea and then be beached to provide a stable platform to engage in the land battle. There were 'landing craft, rocket', which could fire a devastating salvo of 792 missiles, equivalent to 80 cruisers, but they were difficult to aim and slow to reload. All this was to take place in conjunction with hundreds of heavy and light bombers dropping their loads in the area.

The medical organisation of the *Belfast* was reviewed for the prospect of long periods at action stations. Equipment was dispersed between two medical stations and five first-aid posts at strategic points in the ship. Every man was made aware of the first-aid point nearest to his action station, and nine officers in different parts were given ampoules of Omnopon painkillers containing morphine for injection.

* * * * *

Meanwhile the *Belfast* was unwittingly involved in a controversy at the very centre of government. Churchill was always anxious to get as close as possible to the scene of action, and his own (rather short) experience in the trenches of the First World War reinforced his belief that 'generals and other high commanders should try from time to time to see the conditions and aspect of the battle for themselves'. At a final planning meeting on 17 May he approached Admiral Bertram Ramsay, in charge of the naval side of the operation, and asked him to arrange for him to be aboard a ship during the landings – he carefully avoided the strong personality of Admiral Cunningham, the First Sea Lord. Ramsay was reluctant but made a plan for the *Belfast* to pick the Prime Minister up off Weymouth on the way from the Clyde to Normandy. He did not give his reasons for choosing the ship beyond saying that 'nothing smaller than a cruiser is suitable for you during the night and the approach', but the reasons are not hard to deduce. The only British battleships present on the first day would be the *Warspite* and *Ramillies*, both rather slow by modern standards, so it would be difficult to divert them while allowing time to catch up with the rest of the force. They were intended for the fringes of the action to the east of the landing area, whereas the *Belfast* would be right in the centre between 'Gold' and 'Juno' beaches. Destroyers, on the other hand, were unarmoured and rather vulnerable – 154 of them were lost during the war – and this time they would be inshore close to the front line. The *Belfast* was the largest of the thirteen cruisers in the British sector. Only the *Mauritius* came close but she too would be on the fringes of the action. That ship had unrivalled experience of shore bombardment, having supported the landings in Sicily, Anzio and Salerno, but she had a notoriously difficult crew, with an outright mutiny in January that year. The *Belfast* was always a happy ship, and Dalrymple-Hamilton was the ideal admiral to host such a visitor. With his royal connections and experience at the Admiralty, he knew how to deal with distinguished personalities, and he was liked by almost everyone. At sea he would live in his cabin under the bridge and his spacious quarters aft would be available for the guests.

Churchill's plan caused deep concern in high places. General Eisenhower, in overall command of the operation, tried to ban it but was told he had no rights over who was on board a British warship. Churchill's military aide, Major General Ismay, was horrified, 'not so much at the risk involved, but at the prospect of the Prime Minister being cut off from communication with the outside world when critical and immediate decisions might have to be taken'. But initially the King had a different reaction. Over a weekly lunch on 30 May, he asked Churchill where he would be for D-Day and was told that he planned to witness it from one of the cruiser squadrons. The King immediately replied that he would like to come too, as a former naval officer and head of the armed forces. But next day he changed his mind and wrote to Churchill, 'I have come to the conclusion that it would not be right for either you or I to be where we planned in D Day.' Churchill was not deterred and argued about the constitutional niceties of his leaving the country without permission from sovereign or cabinet. On 2 June, as ships from distant ports were already preparing to sail, he called Cunningham to his map room in Downing Street and told him of the plan. Cunningham replied that he would 'risk his wrath and said outright that it was absolutely wrong for him to go'. That afternoon Churchill turned up at Eisenhower's headquarters near Portsmouth where he received another letter from the King: 'I ask you most earnestly to consider the whole question again, and not to let your personal wishes, which I well understand, lead you to depart from your own high standard of duty to the State.' Churchill relented under this pressure and sent a dispatch rider with a message to the King reluctantly agreeing not to go.

* * * * *

At 1055 in the morning of Saturday 3 June 1944, the *Belfast* cast off from E1 buoy in the Firth of Clyde off Greenock and headed out to sea in company with the cruiser *Emerald* to form Force E, with four more cruisers making up Force K, and a group of destroyers. In theory the crew had no idea where they were going, but there was a general air of anticipation and a strong hint when the Royal Marine band struck up the early wartime hit *We're Gonna Hang out the Washing on the Siegfried Line*. They might also have had an indication from the presence of Captain Hugh Kenion of the Royal Artillery, who would serve as bombardment liaison officer. Captain Parham usually preferred to address the crew face to face, but it was not practicable in this case and he used the Tannoy for the only time, telling them they were going on the biggest military exercise the world will ever have known. This was followed by a short address by the chaplain. Lieutenant Commander Charles Simpson felt 'subdued jubilation' at the news, while on Bob Shrimpton's messdeck an aged leading seaman announced that it was time for a cup of tea. They passed many merchant ships and convoys as they headed down the Irish Sea. The weather was terrible, and the ships were off the Bristol Channel at 0820 on the 4th when they received a signal that the operation had been postponed for 24 hours. They reversed course and headed north for the next twelve hours, during which they met many more ships and the destroyer *Ulster* dropped depth-charges on a suspected submarine.

The high command of the operation met in Eisenhower's headquarters near Portsmouth at 0415 on the morning of 5 June and, in the words of Admiral Ramsay, 'the [weather] prophets came in smiling, conditions having shown a considerable improvement. It was … decided to … proceed.' The *Belfast* and her consorts were already heading south, and Land's End was abeam just before noon. They turned east into the English Channel to find even more traffic heading in the same direction and at 1810 they overtook a convoy of landing craft. Able Seaman Jones later wrote to his family, 'When we came along the English Channel … we passed thousands of landing craft, of all shapes and sizes and [as] we passed them, all the boys were cheering …'

At ten in the evening of the 5th they were off the Isle of Wight, where they were joined by the Dutch cruiser *Flores*. They sailed round Area Z, or 'Piccadilly Circus', then down a prearranged route through 'the Spout', which had been swept clear of German mines. At 0120 in the morning of 6 June, Forces E and K parted company and the *Belfast* led the way towards the fifth of ten narrow channels that had been cleared, two for each of the landing beaches. There was some difficulty in finding the buoys marking the entrance to the channel, probably because of the great volume of shipping, but soon they were heading south towards the French coast. Despite the traffic, they only had to leave the channel once to avoid collision with other craft, but they had to make many small alterations of course, while at the same time a cross-tide was pushing them sideways, so careful navigation was needed. There was a break in the cloud, and Dalrymple-Hamilton and Parham were both grateful for the full moon, which made safe passage possible. Large formations of aircraft were heard overhead and at 0320 in the morning anti-aircraft fire could be seen on both bows as the Allied bombers struck. Thirty-five minutes later fires were seen on the port bow. The crew was called to action stations at four o'clock and AB Jones wrote, 'As we approached the coast of France we could hear thousands of bombers overhead and then along the coast there were loud explosions, and great fires.' An hour later they stopped in a prearranged position six miles off the coast of Normandy. The destroyers parted company, and at 0500 the three cruisers formed a line with the *Belfast* in the centre.

Soon they were in radio contact with the spotting Spitfire codenamed 'Quicksand'. These aircraft operated in pairs, one observing the fall of shot and the other covering its tail. Gun crews were called to action as the sky lightened on a momentous morning. The navigators established the exact position of the ship by taking bearings on lighthouses and churches, and the range to Ver-sur-Mer battery, strongpoint WN 34 in the German scheme of defence, map reference 917842 on the British maps, was calculated at 15,700 yards. At 0527 the ship fired the first of four ranging salvoes over her port side, but the cloud had closed in and the aircraft could only see the target occasionally. Nevertheless they began to fire 'for effect' and over thirteen minutes loosed off eighteen armour-piercing rounds and thirteen high-explosive. Down in the engine room, Charles Simpson knew it was something extraordinary because the guns were firing continuously, rather than every one or two minutes. It seemed to last forever – he never knew time to pass so slowly. Visibility had apparently improved by 0555 when the second firing began. The four ranging salvoes were all seen to be within 200 yards of the target and the first 42 rounds fired for effect were also on target. After that the ship shifted position while the aircraft had to go and spot for another ship, and the next 24 rounds were unobserved when firing ceased again after twelve minutes. Four more six-gun salvoes were fired blind in 1½ minutes after 0623 to neutralise the target, and at 0628 the aircraft was available again but only for six minutes as 55 more shots were fired to hit within 200

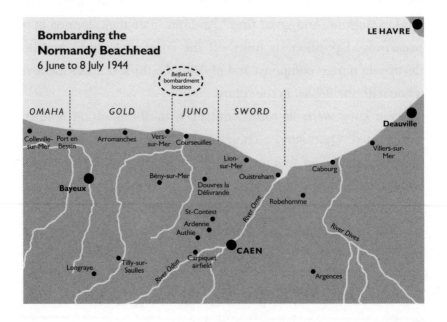

Bombarding the Normandy Beachhead
6 June to 8 July 1944

LE HAVRE

Belfast's bombardment location

OMAHA GOLD JUNO SWORD

Deauville

Colleville-sur-Mer Port en Bessin Arromanches Vers-sur-Mer Courseuilles Villers-sur-Mer

Lion-sur-Mer Cabourg

Bény-sur-Mer Ouistreham

Bayeux Douvres la Délivrande

St-Contest Robehomme

Ardenne River Orne River Dives

Authie

Carpiquet airfield **CAEN**

Longraye Tilly-sur-Saulles River Odon Argences

yards of the target. The *Belfast* shifted position again and fired 24 more neutralising shots in two 1½-minute bursts to keep the enemy heads down. By that time it was 0716 and the landing was almost ready to begin.

Soon they were surrounded by a bewildering collection of landing ships and craft of many shapes and sizes, mostly developed since the evacuation from Dunkirk exactly four years ago, or converted from merchant vessels or warships. Some were designed to land vehicles, such as the 'tank landing craft', or LCTs, that were leading the assault with 'Hobart's funnies', tanks converted to clear beach obstacles and mines or lay bridges. Others carried personnel such as the 'assault landing craft', or LCAs, which were close behind them, each with a platoon of about 30 infantrymen or the equivalent number of specialists. Some were headquarters ships like the *Bulolo*, anchored 2½ miles from *Belfast* with her sophisticated radio and operations rooms to cater for the needs of all three services. Some made the voyage across under their own steam and landed their cargoes on the beaches, like the tank landing craft and the bigger 'tank landing ships', which would land up to 20 tanks each in a later wave. Some anchored offshore to launch smaller vessels such as assault landing craft. These included 'landing ships infantry', or LSIs, such as the *Prinses Astrid* and *Prince David*, converted Belgian ferries, which were lowering their LCAs crammed with men a few miles away.

It is doubtful if many people appreciated the detail of this, not even Dalrymple-Hamilton, who wrote,

> It was noticeable in what good order all the various craft proceeded despite somewhat unfavourable weather and after a long night voyage. All the personnel in the craft appeared cheerful and

unconcerned. There was no shouting or hesitation of any kind. In fact the whole operation as viewed from the *Belfast* appeared to go like clockwork and fully justified the immense amount of work put into the issue of orders for the operation.

Able Seaman Jones wrote to his family, 'We went in first with the invasion barges behind us, and then the first great moment when we opened fire, when we had finished shelling the beach, all the invasion craft surged forward and landed on the beach and they seem to be making splendid progress.' It was not so simple for the men in the landing craft, but they took comfort from the support of ships like the *Belfast*. Austin Baker was a tank wireless operator with the 'funnies':

> The first sight of the French coast gave me a queer feeling … as we slowly drew towards it, passing the big troop ships which lay at anchor, having sent their infantry on towards the beach in small assault boats. There were several cruisers lying there too, firing broadside after broadside inland. We passed within a couple of hundred yards of the *Belfast*. The noise of her guns was ear-splitting. There was a battleship firing in the distance …

Lieutenant R. B. Davies was in command of *LCT 647*:

> Well, we are going in now, the guns of HMS *Belfast* firing over us. Landmarks were clear – we were coming in line abreast, six craft covering a mile of beach, my craft on the left flank … Tanks were manned and revving up, the ramp door eased … all of us dressed and armed and provisioned against an enforced stay ashore, feeling and looking like pirates …

The *Belfast* was ordered to cease firing at Ver-sur-Mer after the landing began. It is doubtful if the bombardment had been as successful as hoped. Dalrymple-Hamilton later reported after visiting the site, 'It was evident that the C.P.B.C. [armour piercing] shell of the cruisers had no effect on concrete gun emplacements and probably that the initial counter battery fire would have had a better chance of success had [high-explosive] shell been used in the hope that splinters would enter the gun house through the embrasures.' Around seven in the morning Parham went down from the bridge to the plotting room and was surprised to hear a voice saying, 'Now then, girls.' The operators were listening to a keep-fit programme on the BBC. Once the constant gunfire had stopped, Lieutenant Commander Simpson allowed his stokers to go on deck one by one for two minutes each to see the action. On his own turn he saw a sandy beach lined with houses and trees, very rough seas with waves seven or eight feet high, and landing craft passing so close that they could hear the soldiers shouting.

Now the *Belfast* was ordered to wait for targets of opportunity as requested from the shore. Communication had not yet been established with the FOBs, but around 0750 her radio operators heard a request from the commander of Force J calling for the bombardment of a battery 1,200 yards inland, just east of the town of Courseulles. They fired sixteen shots blind, despite Commodore Oliver's orders that stated: 'Under ordinary conditions, indirect fire without observation is a most unprofitable expenditure of ammunition.' At 0827, as the army progressed inland, they began another blind fire on request, on a battery of 88mm guns two miles from the shore, near the village of Bény-sur-Mer. At 0955 they began a sustained fire of two-gun salvoes over twenty minutes at a group of machine-guns in the open some way to the west, over a range of 18,300 yards. In nearly four hours of engagement, the *Belfast* fired for a total of 68 minutes using 158 rounds of armour-piercing and 139 of high-explosive.

The effect of the war was brought home to the crew of *Belfast* at 1300 when a motor launch brought seven army casualties on board for treatment by the ship's medical team before transfer to the cruiser *Orion*, where two of them died before being transported back to England. So far the forward observers, bombardment, had not been able to request fire, largely due to radio difficulties. At 1300 the *Belfast* moved closer inshore in the hope of establishing contact, but to no effect. That night, as the men of 48 Marine Commando prepared for a counterattack by panzers massing close by, Captain Jim Tyler tried to get them support. Sergeant Ralph Dye reported,

> We were asked to carry out a shoot from HMS *Belfast* to break up this assembly point, but we couldn't get through to the cruiser on our radios. We crawled outside the perimeter to try to get a better range on our backpack set. One telegraphist was peering at the dials with the light of a pencil torch. I told him he had better put the light out because there were German patrols about. I was right, for the next thing we knew there were mortar bombs homing in on us. We crept back through the wall and Captain Tyler told Colonel Moulton that we just couldn't get through to the Belfast. He was a bit miffed at the news.

✳ ✳ ✳ ✳ ✳

The landings had been successful and even on the American 'Omaha' Beach disaster had been averted despite heavy casualties, but progress inland was slow in the British and Canadian sector. By next morning the 9th Canadian Brigade and the 3rd British Division were only halfway to the city of Caen, nominally an objective for the first day. The FOBs were now in place, and *Belfast* was in contact with No. 71. She opened her day at 0832 by firing 122 rounds of high-explosive at a concentration of troops reported by the FOB near the town of Douvres la Délivrande where the enemy was holding out in the gap between 'Juno' and 'Sword' beaches. It was reported, 'All salvoes after the first were within 200 yards of target and all were in target area. Shoot effective.' They continued to fire in the same area several times, and AB Jones used a lull to write to his family, though he seems to have been a little confused about the geography: 'As I am writing this, the sun is beating down and its a glorious day, as I look to my right I can see the green fields and small forests of Cherbourg which is just about a mile away from the ship, and just over the hill can see small bursts of smoke, where a kind of tank battle seems to be in progress.' It was quiet for the rest of the day until 2335 when they fired blind on the town of Authie, 17,900 yards away, where the Canadians were involved in a particularly savage battle with a brutal SS division. This was probably a 'plaster' as described in the operational orders – a series of five multi-gun salvoes, the first to the estimated range of the target followed by one each 400 yards short, over, left and right. She repeated this with eleven guns per salvo and fired 110 shots in total. It was followed by a 'blind neutralisation' – the results were unknown.

On the 8th the *Belfast* was engaged with the town of St-Contest, from where Canadian forces were being heavily shelled as they tried to advance north-west of Caen. The FOB was in continuous contact from 0515 that morning, but the first shoot at 1428 used air spotting. It was terminated after twelve rounds when the observer reported that too much shot was falling to allow observation. This remained a problem after the FOB took over for the next five shoots, which lasted intermittently until 2051. In all, 284 rounds were fired that day over a total firing time of 136 minutes. It was claimed that apart from the first attempts, each shoot had been 'effective' or 'most effective', but the enemy continued to hold back the British and

Canadians. There was only one ten-minute shoot on the 9th; as Dalrymple-Hamilton reported, 'There were frequently periods on each day during which no targets were engaged.' A defended post was neutralised, all shots falling within 100 yards of the target. Early in the morning of the 10th the *Belfast* spent three hours firing blind at a large number of enemy armoured vehicles sheltering in woods. Two hundred rounds were spread over 800 yards in each direction, and the FOB reported, 'They seem to have landed on the right spot', though he did not assess the actual damage.

So far enemy action against the ships had been slight. The Germans had been taken completely by surprise, and Hitler still did not believe that this was the real invasion. A stick of bombs fell off the starboard beam of the *Belfast* at 1000 on the 6th. She saw a fighter chased off by two Spitfires at 1530, and the *Emerald* had a near miss towards the end of the day. There was no damage during an attack on the 9th, but the medical officer observed, 'Several ratings sustained minor injuries in their hurry to take cover.' The gunners of the multifarious ships offshore were beginning to overreact, and the *Belfast*'s log reported, 'flak all round'. Dalrymple-Hamilton described a 'violent reaction from close range weapons in merchant vessels and assault craft'. On the night of 12/13 June the *Belfast* witnessed a Spitfire being shot at with Oerlikon guns and another example of 'friendly fire' an hour later. Ramsay complained about 'regrettable incidents'. 'Because of the unfortunate weather conditions and low cloud base which have prevailed since D-Day, aircraft have been unable to abide by the instruction ... to avoid flying below 3000 ft while over the restricted area. Also because many of the ships and craft engaged were new to active service conditions.' On the 7th, however, the only damage to the *Belfast* was to the fore bridge from the blast of the ship's own guns. Next day enemy torpedoboats, known as E-boats, were reported at 0244 in the morning, but the warning was soon cancelled and destroyers were reported instead, but no attack developed. That afternoon a destroyer dropped a depth-charge on a suspected U-boat and later an Me 109 dropped a bomb in the area. Early in the morning of the 9th there was an E-boat warning, and bombs were dropped on the anchorage. Just after three, some enemy destroyers were reported and they were sighted bearing 65 degrees from the *Belfast* before they turned away. An enemy bomber dropped her load at 0515, and more hostile aircraft were seen in the afternoon and early next morning.

The crew of the *Belfast* were kept informed of the army's progress by the ship's notice board, though Denis Watkinson thought it was carefully edited to cut out bad news. They could see some of it for themselves and on the 9th they watched blockships being sunk to create a 'Gooseberry' artificial harbour. Next day they saw Spitfires landing on one of the improvised airfields on shore. By that time ammunition was short and at 2000 they weighed anchor to sail to Portsmouth to replenish, arriving just after midnight.

The visit was the opposite of relaxing as ammunition lighters came alongside and shells were carried and stowed by hand. She sailed again in the afternoon of the 11th and was back on station at 1815 after less than 24 hours' absence. It was too late to find any targets that day, and on the 12th they could observe the Prime Minister's visit to the battlefield in the destroyer *Kelvin*. They might well have hosted him had circumstance been different, but very few were aware of that as Churchill passed close astern of the *Belfast* in a barge – Denis Watkinson was slightly surprised that he did not visit them as a flagship. By three in the afternoon they were in action again, firing on buildings in Carpiquet airfield to the west of Caen, which the enemy had fortified. It was found that the FOB was using false reports to spread the fall of shot over a greater area, a practice the sailors deplored. A second shoot on the same target around 0430 led to praise from the Commander Royal Artillery, who was 'very pleased' with the shooting. The next day was spent in short bombardments around the same area to the north and east of Caen, as well as the village of Authie, which they had already shelled on the 7th – for the land war was now bogged down outside the city. On the 14th they carried out a much heavier bombardment of 154 rounds of high-explosive against a newly located enemy headquarters in the unfortunate village of Ardenne. The ship moved west to the 'Juno' area for an afternoon shoot against the village of Longraye south of Bayeux, but after 95 rounds the ship was sent back to England. She missed the King's visit to the beaches on the 16th but was back on station by the 18th. She fired on German positions east of the River Orne on the 19th as the winds began to rise. The *Belfast* herself only recorded winds up to Force 7, which was nothing to a cruiser, especially one that had endured an Arctic winter. It was far more devastating to the tiny landing craft and fragile artificial harbours that were being constructed on the beaches, and it delayed supplies for several days. In fact, winds were gusting up to Gale Force 8 – Ramsay had been assured from records stretching back 70 years that there was only a one in 300 chance of such weather in June – it was the worst summer storm for 35 years. The *Belfast* continued her activity during the night with blind firing by 'X' turret at a group of tanks near Robehomme just after nine o'clock. There was an air raid early in the morning, but by 0350 the log recorded 'all quiet'. There was devastation on the beaches, and from the 23rd onwards the *Belfast* sent parties ashore to help remove damaged landing craft. One of these included Denis Watkinson, who knew fear for the first time as he travelled towards the beach in a seemingly frail landing craft. In the meantime the *Belfast* kept up her fire with five shoots in the afternoon and evening of the 20th. Mostly it was now done with one or two turrets at a time, to save ammunition and wear and tear on the gun barrels.

The initial enemy response against the ships had been feeble, but now they were subjected to everything that German ingenuity could devise to throw at them. The crew of the *Belfast* did not have to share the discomfort and danger of the troops ashore, or indeed the conditions they themselves had endured six months ago in the Arctic winter, but there was no rest. The enemy was still ensconced on the east bank of the River Orne on the left flank of the landing area and was using mobile artillery. Shells were seen to hit the nearby Mulberry Harbour at Arromanches at 1828 on the 21st. It was difficult for the bombarding ships to deal with this as the enemy guns were well camouflaged and highly mobile – by the time an air observer or FOB found the site they would have moved on. The ships had to change position every few hours, which meant that the engineers had to keep the boilers banked and at half an hour's notice for steam. But there was another complication. On 23 June headquarters reported, 'A new type of mine is being laid in Task Force areas.' This was the 'oyster' pressure mine, which was dropped by aircraft at night and set off by the difference in water pressure caused by a ship moving over it. It is estimated that 600 were dropped. They were 'rather a trap', as Parham put it with his usual understatement. There was no immediate remedy except to restrict speed, and cruisers like the *Belfast* were ordered to proceed at no more than four knots in 5 to 10 fathoms of water, eight knots in 10 to 15 fathoms and ten knots in 15 to 20 fathoms. That would not have been such a great problem, except that enemy batteries were making it necessary to change berth regularly. During the afternoon of the 23rd the *Belfast* recorded three mine explosions nearby, while shells fell twice during the night. There were three more mine explosions next morning, including one that sank the destroyer *Swift* a mile away. Some of the casualties were brought on board the *Belfast*, and Denis Watkinson saw bodies in the water. The day continued with more explosions and shellfire, and air raids that night. The cruiser *Arethusa* was mined early next morning but survived. One night Dalrymple-Hamilton agreed that Parham could move the ship among some merchant ships under cover of a smoke screen. After that was completed they overheard German radio operators mentioning the *Belfast* by name and it was presumed they had just missed an attack. It was quieter over the next few days, and there was some relief at 2200 on the 26th when the mail arrived from home. This turned to disappointment and anger when it became clear that the relatives ashore had received no letters from the sailors since the landings on 6 June. Dalrymple-Hamilton was always concerned with his men's welfare and complained to Ramsay. 'He pointed out that this long delay seemed unnecessary and was liable to have a bad effect.' The fault was traced to flying-bomb activity and shortage of staff at the General Post Office in London, so a hundred naval ratings were drafted in to help.

* * * * *

There are signs that the crew was becoming weary of this strange campaign, neither at sea nor in harbour. Most departments needed constant alertness – 6-inch gun crews ready to bombard, AA crews sleeping in the shelters beside the guns in case they had to be deployed during the night, engineers keeping up steam, seamen ready to raise and lower the anchors, and medical teams dealing with casualties brought on board. It was uncomfortable below decks because some of the ventilation hatches had to be kept closed as part of damage-control procedures. The men were never in mortal danger but never entirely safe. They were taking part in a land war they only knew vicariously. They did not observe the fall of shot themselves, and in the case of blind firing they learned even less about its accuracy. More generally, they would never know how much harm their fire really did to the enemy, or how much collateral damage they had done to French civilian lives and property. Dalrymple-Hamilton was consoled that, 'appreciations of the accuracy and good effect of these bombardments were received on more than one occasion from the Army authorities', but he was aware of the growing weariness. On 3 July he reminded Ramsay that by the time she was due for relief in three or four days, 'her ship's company would have been closed up without much relaxation for 20 days'. He suggested she should be relieved immediately and a spare cruiser brought in from Spithead if necessary. The admiral would transfer his flag to his old ship the *Rodney* if a flag officer was still needed in the area, though it is clear that he would rather have gone back in the *Belfast*. In any case Ramsay had to say no: every effort would soon be needed for the army's final push on the town of Caen.

Meanwhile a fourth hazard had developed to add to air bombing, shore bombardment and mines. E-boats and U-boats had been kept out of the area by patrols, but in the early hours of 6 July the first 'human torpedo' attack took place. These had already been used against the landing at Anzio in the previous year, but this was their first appearance in Normandy. Each was an electric one-man submersible craft that carried a torpedo under its hull. Twenty-six set out from Le Havre that night. Their success was limited, sinking two small minesweepers, but Dalrymple-Hamilton 'formed the opinion that the Human Torpedo attack had as its chief objective the battleships and cruisers of the bombarding forces'. He considered it an unacceptable risk that these ships should remain at anchor in the 'Sword' Sector, especially as movements away could only be made on a favourable tide owing to the drastic speed restrictions imposed by the mining situation. He had his way, and the forces moved west into the 'Juno' sector.

On the night of the 7th the crew watched waves of Lancaster bombers escorted by fighters heading inland, and Parham announced that they were heading towards Caen. Early on the 8th they saw heavy bombing and a petrol dump exploding. There was another human torpedo raid in which all 21 attackers were sunk, and in the afternoon the *Belfast* joined the *Rodney*, the cruiser *Emerald* and the monitor *Roberts* with gunfire to support the advance of the troops towards Caen, with *Belfast* concentrating on railways and bridges over the River Odon. The deadlock in Normandy was finally broken, and at midday on the 8th the *Belfast* raised anchor. One can almost feel the relief as the ship left the danger area and increased to 100 rpm and a speed of twelve knots by 1500. That was soon increased to 240 revolutions and 26 knots as the ship headed north to anchor in Stokes Bay near Portsmouth. It was the end of her participation in the Normandy invasion.

9

TO THE EAST

BELFAST WENT TO SCAPA FLOW after the Normandy bombardments, and some of the crew feared they might be sent back to the Arctic. Instead they went south to the River Tyne, where the ship was to be refitted by the Middle Dock & High Shields Engineering Company. Captain Parham was sad to leave the ship at the end of July to return to the naval staff at the Admiralty. It was, he wrote modestly, 'I suppose, the most exacting two years … of her long active life …' He was replaced by another outstanding officer. Royer Mylius Dick had entered Dartmouth in September 1910 and gained a month's extra seniority for success in his examinations. As a sub-lieutenant it was noted that he kept good order in the gunroom, but his Achilles' heel began to appear in the destroyer *Gabriel* in 1917 – he was chronically seasick in small ships. Perhaps this is why he began to specialise in signals, for in that role he was more likely to serve in battleships and cruisers. Between courses he was flag lieutenant to the admiral commanding the First Cruiser Squadron in China in 1926–8 and signals officer of the Mediterranean Fleet from 1931 to 1933. Either because destroyers were now bigger and more seaworthy, or because he had found ways of coping with his seasickness, he was able to serve in the *Dainty* in China in 1936–8 and take command of the cruiser *Basilisk* in the Home Fleet in 1938 with the rank of commander. In May 1939 he was appointed to the staff of Admiral Cunningham in the Mediterranean Fleet, and in the early days of the war he served as one of five duty commanders in the flagship *Warspite*, keeping watch day and night and conducting the routine movements of the fleet. He had spent much of his leave in France and was fluent in the language, so he helped Cunningham conduct the negotiations with the French Admiral Godfroy before the French fleet was destroyed at Oran in July 1940. He was present at the victory over the Italians off Cape Matapan in March 1941. When Cunningham went to Washington as head of the British mission in June that year, Dick went with him as deputy chief of staff, for the admiral knew him as 'a brilliant officer'. When Cunningham was given responsibility for organising Operation 'Torch', the invasion of North Africa, Dick became his chief of staff with the acting rank of commodore, despite his relative lack of seniority. Cunningham wrote, 'Roy Dick is surprising even me, and all the high-up Americans think he is a great man.' His language and negotiating skills proved useful yet again when the landings took place in French territory. He was present at the Casablanca conference in 1943, and afterwards, according to Cunningham, 'The Foreign Office was set up in Roy Dick's bedroom!' He stood beside Cunningham to watch the surrender of the Italian fleet in September 1943. Dick was briefly appointed to the cruiser *Royalist* in June 1944, then to the *Belfast*. He had to give up his acting rank of commodore first class as well as his role at the centre of affairs, but a period in command of a battleship or cruiser was essential if he was to progress any further in the navy. However, Midshipman James Eberle thought that 'he found it difficult to relate to sailors and did not therefore win the confidence of the ship's company'.

Tosswil remained as executive officer, while the new chief engineer was another decorated officer. John Witham Esmonde was a member of an aristocratic Irish family that claimed descent from William the Conqueror. He had won the Distinguished Service Cross for service in the destroyer *Zulu* in the *Bismarck* action when 'the ship's machinery was handled with great skill' and 'he showed great devotion to duty and coolness under fire'. His brother Eugene had led the disastrous attack on the *Scharnhorst* and *Gneisenau* during the Channel Dash of early 1942 and was awarded a posthumous Victoria Cross for it, so it was significant that John was now serving in a ship that had done so much to sink the *Scharnhorst*.

Though most of the *Belfast*'s crew were dispersed, a certain number stayed behind to supervise the repairs on the River Tyne, especially in the engineering department. The senior engineer Charles Simpson was among those who remained, along with ERA Ronald Jesse, Bob Shrimpton from the anti-submarine department and seaman gunner Denis Watkinson. Archie Jarvis, a signaller from Merseyside, was pleased to be drafted to the *Belfast* in October 1944 as he had a long-standing school friend on board. Coming from a destroyer, he was happy with the space available. He was to live in the former boys' messdeck, with its toilet and shower room incorporated – though these could not be used in dock: it was necessary to leave the ship and climb up and down ladders to the toilets ashore, but most men kept tins close to their bunks, and these had to be emptied early in the morning before the shipyard workers arrived at eight. Most of the crew lived on board the ship during the refit, though they were allowed leave ashore on many nights. Radar operator Jake Jacobs was accommodated in the former hangar. As a Londoner, he had a culture clash with the natives and their accent. One night he saw a girl home to Gateshead then asked the way to his lodgings in Newcastle. He could not understand the directions and spent the night wandering around.

The engines were stripped for reconditioning after thousands of miles of steaming. Much of the piping for steam heating for Arctic conditions was ripped out and replaced with fans and trunking for better ventilation – though air conditioning was only used for selected compartments.

* * * * *

With the war in Europe apparently drawing to a close, it was likely that much of the Royal Navy, including the *Belfast*, would now be deployed to the Pacific. On 25 October 1944 the Japanese initiated a terrifying new weapon when they launched the first kamikaze suicide bombers against the United States fleet during the Battle of Leyte Gulf. Unlike normal bombers, kamikazes could not be deterred or put off their aim by heavy gunfire: each one would have to be shot down before it reached the ship. In view of this threat, more short-range weapons and anti-aircraft guns would be necessary for a ship heading for the Pacific. Two mountings of medium-range guns, the 4-inch, were removed from the aftermost positions. The others were converted to remote power control or RPC. Two 8-barrelled 'pom-poms' were mounted on either side of the bridge, also controlled by RPC and by Type 282 radar. In addition there were four 4-barrelled 'pom-poms' located on each side, aft of the forward funnel, abreast of the high-angle director tower, aft of the forward 'pom-pom' mounting and on sponsons aft of the high angle-director tower. For shorter range the ship was fitted with a dozen twin Oerlikon guns.

Radar had been transformed in the two years since *Belfast*'s last refit, and she was one of the first ships to form part of 'Bubbly', a crash programme to provide the best radar and information systems for ships going to the Far East. Most of the new radar sets had plan position indicators, or PPIs, and they could be sited where they would be most useful: for example, the Type 274 gunnery radar was in the transmitting station. The PPI was combined with the Skiatron, which projected the radar picture on to a screen for plotting. Beam switching was now used on many sets: this was a device that oscillated the beam 25 times a second to give a much more accurate bearing as the edges of two beams overlapped. Sets were now usually rotated continuously, removing the need to reverse direction after each full circle.

Type 277 radar, a high-power set on the ten-centimetre waveband, was fitted for surface warning, replacing the well-used Type 273. It could also find the height of an aerial target up to 40 degrees by elevating the parabolic reflector aerial. Type 281 was the long-range air warning system, which could detect high-flying targets up to 110 miles away. It had a beam-switching device that gave an accuracy of one degree, but it needed efficient maintenance to keep up its performance. Type 274 was fitted to control the 6-inch armament. It was considered 'an integral part of the fire control arrangements'. As well as measuring the distance of the target, it could 'spot' the fall of shot, not just telling the gunners whether the splashes were over or short, as visual observation would do in good conditions, but also their actual distance away from the target. Type 282, with its 'fishbone' aerials on top of the director, was used to direct the 'pom-poms' with a maximum range of 6,000 yards and 50 yards' accuracy. Type 283 controlled the anti-aircraft barrage for the main and secondary armaments, with a range of zero to 7,000 yards and an accuracy of 40 yards. Type 285, with fishbone aerials mounted on the directors, was for high-angle anti-aircraft fire. It could operate at a maximum range of 40,000 yards, and beam-switching allowed it an accuracy of 15 to 30 minutes, a quarter or a half of a degree. Type 293Q was to be used for close-range height finding and surface warning. With such equipment searchlights were no longer necessary and they were removed.

The ship also had a new coat of paint and a totally different scheme of camouflage as the disruptive scheme was found to be ineffective. Instead of the variegated colours of the older system, she had a long, simple rectangle in dark paint near the centre of the ship with the rest in lighter grey, a system known as the 'standard light tone scheme'. Before sailing she had the usual inclining test in dock on 14 April, though weather conditions were not ideal and only 1½ hours were available because of the tide, and some readings had to be disregarded after it was found that the ship was still being held by a wire. It was found that her weight had increased by 520 tons since 1942 – but only 234 of these could be accounted for.

* * * * *

By the time she was ready for sea on 18 April 1945, the European war was nearly over, as Allied armies advanced into Germany; the Soviets reached Berlin two days later, and Hitler killed himself at the end of the month. This was a difficult time for the navy as selective demobilisation began. According to Admiral Sir Algernon Willis, Dick's predecessor as Cunningham's chief of staff, 'We have seldom got through a major war without some breakdown of morale varying from serious mutiny down to vociferous expressions of dissension and dissatisfaction.' He knew that naval mutinies had started off the social breakdowns in Russia and Germany at the end of the last war, and the peacetime Invergordon mutiny of 1931 had forced Britain off the gold standard and undermined the confidence of naval officers. There were likely to be more specific problems if the war in the Pacific went on for years:

… some of the ingredients which go to make trouble of the type referred to seem likely to exist when the Germans are defeated and the full realisation that for the Navy this will mean an even greater effort in order to defeat Japan is brought home to the personnel. We shall no longer be fighting for our existence, the homeland will no longer be in danger, many of the other two services will be released to industry and at the same time personnel of the Navy, which must be kept at full strength, will be required to do more foreign service than ever.

Every effort was made to find men for the British Pacific Fleet. Arriving at Chatham just before the end of the war in Europe, Ordinary Seaman George Melly was confronted by a petty officer who said, 'We'll have you out East before the fuckin' week's out' – though in fact he managed to avoid the draft by taking the advice of old hands. Regular sailors whose time had been extended due to the war were being released, as were some of the older wartime entrants, who had often become experienced petty officers and leading hands by this time. An attempt to persuade men to transfer from HO to continuous service engagements was a dismal failure, with only 1,694 applicants out of more than 800,000 men in the navy. On the other hand, many young men who had signed on for twelve years at the height of the war were having second thoughts and applied to transfer to HO engagements: at first the Admiralty treated them sympathetically, but the numbers were so great that they were only allowed in exceptional cases. Meanwhile, according to Louis Le Bailly, 'Some were determined to avoid their Pacific drafts and most of the regular petty officers, artificers and mechanicians were survivors who rightly felt they had done their bit. There was also an infusion of Barrack Stanchions, men who, thus far, had avoided sea service. As the war in Europe drew to a close they had not been rumbled …' This was not the ideal material from which to build a crew.

The *Belfast* finally left Shields on 6 May but headed for Rosyth for further repairs and entered the main basin at 1110 on the 7th. The men were given three or four days leave but there were no travel warrants to take them home by train unless they could purchase them unofficially. They were mostly in Rosyth in the morning of the 8th when they heard that the European war had ended. Captain Dick cleared the lower deck and told the men the news, but he was annoyed when they cheered. Jake Jacobs used his leave to go to Edinburgh. With his knack of finding feminine company in any circumstances, he got together with a tough ex-land girl and joined a procession through the city led by bagpipers. But he failed to get away from them and again he spent the night on the streets.

A group of midshipmen joined on 22 May after the long train journey from the south via King's Cross Station in London, breakfast at the North British Hotel in Edinburgh and the train across the Forth Bridge to Inverkeithing. They included David Mudford and the future admiral James Eberle. On joining they were shown the chart and plotting rooms where most of them would work and the gunroom where they would live – it was overcrowded at the moment and some of them would have to sleep in the chest room. They met some old friends, including the sub-lieutenant of the gunroom, M. B. H. Kersey whom they had known at Dartmouth. Mudford was appointed 'tanky', or navigator's assistant, which involved much time on the bridge and gave him an insight into the ship's planned movements. He enjoyed it even though it had to be done in addition to the usual midshipman's duties. Conditions in the gunroom improved after a few days when three midshipmen (E) left the ship and there was more space. They had already heard a 'buzz' that they were going to the Far East, and Eberle was pleased at the prospect of more action, while having time to visit his girlfriend in Bristol when the ship was in dock.

On 11 June they left the Rosyth basin at last and headed straight to Scapa Flow for more exercises. There was difficulty mooring to a buoy in a gale – the blacksmith and 'buoy jumper' were swept off the buoy in the wind. The ship's whaler picked up the buoy jumper and a lifebuoy was thrown to the blacksmith, who was picked up by a motor fishing vessel. On the 14th they began exercises in the Pentland Firth, which Mudford considered to be 'fully comprehensive' – though there was still a great deal to learn. Mudford had served in the battlecruiser *Renown*, which he thought was one of the most unorthodox ships but one of the happiest. In contrast he felt that the spirit of the *Belfast*'s company was 'undoubtedly bad' at this point. His captain did not agree.

At 2330 on Sunday the 17th they slipped their buoy and headed for Malta to work up more fully. After two days of bad weather they were at Gibraltar for refuelling on the 21st; they anchored outside and there was no shore leave. Mail and new charts were brought on board, the ship refuelled from an oiler and then headed out in the dog watches that afternoon. There was something of a holiday atmosphere, and they were warned against the dangers of sunbathing. Some looked on in envy as they saw two troopships bringing men of the Fourteenth Army home. To Bob Shrimpton it was an 'incredible change' in the climate from the days in the Arctic. There was a smooth voyage to Malta, interrupted by a range-finding exercise with the fast minelayer *Manxman*, which played the part of a Japanese cruiser ferrying troops to Sicily. All was not well with the new command and control systems during an air exercise, as Mudford wrote in his journal:

There was a certain amount of confusion in the compass platform throughout as various voices kept floating over the air on the intercom and SRE without announcing who they were or who they were addressing. They were reporting five different raids and there were eight different raids plotted on the LOP in the RPR, some in true bearing and miles and others in relative bearing and thousands of yards. It was at times extremely difficult to follow and I think the use of these co-ordinates will have to be cut down considerably before perfect efficiency and clarity can be obtained.

* * * * *

Arriving at Malta, they entered Grand Harbour in Valetta – Jake Jacobs noticed the brightness of the colours after drab, wartime Britain. Despite the dramatic surroundings, it could be a difficult experience for the ship's officers in front of the crowds that might be watching from viewpoints on shore. Mudford noted, 'When coming to a buoy in this ship, if there is a strong wind blowing many factors have to be considered. Of primary importance obviously is getting the bow near the buoy with the ship stopped. An extremely close second however is getting the picking up rope to the buoy and as this is done by means of a whaler much consideration must be paid to it.'

For most of the crew this would be their first experience of a real 'run ashore' in a traditional naval port. Those who had stayed on during the refit had only known the cold and unfriendly northern harbours, while most of the younger seamen had never been abroad. Malta had been severely damaged by bombing in the war, and there was a strong nationalist movement that wanted the British to leave, but for the moment they were happy to entertain the sailors as they had done for more than a century. Ashore, the men encountered a deeply religious people with the women often dressed in black, but that did not stop them enjoying themselves. In The Gut, in the capital Valetta, they found clubs such as the *Diamond Horseshoe* and the *Union Jack* with female impersonators known as 'Sugar' and 'Playful Bobby'. Jacobs got very drunk and played the piano. He found his way back to the jetty, but the last liberty boat had left. He hired a traditional Maltese 'dgiasha' to get back to the ship but had an altercation with the boatman when he found that he had no money left – then he discovered that his pay book had been stolen. Disciplinary action awaited him. Officers' Cook Bernard Thomson had used his white uniform in the galley and had to go ashore in his blues, which made him stand out, especially since it was the hottest day for five years. Midshipman Mudford played tennis in the Marine Club. He also visited some of the tunnels where the people had spent many days at the height of the war: 'Most of the tunnels are made by man, not by nature, and are deep and strong enough to withstand any bombs which have been produced. Off the main tunnels have been built small tunnels which lead into great underground rooms many of which have been fitted out as workshops and minor factories.'

But they were at Malta to work up, and on Monday 1 July they began their exercises. Now that peace was restored to the Mediterranean the area was 'extensively used as a working up base and has all the facilities as such'. Mostly they anchored in St. Paul's Bay to the west of Valetta in the evenings, and Eberle remembered an incident when the forecastle officer allowed the anchor to be caught twice in succession under the bow when it was being raised, to the captain's fury: 'I had never before seen anyone quite as angry and agitated ...' More happily, the officers and ratings competed at water polo. They had a night-encounter exercise with the destroyer *Jervis* and motor torpedo boats, and they were 'attacked' by aircraft on 14 July when Mudford noted, 'We fired 6" and 4" barrage ... there is much improvement in barrage shooting.' They practised station keeping with the monitor *Abercrombie* and fired the 4-inch guns and 'pom-poms' at a 'Hong Kong', or splash target. There were more signs that they were going to the east to cooperate with the American fleet when a chief yeoman who had specialised in American signals gave a lecture to the executive officers.

Mudford followed the general election which was going on at home, and on 2 July he recorded,

> Last night Mr Churchill made the last of the pre-election speeches. He spoke well but a lot of the drive of his war speeches was lacking. He brought out that the Labour party had been treacherous and that it would not tolerate any more coalition of the parties if it came into power. This I consider he was justified in doing as Labour, evidently, when in supremacy, has not played the game by Churchill and the national government since the campaign began.

The new ventilation systems were not entirely adequate, and one Sunday Captain Dick addressed the crew after divisions. 'Amongst other things he said that everything would be done to better the ventilation on the messdecks. Work on this has already started and a large ventilation mushroom has been put in on the port side of the boat deck which will supply air to the Royal Marine barracks. I think the barracks is probably the worst ventilated place in the ship (apart from the after HACP).' Though he was conservative in many ways, this caused Mudford to think more about the condition of the lower deck:

> When I go forward through the port waist and see messes of ratings, in particular Royal Marines, sitting on the deck and eating meals

with their fingers it rather horrifies me to think that they cannot even have meals in comparative comfort. However thoughtless, smug and plutocratic an officer is I cannot believe that he can return to his mess, after seeing the 'troops' living under such conditions, sit in a comfortable chair with a fan blowing on him and a whisky-and-soda at his elbow, and think to himself, 'Well I expect they come from poor backgrounds and are used to such things.' ... This is the British Navy, probably the most famous and romantic service in the world, and everyone who enters it should be improved mentally and physically by the time they leave it.

Standards of living ashore were levelling out, he believed. The working classes were moving closer to the middle classes, but 'the British Navy does not appear to have taken this into consideration ... The Americans can do it, why cannot we?'

As working up drew to a close, the ship was moored alongside the small cruiser *Orion* in Grand Harbour when the gunroom was raided by the *Orion*'s midshipmen in a typical prank. They stripped it down to the bare bulkheads as Mudford lamented. 'The dart board, pipe rack, clock, carpets, pictures and the barber's pole had vanished.' Next day they launched a counterattack 'with partial success' during the quarterdeck and wardroom farewell party.

Everyone knew that the greatest threat to the ship came in the terrifying form of kamikaze suicide aircraft, and the high command issued instructions on how to deal with them. Captains should use maximum speed and manoeuvrability consistent with fire control. Lookouts should be restricted to their own sectors and avoid sightseeing; they should look up, especially when low cloud cover might bring a sudden attack. Early recognition was needed as well as a method of identifying friendly aircraft. Unnecessary personnel should stay below; those above should be properly clothed. Fire-fighting equipment should be well placed, and there should be a drill every morning. This was worrying enough, but most people felt that there was no real answer – the best hope was that the kamikazes would concentrate on the aircraft carriers and ignore a cruiser.

* * * * *

On 25 July they left Grand Harbour in company with three 'Hunt' class escort destroyers, which Mudford lamented would reduce average speed considerably. They continued to exercise and had to fight off a mock attack by motor torpedo boats. Off the North African coast they landed marines in an exercise, and Denis Watkinson took his usual place in a motor boat towing one of the ship's whalers. The marines jumped into the water and landed, then after the exercise they came back on board by scrambling up nets. At 1900 on the 26th the BBC announced that the Labour Party had won the election with a large majority. Midshipman Mudford was concerned: 'For the first time in history labour is on power as well as office. I cannot pretend to like it.'

They arrived at Port Said at 0720 on the 27th, and in his role as tanky Mudford went ashore with the navigator's yeoman to return charts and pilot books of the Mediterranean. After waiting 24 hours for a gap in the traffic they entered the Suez Canal at 0940 with the escort destroyer *Eggesford* a short distance ahead. Someone in a crowd of soldiers on shore shouted 'What ship?', and one of the crew, referring to the recently liberated concentration camp and its notorious commandant, answered 'Belsen', and another made it even worse when he added, 'and we've got the Beast of Belsen on board as well'. Captain Dick, already in an anxious state, ordered the arrest of the man, but he could not be found among the crowd. Denis Watkinson was intrigued to see camels on shore. They changed pilots at the first lake and saw the famous old battleship *Queen Elizabeth* moored in the Great Bitter Lake. Mudford was unsentimental and thought that she would provide enough scrap for a dozen destroyers, but instead, 'we waste money and material to build new ships while leaving old and useless ships to clutter up and rot in our busy ports'. The signal 'Hands to bathe' was piped, and Mudford found 'the water was terrifically warm and very buoyant ...' Bernard Thomson was beginning to feel trepidation about what was ahead, along with 90 percent of the crew, he thought. They had all heard stories about Japanese cruelty and their suicidal bravery. For now, they were enjoying good weather and getting a suntan despite advice to the contrary. It was like life on a liner – but soon they would have to face a fanatical and desperate enemy.

On Saturday morning the officers were told of their programme as far as Colombo in Sri Lanka, which was then the British colony of Ceylon. They were to arrive at Aden for refuelling on the 31st. Once there, Mudford regretted that they lost Chief Yeoman Heath 'who is now age and service group 22 having finished his twelve years' service. All the gunroom were very sorry to see him go as he was a very nice fellow and has taught us a lot.' They left next morning, and at sea they made a speed of 22 knots and continued to exercise their close-range weapons with mock attacks by Spitfires and Baltimore bombers.

The men were suffering increasingly from the heat during the voyage, and equipment and techniques were barely adequate. It was necessary to wash white uniforms regularly, and if any soap was not washed out the man was likely to get 'dhobi rash' – Jake Jacobs found that the top layer of his skin was burned off and he got no sleep. The sick-berth attendant put iodine on his penis which was 'like a walnut' next morning, and he washed his clothes carefully after that. The ventilation of the messdecks was still inadequate despite Dick's efforts, and the men often suffered from 'prickly heat'.

They arrived at Colombo shortly after 0700 on Monday 6 August, dropping both anchors and swinging through 90 degrees to moor the stern to a buoy. As it was no longer an operational area, lights were at 'full brilliance' again. The harbour was packed with merchant shipping and a large number of small naval vessels that seemed to be preparing for an invasion of the Andaman Islands, Malaya or the Nicobar Islands. The lower deck did not enjoy the visit because there were no facilities for them. Jake Jacobs, however, was interested to see boys playing football with bare feet and found a family friend who invited him to his bungalow. He had his first curry there and nearly choked. Mudford and his colleagues went around the docks. 'The rubber plantations have now got over their worst difficulties and are starting to make up for lost time. There were many large storage sheds absolutely packed with rubber awaiting transportation to New York.' But already there were signs of political trouble. 'The violently anti-European party, which has been in prison throughout the war, has just been released … its leaders are touring the country and are collecting vast crowds which frequently number over ten thousand.'

Before they sailed from Colombo, Signaller Archie Jarvis noticed that messages started flowing, which showed that something important was happening. The crew soon received momentous news, though not everyone was able to appreciate its scale. An atom bomb had been dropped on the Japanese city of Hiroshima with devastating effect. To most of the men this came out of the blue – Denis Watkinson registered that 'some bomb had been dropped' – and most of them had no idea what it was. They were fortunate to have Instructor Lieutenant Harold Robert Jones, BSc, on board. He had worked on radium at Birmingham University and he had read newspaper articles in Malta which hinted that a new 'secret weapon' might be under development. He wrote to his wife asking her to send on his notes, and by chance they arrived in Colombo just in time. He offered the captain a talk to explain nuclear fission. According to Mudford,

> … our 'Schoolie' was at Birmingham University at the beginning of the war, reading science, and had been in the Birmingham lab which worked to solve the 'splitting of the atom'. We actually developed the process to a far greater extent than any of our allies, but owing to limited experimental gear and insufficient available scientists we turned our knowledge over to the Americans to complete. Lieutenant Jones gave a talk to the officers in the wardroom on Wednesday night on both the theory and the practical application of the splitting of the atom.

He described the theory in some detail, in possibly the first talk of its kind in the world. Mudford noted it all down, musing, 'The possibilities of this discovery are fantastic. They have already been shown as far as war is concerned … but the commercial aspect of it is hard to conceive.' Jones also gave two talks to the lower deck in the hangar, and ERA Roland Jesse found it 'quite stirring', while Archie Jarvis still didn't understand it. Stores Assistant Frank Briggs thought that Jones did very well in introducing things like neutrons and protons, but still found it difficult to follow.

* * * * *

They sailed south towards Australia, and on Wednesday 8 August they crossed the Equator, 'the line', at 1658¾, as recorded precisely by the navigation officer. This was considered too late in the day for the traditional saturnalia, but next morning 'Neptune with all his train came aboard and was enthroned on A turret. After the captain and commander had been "knighted" the proceedings went forward. The list included many who had crossed the line before but had [no] warrants to square off.' To Archie Jarvis it was 'a great laugh'. Jake Jacobs did not mind being 'drowned in the bloody bowl' made of canvas, especially since the officers were not spared the ordeal.

On 10 August as they approached Fremantle, Japan announced it was prepared to accept unconditional surrender. Archie Jarvis was

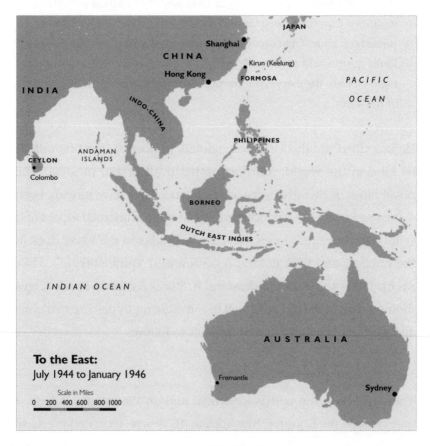

probably in the great majority in being very pleased that he might get home soon. Jake Jacobs and his colleagues were surprisingly indifferent – an officer and a steward had been found in a compromising position in a cabin in the cruiser *Black Prince*, and that was the talk of the fleet. ERA Roland Jesse was ambivalent, half pleased but half regretful that all the working up was to no purpose. 'Schoolie' Jones wondered if it meant they would go home soon but was told, 'last out, last back'. Nevertheless it was a heady moment as they arrived at Fremantle, with the war just finished and a welcoming, English-speaking population. Wednesday the 16th was considered 'V-P' or Victory in the Pacific day, and as soon as all essential work had finished the men were allowed ashore from 1030 till 0815 next morning – though Commander Tosswil warned them that they would be slipping her anchor within three or four minutes of that time, so they should not be late back. The majority of them, according to Mudford, went to Perth, twelve miles away, but some stayed in Fremantle where 'there was less rowdy fun but no lack of entertainment'. Jacobs was surprised by the ice-cold, almost tasteless beer and like most of his comrades he was shocked by the law that closed all the pubs at six o'clock. Bernard Thomson went to a civic reception where they were issued with fruit and chocolate and every sailor was taken home by a family. Not all the men were well behaved, and Mudford commented coyly, 'I think it will be better for me to leave well alone and to make no effort to recapture some of scenes which occurred there and which will probably not reoccur until next victory day.' But, he went on, 'We were very fortunate in leaving only two hands behind … a fair indication of the improvement in the ship's company's spirit since we left the UK.'

There were rough seas on the way to Sydney, but soon Archie Jarvis enjoyed the 'wonderful experience' of sailing through the

Heads into the great harbour. They anchored at the south end by the famous bridge. The ship's anti-aircraft armament was increased yet again when five single Bofors guns were added, replacing some of the twin Oerlikons. These were generally reckoned to be the most effective anti-aircraft guns of the war, but they were in short supply and there were less than 1,400 of them in the navy at the end of the war, more than a third of them in defensively equipped merchant ships. The shell diameter, 40mm or 1.575 inches, was the same as the 'pom-pom', but the muzzle velocity was higher, at 2,890 feet per second compared with 2,400, and a range of 10,750 yards compared with 6,800.

The midshipmen were preparing for their seamanship exams and despite all the distractions 'Schoolie' Jones got them through – no one got a first class mark but most got seconds. Able Seaman Jarvis had brandy in a pub, but he was not used to it and his head hit the table. Denis Watkinson spent a week in the Blue Mountains as the ship was serviced, while Lieutenant Commander Simpson went to the famous Bondi Beach with a party of officers. Able Seaman Jake Jarvis found himself with a party that included celebrities and bankers and was pleased that there were no class distinctions in Australia – it would never have happened in England. And, true to form, he met a girl in a dance hall who took him into the Blue Mountains.

* * * * *

They sailed on 30 August with a more serious purpose in mind. The widely-scattered Japanese forces had not all surrendered formally, and there was a strong possibility that some of them would resist. Britain had been humiliated by numerous defeats in the early days of the Pacific War, most notably the surrender of Singapore, so one of the *Belfast*'s jobs was to restore the prestige of the Empire in the Far East. More urgently, there were thousands of captives – military prisoners of war and civilian internees – in camps all around the region, often badly treated, starved and in need of medical attention as well as liberation.

The first call was to be at Formosa (now Taiwan), but rough weather was encountered on the way, on the fringes of a typhoon. Mudford noted the colourful behaviour of the first lieutenant, who was apparently steeped in naval history:

> No 1 who had been leaning over the front of the bridge playing sea dogs with himself and his imagination, waited till the squall had reached its greatest fury, then stripped off, except for his short and socks, tore down the wind screen and strutted about the bridge bare footed tugging at his beard and smoothing his dripping and drooping moustaches!!
>
> Then the shouting started
>
> 'Snottie, warn the captain visibility is down to ½ a mile. No immediate danger.' [the ship was 240 miles from land and no shipping on the radar]
>
> 'Messenger, fetch my glasses!'
>
> 'Drummer, find the duty petty officer'
>
> 'Officer of the watch, What's your ship's head? – how much wheel is she carrying?'
>
> I could read his imagination like an open book. He was the mate of a privateer in a land locked harbour with a coast guard cutter pulling out to them.

By 0900 on 10 September they were in sight of Formosa, and 'a damned miserable sight it was too!' according to Mudford. Officers' Cook Bernard Thomson was amused by a Japanese harbour pilot who came on board dressed 'like an admiral of the fleet' in a cocked hat with plumes and guided them through a minefield. They entered Kiirun harbour an hour later, and *Belfast* was to regain her status as a flagship under Rear Admiral Reginald Maxwell Servaes. The opposite characters of Admiral Burnett and Captain Parham had complemented each other in the Arctic, but now Servaes and Captain Dick had a good deal in common. There was never any doubt about the admiral's 'brains': he had gained firsts in all five subjects at Dartmouth in 1913 with a £10 prize and two months' seniority. His references were glowing throughout his career, though some thought he seemed rather slow and lethargic and others that he was too argumentative. In 1940 he was at the Admiralty, where he took charge of the defence of naval bases against invasion and saboteurs. He commanded the *London* in the Arctic, and she was considered 'the most efficient ship in the First Cruiser'. In 1943 he was the naval member of a delegation to Portugal, which culminated in them being allowed to use bases in the Azores. It was reported, 'He has good judgement, is extremely loyal and though apt at times to get a little heated in argument, is not afraid to press his honest opinions however unpalatable he may know them to be.'

On entering the harbour, the *Belfast* came alongside the *Berwick*, which was flying Servaes' flag. A brow, or gangway, was passed between the two ships and the staff transferred the admiral's goods and papers. The *Belfast* shifted berth and later the admiral came on board. Mudford saw him taken below by the captain, after which the midshipmen 'heaved a sigh of relief and stayed off for a time in the gunroom'. Servaes and Dick would need all their skills on the mission that was to follow.

The situation was confused to say the least – the local Japanese had not yet signed their surrender. Mudford noted, 'On our starboard side there is an imperial flag flying from the signal station, a Yank flag on the house adjacent to it, a Chinese flag on a junk alongside, while the task group of course flying the white ensign and the oiler flying a blue ensign. Damned annoying.' British and Allied prisoners of war in the area had been employed in terrible conditions in copper mines, and Mudford was told reliably, 'There are over 100 ex POWs in the hospital ship suffering from malnutrition and the authenticated stories of their existence in Jap hands are atrocious … They were treated as slaves and if they failed in their presumed duties they were beaten, often to death.' To Lieutenant Commander Simpson they were 'walking skeletons.' They were taken straight to the hospital ship, so most of the *Belfast*'s crew saw little of them, but they were shocked and outraged by what they heard. The war artist Jim Morris, who had entered the port in the *Belfast*, did a sketch of them.

They did not stay long but slipped and proceeded to sea astern of the cruisers *Bermuda* and *Argonaut*. They were to rendezvous with elements of the United States Seventh Fleet to enter the great port of Shanghai. On the way they passed another typhoon, which Mudford relished:

> As we plunged into the head sea it was a fine sight to watch the cruisers crashing into the swell and leaping up again with solid sheets of spray flying clear by the painting strakes. The destroyers were not doing so well as the swell was too long for them and they were buried in the seas right up to their forecastles and up to the foremost guns.

* * * * *

Modern Shanghai was largely a British creation. It was one of five 'treaty ports' forcibly opened up to foreign trade after the Opium War of 1842, at the same time as Hong Kong was annexed to the

British crown. It was near the mouth of the Yangtze River, which allowed access to 750,000 square miles of land and a population of 180 million. The great river itself was too wide to offer shelter, so Shanghai was developed fourteen miles up its tributary, the Whangpoo (now the Huangpu). The British Concession was north of the old Chinese city and stretched four miles inland from an acute bend in the river known as the Bund, with a spectacular built-up waterfront. The French concession was south of that, and there was also a great deal of American trade with the city. It was a vibrant international community with great extremes of wealth and poverty, and before the war it had been the sixth busiest port in the world. In those days there had been a system of 'extra-territoriality' by which residents in the concessions were only subject to the laws of their own countries; but that had ended by an agreement with the Chinese nationalist leader Chiang Kai-shek. The city had been occupied by Japanese invaders since 1937, and after Pearl Harbor the numerous British and American citizens had been interned.

By 13 September the *Belfast* was within striking distance of Shanghai but six hours from the entrance to the Yangtze River when they received a signal from the American Admiral Kinkaid ordering them not to enter until reinforced by his squadron as they were not considered strong enough without support. Mudford commented that the force was already strong, consisting of the aircraft carrier *Colossus*, three cruisers and three destroyers. They were 'all pretty fed up at receiving this signal …' but Servaes had to conform and reduced the speed to eight knots. They were 50 miles north of the Yangtze at dawn when they met the American ships, the cruiser *Nashville* of 1937 and three *Fletcher*-class destroyers. Mudford and his colleagues were 'damned angry at being kept waiting for this junk outfit the yanks had the nerve to call a squadron'. They were ordered to anchor to await the arrival of the transport *Rocky Mount*. Servaes was called on board the *Nashville* but according to Mudford he was, 'so angry at being fouled by him that he refused to go unless given a direct order to do so'. He was no more pleased when he had his orders from Kinkaid:

> He said that *Belfast* must berth at the head of the line, as the buoys off the Bund would not take her, which statement I found after proceeding up river to be incorrect. This plan gave the three best berths off the Bund, including the British buoys, to the three American flagships, with the *Belfast* some little distance up the river, not visible to the crowds which throng the Bund. A comparatively minor matter such as this counts a great deal in the East.

Moreover, the other British ships, led by the *Bermuda*, were not to be permitted to visit other ports in the area to restore prestige and rescue prisoners. Chiang Kai-shek had proclaimed that 'while American ships were very welcome in every Chinese port British ships were not [repeat] NOT and he complained of our entry into Shanghai … Kinkaid received the impression that the General-issimo's attitude which is based on his resentment over Hong Kong and suspicion of Imperialistic motives is unlikely to change in the near future.' Americans had only appeared in China as traders; the British had humiliated the Chinese during the Opium Wars of 1839–42 and 1856–60, and that had not been forgotten.

The ships began to sail up the Whangpoo River to Shanghai with the *Belfast* in the rear, but there was not enough water on the bar for her to cross so she had to wait for the afternoon flood tide. The river was winding but not as difficult as it had been because the banks had been built up in the last few decades. However, the Admiralty handbook warned that only the position up to 1937 was known about, and 'conditions in many places must be radically different, especially with regard to port facilities and communications'. Moreover, the *Belfast* was the largest British warship ever to enter the port. On the way up it seemed that Chiang Kai-shek's dislike of the British was not universal. According to Mudford they were, 'warmly received. Everything and everyone hooted, yelled, clasped, threw fireworks etc, and we let off an occasional blast … to prove that we British were not impervious to applause, and in addition we were flying our real silk ensign while the band struck up on X gun deck. On every boat, ship, house and factory there were flags flying and I am glad to say that next to the Chinese national flag the union jack was most in evidence.' American sailors were seen to dance on their decks to the Royal Marine band, but it was not easy to bear as they approached the city. 'As we came round the bank into sight of the main Shanghai water-front we saw *Nashville* and *Rocky Mount* lying in the two pre-war British flagship berths. This did not add to our delight and when we found that our berth was in front of the French settlement … away from the berth that was ours by right.' Nevertheless Servaes took comfort in his belief that, 'It was in some ways an advantage that *Belfast* came up harbour by herself later in the day. Particular care was taken in regard to ceremonial with the ship's company fallen in and guard and band paraded … The U.S. ships being by this time berthed, *Belfast* passed between them and the Bund which meant passing the latter packed with spectators at relatively close quarters.' Even Mudford took some comfort from the fact that, 'In our light paint and lighter superstructure we were by far the best looking ship in harbour and made the Yanks look like urchins.' She moored with two anchors upstream and her stern to a Japanese buoy.

Teams to deal with the internees had been landed in three-seater Barracuda aircraft from the carrier *Colossus* while the British consular team was re-established in the city. It was soon discovered that there were around 6,000 internees in camps near Shanghai and 4,500 further away. Their condition was 'somewhat uncomfortable' according to Servaes, but in general they had been treated far better than the prisoners of war on Taiwan. Only about 400 of them expressed a wish to be evacuated to the United Kingdom, but for the moment the others were not able to go back to their pre-war homes in the area, as they were often occupied by Japanese, Chinese or Americans. They would remain in the camps for now, but each of the ships in harbour would adopt one of the camps for entertainment purposes. In Lunghau Camp, thirteen-year-old James Maas knew that something was happening as the guards disappeared, but the actual release seemed an 'indefinite affair' even though he was able to make a trip into Shanghai with friends and visit a swimming pool.

On Monday 2 November the ship was opened to visitors of British nationality, and according to Mudford it was 'so perfect' that for the rest of the week all the ships of the squadron were open. 'The drill was to embark guests in any available boats at about 1400, show them round the ships and give everyone a 5/3*d* [26*p*] voucher for the canteen, giving them time on board and return them to shore at about 1700. The chief thrill they got out of it was being on British territory, but a close second was the navy "flannel".' Children's parties were held on the ship, to the delight of the seamen who could be sentimental on occasion and often missed their own families. They used their ropework skills to the full to rig up swings of various kinds, drawn by the artist Jim Morris and recorded by official photographers. Jake Jarvis thought the ex-internees were 'bloody well dressed' and met a young man with 'a plum in his mouth' whom he believed was J. G. Ballard – at the time fifteen years old, who later wrote *Empire of the Sun*. Young James Maas had already visited the USS *Nashville*, where he was plied with ice cream, but he enjoyed the event on *Belfast* too.

The midshipmen went ashore soon after their arrival. Mudford noted, 'We went to a very Chinese restaurant where we had a very Chinese meal, which I conceived was excellent in quality but poor in quantity …' According to Eberle, 'much of our time was sent trying to use chopsticks to shove bean shoots and pak choi (a sort of cabbage) into our mouths from a small chow bowl held close to the chin. We drank copious quantities of Chinese rice wine (shaoxing) and beer (pijiu), and by the time we had finished our meal, we found it difficult to distinguish between the two.' After a few days the midshipmen were found jobs away from the *Belfast*. Mudford went to the landing ship *Glenearn*, a veteran of many operations including the Normandy invasion, which was now being used to transport ex-internees. He was more worried about their mental than physical condition: 'The one thing that really stood out with all those internees was the way the normal British ability to take charge had been driven out of them. You could take charge of them alright …' Eberle and his friend Chambers were sent to the British Consulate where they were employed creating files on potential war criminals, though he was not sure it really did much to help the process. The midshipmen were drafted away from the ship in October to get 'small ship' time in destroyers, and Eberle and Chambers were happy to go to the more relaxed atmosphere on the *Tuscan*. Meanwhile the crew on board the *Belfast* endured a peacetime routine of cleaning, polishing and painting.

* * * * *

Admiral Servaes was increasingly unhappy with his role. He felt that 'this rather shoddy Paris of the East' was doing 'no good to either ships or men'. He did not want to give the impression that the Allied warships were based at Shanghai permanently, and moving them around would help dispel that. He wanted his crews to go to sea and exercise gunnery and other matters before they became rusty. Anxious to visit the other ports of China before winter set in, he proposed to leave the *Bermuda* and two smaller ships while he went on tour with another cruiser and two destroyers. Admiral Kinkaid stood in his way, and Servaes was disappointed when he was ordered to remain at Shanghai. He decided to retain the *Belfast* as his flagship and the *Bermuda* went on tour instead. Meanwhile American ships were moving freely in the area, even at Wei Hai Wei, the pre-war British base to the north.

Servaes attempted to establish relations with the Chinese at all levels. On 19 and 20 September he called on the Mayor of Shanghai, then on Admiral of the Fleet Chen and General Tang en Po (Tang Enbo). On the afternoon of the 20th a hundred thousand Chinese assembled on the Bund and from these 20 'of all ages and both sexes' were invited to tea on each of the flagships. On 10 October, the Chinese National Day, American and British sailors and marines paraded through the streets. Servaes was pleased that a contingent of 200 men from the *Belfast* and the destroyers 'undoubtedly made a markedly favourable impression'. At receptions and the theatre afterwards he found 'the atmosphere at all these functions was extremely cordial and recognition of the British as well as the United States' war effort was gratifyingly noticeable.' Two days later he arranged the 'gala premiere' of Noel Coward's 1943 naval film *In Which We Serve*, which had already proved a great success in Britain and America. The band of the Royal Marines played the Chinese

National Anthem, and there were readings from Churchill's *Onwards to Victory* before the film began. During the showing Servaes noted that, 'The Chinese seemed impressed by the film and some of them were enthusiastic and genuinely moved.' During their own Navy Day at the end of the month, the Americans replied with a showing of *The Fighting Lady*, a documentary about aircraft carriers in combat.

When General Tang en Po gave up his command early in December he visited the *Belfast* bearing gifts of ham, tea and Chinese embroidery. Admiral Servaes could only reply with 'a supply of a popular brand of Stomach Powder which seemed to give him particular pleasure as he has recently been in hospital suffering from stomach ulcers'. When Admiral Chen visited on the 12th he was shown around the *Belfast* 'with the intention of demonstrating the complications of a modern warship in the hope that it might bring home the need of British naval advice in operating the warships which are being given to China'.

Servaes was pleased when Admiral Kinkaid was replaced in December, for he believed that Vice Admiral Barbey was 'a man of much higher capacity than his predecessor, and is most well disposed to the Royal Navy'. But he tended to criticise the maritime arrangements, which were completely in American hands: there was no proper pilot boat in the estuary, no night work was allowed on heavy ships, and at the root of it all there was poor organisation in the port director's office. He was, however, not present to enjoy the British *schadenfreude* on 23rd December when the USS *Blue Ridge* failed to secure to her buoys and was swept down the harbour.

* * * * *

There was still instability in the crew of the *Belfast*, and on 18 October all the men in the age and service groups who could be spared without immediate replacement had been sent by ship to Hong Kong for passage to Australia then home. Often there were good relations with the Americans on shore and in their respective ships. Bob Shrimpton enjoyed their supply ships, like enormous floating supermarkets. Jake Jacobs reported that the Americans discovered how primitive the British ships' cinema equipment was and lent them a second projector so that the show did not have to pause when reels were changed, as well as sending them the latest Hollywood films such as *State Fair* and *National Velvet*. But underlying this was an increasing tension. The chagrin of the admirals and captains may well have filtered down to the crews. The British sailors resented what they saw as the Americans' boastfulness – they had won the Pacific War with practically no help from the Royal Navy, while the British believed they had been in the war longer and had taken on the brunt of resisting the Nazis and fighting the Battle of the Atlantic. They were scornful of American amenities such as ice cream and Coca Cola machines, and despised them in that their ships were 'dry' or free of alcohol. Perhaps the sorest issue of all was the pay of the American sailors, who got three or four times as much as British sailors in equivalent rates. This meant that prices were often higher than the British sailors could afford. There were other niggling issues – at one point the American authorities forbade football matches on the racecourse on Wednesdays, Saturdays and Sundays so that they could play golf, though that was rescinded. Matters came to a head early in December when there were several fights between British and American sailors ashore. Servaes believed that relations were 'remarkably good' on the whole and that the trouble was caused by 'specific gangs of hooligans'. This period entered the *Belfast*'s legend and was later described by old hands to William Hope, who was no stranger to trouble himself: 'I had heard many stories from my shipmates about the 'Battle of Shanghai', when it was alleged that Americans sailors searched the streets of Shanghai for British troops with the intention of beating up the Limeys.' Jake Jacobs learned to stay well away from groups of American sailors who usually outnumbered them, though he thought they were all right on their own.

The *Belfast* left the harbour on 18 December to visit Hong Kong, where Servaes was to consult with his superiors. On 21 December they joined the destroyer *Terpsichore* for exercises and then entered the harbour of Hong Kong. On 23 December they were visited by Admiral Sir Bruce Fraser. Captain Dick had apparently won the trust of the crew over the voyage. Radar operator Charles Quinlain described how he and his friend were standing on the upper deck trying on civilian suits they had bought in Hong Kong and the captain came and talked to them. As a 'punishment' for being out of uniform they were ordered to follow him round during the Christmas celebrations, getting a drink in every mess. On 28 December they sailed again for Shanghai. They berthed at the French buoys on 31 December and Servaes resumed his duties as Flag Officer Force S. By this time most of the internees had been settled one way or another, and by January 1946 there were only 307 left, mostly with ambiguous claims to British nationality, and they were concentrated in Ash Camp. When the *Belfast* sailed from Shanghai on 17 January 1946, there were few regrets.

10

SHOWING THE FLAG

While most of the Royal Navy's sailors worried about how soon they would be demobilised and how many civilian jobs would still be vacant by the time they got home, the senior officers had to face a new world in which their role was vastly reduced. Britain was almost bankrupt and dependent on American loans, so the navy was inevitably reduced to far below what the admirals considered desirable. The new Labour government was against 'imperialism' and was already planning the independence of India, but it did not intend to abandon Britain's status as a world power. That meant a naval presence in the Pacific.

'Showing the flag' meant different things in different places. To a defeated enemy like Japan it might be an assertion of power. To an isolated town in a 'white Commonwealth' dominion like New Zealand it would be a reminder that they still had ties with the mother country. To a colony like Fiji it reassured the European ruling class that they had not been forgotten in London, and reminded the natives of British power. Though it had resonances of Victorian naval might, which seemed obsolete in the days of American supremacy, it still had some effect in places with a strong community spirit, or which were lacking in regular excitement.

The *Belfast* now had to deal with the legacy of British imperialism in the western Pacific. With the defeat of Japan, there was no clear enemy in the region, though the attitudes of the different nations varied greatly. Australia and New Zealand were dominated by white, English-speaking people of British descent, and they still tended to look towards Britain for trade, moral support and military cooperation. The Australian people still bore a certain amount of resentment about their sacrifices in the Dardanelles during the previous war, bitter sporting rivalries such as the 'bodyline' cricket test series in 1932–3, and the alleged arrogance of the 'Poms', but

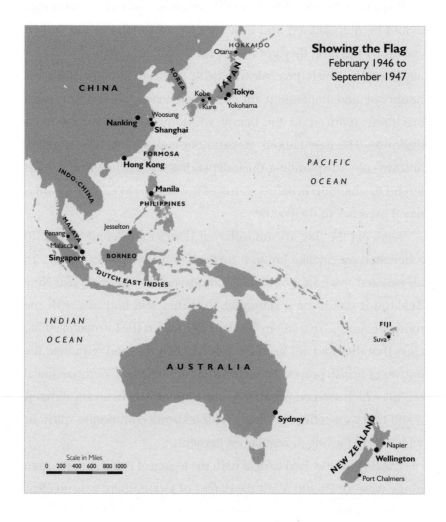

Showing the Flag
February 1946 to
September 1947

that led to nothing worse than joking. Their government was anxious to secure relations with Britain as a source of emigrants whose numbers would make the country far more secure against invasion in the future. China, of course, was greatly changed, as the officers and crew of the *Belfast* well knew, but with the defeat of Japan the British were expected to provide part of the occupation forces – it was still unclear how this would work out.

* * * *

Servaes described the voyage from the Yangtze late in 1946 as 'a pleasant trip south, during which opportunity was taken in the ship to carry out intensive training, vocational training and current affairs courses. A full programme of sports and physical training was also carried out.' They conducted trials by steaming on two propeller shafts instead of four and found 'a considerable saving on the authorised speed of 14 knots resulted although the average speed was 14.20'. On 1 February 1946 they arrived back in Sydney for more repairs. Eight days leave was granted to each watch in turn. Jake Jacobs went ashore and found his girlfriend of the last visit. They went inland to the mining town of Lithgow, 90 miles away. It was 'like a cowboy town', where they proved very popular in the pub, but it was a long way to go to get a drink and the last bus left at five in the evening. The ship had her torpedoes and depth-charges landed, anti-submarine warfare not being regarded as a priority in the Pacific. Twin Oerlikon guns and their blast screens were removed from the quarterdeck, possibly because the area would be needed for entertaining in the ship's new role. Ventilation was improved in various small ways, and air conditioning was fitted to the main switchboard. The ship was put into Woolwich Dock from the 14th to the 19th for essential repairs to the hull. There were many delays due to strikes among the dockyard workforce.

The *Belfast* was to form part of the reduced British Pacific Fleet. As planned in 1946, this would consist of two light fleet aircraft carriers, which would be shared with the East Indies Fleet in the Indian Ocean, four cruisers (one provided by the Commonwealth navies), eight destroyers, twelve escort vessels and ten submarines. In practice the carriers were rarely available, and Admiral Fraser recognised that the service would fall hardest on the cruisers, which were large enough to make an impression during port visits. Each might have to stay out there for more than two years on each commission. Since the war-built cruisers of the 'Colony' classes were more cramped and were considered uninhabitable in tropical conditions, the only suitable ships were the ageing pre-war 8-inch cruisers of the 'County' classes, and those of the 'Town' classes, which for these purposes included the *Belfast*. The naval staff in London juggled with the various ships available to find suitable reliefs, but it was not easy.

* * * * *

Meanwhile there was turbulence in the manning of each ship. According to Admiral Fraser, 'At the end of 1945 and during the first month of 1946 the flood of Age and Service Group reliefs was in full spate.' A hundred ratings left the *Belfast* in Sydney on 14 February to be replaced by 71 others; 91 more left on the 23rd and were replaced by 56. Officers left and were replaced in small groups throughout the period, while small numbers of specialist ratings arrived. It is not too much of an exaggeration to say that the disorder on the messdecks and wardroom reflected the chaos and uncertainty of society outside, in the Pacific as much as anywhere else. Flying was rarely available for the journey home and was often not considered safe – when the government ordered that surplus naval doctors be flown home to ease the medical situation at home, some of them protested that they had already risked their lives enough during the war. The great majority of released servicemen would face a wait in the manning bases in the region – HMS *Golden Hind* at Sydney and the unfortunately named HMS *Terror* at Singapore – followed by a long troopship voyage. Archie Jarvis was one of those who left that month when his age and service number 52 came up. He was drafted to the *Golden Hind* for a month, where he did very little except visit Sydney and become involved in a rum racket made easy by the wildly fluctuating numbers in the messes from day to day. He was then drafted to the aircraft carrier *Implacable*, which was in dry dock at the time; when she was finally ready to sail in June there was a dance on board, to which friends from Sydney were invited. Next morning they waved from the dockside as the ship carrier left. During a 28-day voyage the men were expected to keep watch, though no aircraft were operated, and they arrived in Portsmouth early in July.

Replacements from the United Kingdom were sent first of all to the *Golden Hind* at Sydney until the spring of 1946 and to HMS *Terror* at Singapore from then onwards. One of them was William Hope, who was serving his second gruelling period in detention quarters when he was taken to Southampton in handcuffs and put in a cell on board the liner *Aquitania* for the passage to the Far East. He was let out 24 hours after sailing and told that the rest of his sentence would be remitted when he reached the *Golden Hind*. This Here was a 'sailors' paradise' with only light work in the dockyard until he was drafted to the *Belfast*: 'to join her I had to take passage in *Chaser*, a banana-boat aircraft carrier to Hong-Kong, but *Belfast* had sailed to Shanghai, so I was transferred to HMS *Argonaut*. But navy communications were up the creek because *Belfast* had sailed again; however, a month of travel and passage in *Manxman* I caught up with *Belfast* in Hong-Kong ...' Joining the ship he began to settle down. 'Life on board a cruiser ... was a bit more pusser than life in a destroyer; it was more like living in RN Barracks; however, I soon got used to the routine and having proved to the Master-at-Arms that I was no 'Skate' ['Ne'er-do-well, workshy individual'] I settled down to enjoy life ...'

* * * * *

The *Belfast* sailed from Sydney on 25 February and arrived at Port Chalmers, near Dunedin, in New Zealand, on 6 March for a four-day stay. According to the local newspaper, 'Although visibility was restricted by low clouds, spectators from vantage points on the road leading from Carey's Bay to the Heads had a fine view of her formidable armament as she steamed close to land at the point where the channel sweeps round Deborah Bay.' A special train arrived at Port Chalmers with 'people hanging on the buffers'. The ship was open for visitors, and one officer complained, 'It felt like being in a zoo. We were at tea, and they kept staring into the ward room as if expecting us to pour our tea into our saucers and fan it with our hats.' The city gave the ship a welcome and, according to the local newspaper, 'The men compared Dunedin more than favourably with Sydney, which they found hard.' Moreover, 'Dunedin girls are the subject of much wistful reminiscing in all quarters of the ship.' But to Servaes the visit was only a qualified success – 'much of its value was lost by the necessity of berthing the "Belfast" at Port Chalmers.' He recommended a smaller cruiser of the 'Colony' class for future visits.

She made a ten-hour visit to the capital, Wellington, berthing at Aotea Quay. There was no time for ceremony, leave or visitors except for an unofficial visit by Commodore Faulkner of the New Zealand Naval Board. She refuelled and left at 5 p.m. The visit to Napier was perhaps the most successful of the cruise. The Royal Navy was already very popular there – people remembered the visit of HMS *Hood* during her round-the-world voyage in 1923, and in 1931 the cruisers *Diomede* and *Dunedin* had provided assistance after an earthquake. One more cruiser was neither here nor there in a great port like Sydney, the visit to Dunedin had gone off at half-cock, and Wellington was too short, but it all came together at Napier. It was the main port in Hawkes Bay and was based on the wool trade. It had a population of 19,000, but 15,000 people were estimated to have visited the ship, many of them travelling a long way from farms and small towns. Unlike the *Hood*, the *Belfast* was able to berth alongside, so no boat trip was needed. Once on board, 'the children's enthusiasm at their first visit to a war ship saw the sailors assisting the boys and girls to "man the guns", and they played "battle" with the youngsters, with everything on the ship that was made to move in action.' There was a sports programme including tug-of-war and water polo, cricket matches with local teams, football matches for adults and boys and a dance with the admission price of 2/6. A trip was arranged to the town of Hastings a few miles away where there was a 'Maori Show'. But a march planned for the morning of 11 March was cancelled as the ship had to sail. The mayor begged Servaes and Dick to stay for one more day, but the officers 'regretted that through the exigencies of the service such a course was not possible'. When she sailed in the morning of the 11th, thousands of people gathered on the wharf and cheers rang out as the ship cast off and slowly drew away. The sailors cheered, the band played

Heart of Oak and Captain Dick waved from the bridge. According to the local newspaper, 'As the ship rounded the buoy in the fairway the faint strains of the band music could still be heard. The crowd lingered on the wharf until the *Belfast* rounded the mole and headed into the bay. Crowds subsequently gathered along the marine parade and watched the cruiser until it disappeared into the haze.'

On 15 March the ship arrived at Suva in Fiji. The islands had been under British rule in one form or another since the 1870s. People of European descent, including Australians and New Zealanders, were most likely to feel the benefit of the *Belfast*'s visit, though they formed less than three percent of the population. The ethnic Fijians had contributed large numbers to the armed forces during the war, while the Indians had generally held back on the advice of their nationalist leaders. For a colonial people, the Fijians were comparatively happy because their possession of the land was secure, and their only fear was that the Indians who had been brought in to work in the sugar plantations were overtaking them in numbers. The islands were some way south-east of the main Japanese attack during the war and had not been occupied, but they had never felt secure. A local newspaper reported, 'Now that the war is over and ships of the Royal Navy are again moving more freely in southern waters, we can expect to see more of the White Ensign. It reminds many of us of the happy pre-war days when visits by the Navy meant a round of social functions and entertaining, and we are also reminded of the more anxious days of war when the sight of a British cruiser was a great encouragement to people in the islands, whose defences were necessarily somewhat limited.'

The ship berthed alongside King's Wharf, accepting the risk of infection by copra bugs. The officers had a yacht race against the Suva Yacht Club, but local knowledge prevailed against professional expertise and the *Belfast* team lost by a very narrow margin. Most of the visit was aimed to support and encourage the European rulers, but there were some nods towards native tradition. During various bus tours, officers and men were shown 'a glimpse of Fijian village life'. During a parade on Sunday the 19th, the paramount chief Ratu Mara (later Ratu Sir Kamisese Mara) took the salute alongside Captain Dick. Bob Shrimpton was in charge of the shore patrol and was fascinated by the local police with their red sarongs. After a tour around the drinking dens, they were taken to the police barracks and served rum from an enormous pot, which made 'the world spin'. In general there was no shore accommodation for the sailors, but they were put up for the night in the cells. The ship sailed from Suva on 20 March, with a Fijian military band playing and singing the farewell song *Eisa Lei*. Servaes concluded, 'This brief cruise was of great value to those on board, particularly to the large number whose horizon had previously been bounded by Sydney …'

* * * * *

The next task was to sail to Japan for Servaes to take charge of the naval element of the Commonwealth occupation forces, which controlled the southern part of the main island of Honshu, an area of ten million people and 20,000 square miles. In January 1946 it had been agreed that, 'A squadron of the British Pacific Fleet, which includes ships of the Royal Navy, the Royal Australian Navy, and the Royal Indian Navy is stationed in Japanese waters under operational control of the admiral commanding the detachment of the United Sates fleet.' The voyage from Sydney to Japan was 4,000 miles long and would take more than twelve days, for the ship was not allowed to exceed her economic speed in peacetime. It was nicknamed Operation 'Insomnia', and entertainments were devised. There were sports such as deck hockey in the late afternoon, followed by cinema shows, recorded radio plays, radio broadcasts on the ship's system and a quiz. There was a talk at 2030 each evening, then several members of the ship's company, including some of the boys, made their choice of gramophone records in the style of the BBC radio programme *Desert Island Discs*. As well as his duties as 'schoolie' and giving one of the talks, Bob Jones was squadron meteorological officer. He noticed how the barograph was going up and down, the wind went round to the west and thought it was the sign of an approaching typhoon. He told the captain and then the navigating officer, Meares, who dismissed it as it was out of season; then at seven o'clock that evening an American aircraft reported a typhoon exactly where he had suggested.

The days when Stoker Fursland could say 'I never had better grub' and Richard Wilson could write that 'The food, etc, here is very good' were over. By 1946 there was widespread discontent with food in the navy, inspired perhaps by greater expectations now that the war was over or by contact with the Americans. Admiral Fraser pointed out that American morale in the Pacific war depended on good entertainment, a fast and reliable mail service and 'good food, which includes, for the Americans, ice cream'. He went on, 'All these might have been regarded by us as soft and slightly ridiculous, had it not been found by experience that men fight harder and longer when so treated.' Herring in tomato sauce was still very unpopular, and Jake Jacobs claimed that he usually threw his overboard. The *Belfast* somehow missed out on a survey of attitudes to food in the spring of 1946, but the captains of other cruisers sounded out lower deck feelings. In the *Argonaut* of the Fourth Cruiser Squadron, tinned herrings, salmon, soya link sausages, tinned blueberries, Lima beans and prunes were also unpopular, but her captain suggested that things such as honey, tinned tongue and tinned fruits except blueberries were well liked and available on the Pacific station. Pineapple rings were especially popular and were used for sandwiches in action messing. The captain of the *Bermuda* though the situation was more complex: 'Opinions vary throughout the ship's company and while, for example, herrings in tomato sauce can be said to be generally disliked by ratings, they are comparatively popular with officers. No one likes everything and every one dislikes something … In *Bermuda* for instance it is a waste of time serving excellent tinned asparagus as a vegetable, but ratings have been known to buy tins of asparagus from the canteen, and tins of cream to eat with it.'

The Reverend Donald Young was appointed Chaplain to the *Belfast* in February 1946, succeeding J. D. Duden. He was happy with his cabin, No. 2, 'very conveniently situated – opposite the Commander's Office and at the for'ard end of the Senior Officers' Flat'. The shipyard at South Shields had produced an altar table in unstained oak, and various other items were made on board including a set of copper tubular bells made in the engineer's workshop of the ship, rigged every Sunday in harbour and broadcast over the ship's warning telephone system. The chief yeoman of signals made up bunting with a plain red cross to hang across the cinema stage when it was used for services, and other items such as a silver crucifix and blue-jean altar covers were bought from church funds, while the various flower vases were 'of indeterminate origin'. The navy was still an English institution in the sense that *King's Regulations* demanded: 'Divine Service is to be performed every Sunday according to the Liturgy of the Church of England,' with the proviso that 'Roman Catholics, Presbyterians, Methodists, and others, who entertain religious scruples in regard to attending the services of the Church of England, are to have full liberty to absent themselves from these services'. Each Sunday, Young conducted Holy Communion at eight and eleven in the morning in the ship's chapel, but the 34 places were never filled. Matins were held at ten on the quarterdeck in good weather, or in the cinema and were much better attended. Evensong was held at five after evening quarters, also in the chapel. There was a weekday routine of Holy Communion at 7.30 in the morning and evensong at five, but only if piped. The chaplain also broadcast a two-minute epilogue each evening at 10 p.m. over the ship's loudspeakers when at sea.

* * * * *

The ship arrived at Yokohama in Tokyo Bay in the afternoon of 1 April, and Servaes took over from Rear Admiral Archer. There were reports that a tidal wave had struck Honolulu nearly 4,000 miles away and was expected to hit Japan within 24 hours. Two successive two-foot rises in the water level were recorded on the coast, but the effect was dissipated and it was not felt in the Bay. There was diversion of a different kind on the 3rd when the merchant ship *Samwater* arrived with her boatswain insane and violent – a medical officer and a party of marines were sent to escort him to hospital.

General Northcott, the Australian in charge of the British Commonwealth Occupation Force, enforced a strict rule against fraternisation – a policy that was applied much less by the Americans. Service personnel were told that, 'Every member of the BCOF must bear in mind that he is present in Japan in a dual capacity. He is not only a sailor, soldier or airman. He is a representative of the British Commonwealth of Nations and all that stands for in the world.' He was expected to remember Japanese atrocities during the war, and to keep dealings with the people to an absolute minimum. Despite these conditions, many of the *Belfast*'s men travelled to Tokyo, which was an 'absolute shambles' according to Jones. It was believed that a couple of packets of cigarettes could buy almost anything, but Jones was disappointed when he offered them to a postcard seller and got the reply that he didn't smoke. Chief Petty Officer Telegraphist A. M. Long was fatally injured in a motor accident and three ratings were hurt. On the whole, thought Servaes, 'The facilities for libertymen at Yokohama are very restricted.' There was only the White Ensign Club, which sold no food and only bottles of beer, while its accommodation was in need of improvement.

Servaes decided to make a cruise around Japanese waters with the consent of the American Admiral Griffin. The *Belfast* sailed on 10 April with the Australian destroyer *Warramunga*, leaving a captain in charge as senior British naval officer (afloat). On the way to Kure, the *Belfast* exercised at refuelling the destroyer, a relatively new technique, which was essential to improve the range of British ships. It was considered successful despite 'rather unpleasant weather conditions'. They arrived on the 12th, and Servaes visited Hiroshima. He was almost as sceptical as his gunnery officer had been – 'One pile of rubble, ashes and twisted girders looks very much like another but Hiroshima is certainly flatter than the other Japanese cities that I have seen, which is saying a good deal.' Some of the officers and men took the train to the devastated city, which was especially poignant for Bob Jones. They found a flattened site with only a few pillars from major buildings such as banks still standing. People were living in holes in the ground and some were wandering around. No one, even Jones, was aware of the problems of radiation at that time. In stark contrast, according to Servaes, 'The island of Miyajima, the Shrine Island, is a delightful place and well worth a visit to see the many and beautiful shrines and the lovely view over the Inland Sea from the top of the wooded heights behind the town.'

On 17 April they sailed for Kobe and arrived next day. The wind was too strong to enter the harbour until it moderated towards evening. The American port director was friendly and provided maps, a small guide book of local entertainment and details of trips to Kyoto. There was a party for officers on Easter Sunday in the American naval mess, which the *Belfast* returned with a dinner party next day. They sailed on 23 April and carried out various exercises, resisting a massed attack by more than 30 American aircraft. Servaes was fascinated to see ten-mile long streaks of pink plankton in the water. Back at Yokohama on the 24th, Servaes was offered the much greater size, imposing appearance and communication facilities of the battleship *Anson*, sister to the *Duke of York*, which had arrived on the station. He transferred his flag to her on 1 May but agreed that the *Belfast* and her near-sisters had great attributes even though 'the best type of cruiser for permanent employment on this station is the "Town Class", which have the good habitability, including deck space, the long endurance, and the impressive appearance, which are all of importance in the Far East'. He liked the *Anson* but later wrote, 'It is most unfortunate that the great size and deep draught of these impressive ships precludes their continued employment in this part of the world where the harbours they can enter are so few and far between.' She was sent home soon afterwards.

Many of the British and Commonwealth officials were unhappy about General MacArthur's style of governing Japan, his autocracy combined with a desire to build relations with the defeated enemy, but on the whole Servaes was optimistic about Japan's future:

Under the firm guidance of General of the Army Douglas MacArthur, Japan will be one of the first war ravaged nations to re-establish its internal economy and stand again on its own feet. Whether or not the nation's conversion to the principles of democracy is sincere and permanent I cannot hazard a guess, but the mass of the Japanese people seem to be entirely happy under their present conditions of life and treat the occupation forces with the utmost courtesy and respect.

* * * * *

Next day the *Belfast* left for Hong Kong. From the operational point of view this was a very fine harbour, consisting of the island taken from the Chinese in 1842 and supplemented by the much larger mainland areas, the New Territories, leased since 1898. It was well placed for trade up the Pearl River and with the city and district of Canton. There was a long waterfront that could be used for commercial shipping and a naval dockyard near the centre of it. It was surrounded by high hills, which restricted development but protected the port from the worst of the typhoons. The rise and fall of the tide was only about eight feet, so there was no need to build wet docks for ships to load and unload as was done in British ports such as London and Liverpool: ships could enter and leave at any state of the tide.

To the lower deck Hong Kong offered a different prospect – of cheap drink, highly skilled Chinese prostitutes and exotic adventure. The British were gradually regaining respect since they had surrendered humiliatingly in 1942, and they were much more attractive than the Japanese occupiers had been. They offered peace and stability, and the colony was flooded with refugees from China. Despite his past record, William Hope often found himself part of the shore patrol in Hong Kong, perhaps because he was 6 feet 2 inches tall. On 'bag-shanty' patrol in the brothel district, 'Twice each evening we would raid one of these establishments, kicking down doors and charging in we opened every cubicle; the unfortunate men were all lined up, in all states of undress, mostly naked but still wearing shoes or boots, collect all their pay-books and of course report them.' There was still conflict with American sailors.

> We always worked in conjunction with the American Military Police as it was easier to get around in their Jeeps. This particular evening we were called out to quell a riot in one of the well-known drinking houses, as usual the trouble involved British and American sailors; aided by troops from the local barracks. The MPs steamed in wielding their batons and when it was soon evident that the batons were aimed at the British sailors, this only inflamed the situation, so just to even matters we got stuck in with sticks … needless to say the metal ends only found American bodies. Order was eventually restored, with quite a few arrests and a few cases for the hospital truck.

* * * * *

After that the *Belfast* sailed to Singapore for a slightly more extensive refit, arriving on 16 May. The great naval base had been built up in the 1920s and '30s as the centre of British power in the Far East, but its completion was delayed by financial stringency. She entered a dock that had once held the liner *Queen Mary*, and the *Belfast*, small by comparison, was placed on one side of it. There was the usual problem with accommodation, in that the toilets could not be used and it was a long walk to the facilities ashore, until the men were moved into the fleet shore establishment. Frank Briggs was far more comfortable there, with good meals produced by Chinese cooks, swimming pools, tennis and cricket. He got news of his release from the navy and went into town with a group of petty officers to enjoy lunch, tea at the famous Raffles Hotel followed by a night at the cinema.

On June 1946, Lieutenant Commander Hugh Boyce joined the ship. Born in 1911, he was the son of a petty officer and had served an apprenticeship as an electrical engineer with Clarks shoe company. He worked on power supplies in South Africa but was eventually allowed to leave his reserved occupation to join the navy in 1940. He was commissioned in the special branch for specialist officers, which excluded him from any command role, but in 1944 he played a leading part in clearing the approaches to Antwerp of magnetic mines, greatly improving the supply position of the advancing Allied armies. But it was not his humble origins that made Boyce's appointment to the *Belfast* a milestone in naval history – he was the first fully qualified electrical officer to take up post on board ship. Until then the ship's electrics had been handled by torpedo officers such as 'Andy' Palmer, but few of them had the depth of knowledge and understanding to cope with the latest electronic equipment. The formation of a specialised electrical branch was long overdue, but it was not set up until after the war was over, on the same basis as the engineering branch – and it would take some time for sufficient numbers to be trained. Boyce was already experienced in naval culture as well as electricity, and he was also the electrical officer for the Pacific Fleet. Meanwhile the non-electrical part of the torpedo branch was merged with anti-submarine, though that did not affect the *Belfast* much because her torpedoes and depth-charges had been put ashore in February.

Around this time Captain Dick had a list made up of the regular navy ratings on board, showing a total of 202 men. The normal peacetime complement was 837, but if officers, marines and boys were deducted there should have been 650 adult ratings, so regulars were nearly a third of the complement. All but eleven of them were 'continuous service' men who had signed on for twelve years and were perhaps in their second period of ten years to qualify for a pension. The remainder were 'special service' men who had signed up for five years. Only two of the 202 men were due for release by October that year, so the drafting authorities in Portsmouth had done their job in only sending men with some time left on their engagements. Seventy percent of the regulars were above the rating of Able Seaman or equivalent, and more than half of them were chiefs or petty officers. There were signs that at last the ship was beginning to build up a stable core of leaders and technicians on the lower deck.

On 8 June the ship's company led a King's Birthday parade in Johor Bahru, north of Singapore. The parade was headed by the ship's marine band, then a naval detachment from the *Belfast* followed by more sailors from the base HMS *Terror*. There were numerous army and RAF detachments, and the 'mechanised column' was a highly varied collection of vehicles including a compressor lorry, a bridging vehicle and a machinery lorry. In the dock, ventilation was improved with more trunking and fans, while scuttles that had been blocked off in wartime were re-opened and new ones were cut. Extra derricks were fitted on 'B' gun and on the quarterdeck to improve facilities for re-ammunitioning at sea. Communications were improved with a back-up radio telephony system, and the admiral's quarters were upgraded.

Captain Dick was relieved and left the ship by car on 8 July, with the crew standing on one side of the ship cheering him. The new captain was Henry B. Ellison who, like Dick, had done well at Dartmouth with five firsts and a £10 prize. Born in 1900, he had trained as a gunnery officer and served mainly in battleships and cruisers. He had a broader mind than many officers, and in his youth he was commended for his study of naval history, ethnology, natural history of the sea, psychology, science and mathematics. He was on shore duties for most of the war, commanding the gunnery school at Chatham from 1943, then taking part in a mission to study enemy gunnery after the war. He had never commanded a ship at sea, so this was his chance to establish his claim to the higher ranks. Charles Quinlain thought he was more strict than Captain Dick.

* * * * *

The *Belfast* became a flagship again on 29 July when Vice Admiral Sir Denis Boyd came on board. He was yet another outstanding officer, best known for commanding the carrier *Illustrious* when her Swordfish aircraft launched the devastating attack on the Italian Fleet in the harbour of Taranto in November 1940 – a much-needed boost in Britain's darkest hour. Born in 1891, Boyd qualified as a torpedo officer and served in the cruiser *Fearless*. After the war he was first lieutenant of the *Hood* during her round-the-world voyage and served as torpedo officer for the Mediterranean Fleet from 1928 to 1931. His first command was the destroyer *Valentine* in 1932; then he served in the tactical division of the naval staff at the Admiralty. He was 'a great believer in physical fitness, which for a man of his age he is inclined to overdo', and he did not neglect the mind: his knowledge of professional questions was 'the result of careful study'. Like many others he had had his brushes with authority. In 1936 his destroyer *Keith* collided with a merchant ship and he was partly blamed in that he should have reduced speed sooner, and three years later he was censured for employing a blacklisted Maltese paint contractor.

Though he never learned any flying skills, Boyd was closely connected with naval aviation after he took command of the *Illustrious* early in 1940. After Taranto he was promoted to rear admiral commanding the aircraft carriers in the Mediterranean, then he took charge of the carriers in the Eastern Fleet based in the Indian Ocean. Early in 1943 he took his seat on the Board of Admiralty as Fifth Sea Lord and head of naval aviation. His references were glowing throughout his career. Admiral Cunningham thought he was 'a fine officer, with a strong personality and character. Highly intelligent and well read and can express his views clearly both verbally and in writing.' Only his most recent commander, Admiral Sir James Somerville, had any criticism – Boyd was too lenient with officers and men, and so self-opinionated that he found it difficult to accept any other point of view – but these, the admiral said, were minor defects.

Boyd had the title of Commander-in-Chief of the British Pacific Fleet, but this was not nearly so grand as it would have been two years previously, when it consisted of 142 warships including 4 battleships and 17 aircraft carriers, supported by 94 supply vessels. The Royal Navy as a whole had now been reduced to five battleships, the four surviving members of the *King George V* class and the new *Vanguard*. Even these were too expensive to man and they would soon be laid up, except the *Vanguard*, which mostly served as a Royal yacht or static flagship. The navy had a large force of aircraft carriers but few aircraft to equip them, and for the moment there was nothing to spare for the distant Pacific as major forces were maintained in the Mediterranean and home waters. Destroyers were glamorous vessels in warfare but made less impression in harbour, while frigates and minesweepers were even smaller. This meant that a large part of the burden in the Pacific would fall on cruisers. The

Belfast, of course, no longer carried aircraft. It was ironical that Boyd had made his name as a carrier commander but now he had no aircraft under his command. American carriers had won the Pacific war, but now Britain only had cruisers to show the flag in the great ocean.

Boyd began a cruise round his region on 15 August, sailing in the *Belfast* and leaving his staff in Hong Kong to deal with routine matters while he spoke daily to them by radio and made decisions on policy. The first call was at Yokohama, where Boyd conferred with various dignitaries including General MacArthur and the head of the British liaison mission, who put him up in his house, while General Eichelberger, commanding the US Eighth Army, allowed him the use of his personal railway coach for a journey to Nikko. Relations with the Americans were now excellent, 'indeed everybody, both senior and junior, was most kind, hospitable and helpful throughout'. On the night of the 24th the *Belfast* hosted the first of many cocktail parties during the trip, with 142 guests including representatives of all the countries with an interest in the area, including China, France and the Soviet Union, as well as members of the commission prosecuting alleged war criminals. The *Belfast*'s quarterdeck was now cleared of obstructions such as depth-charges and anti-aircraft guns, while capstans and bollards still retained a nautical flavour. The after 6-inch turret loomed over the area, one deck higher than it would be on any other cruiser, but any effect that might have had was probably obscured by an awning to protect the visitors from the sun. Wardroom attendants and marines were available to serve drinks.

The next call was at the port of Otaru on the northern island of Hokkaido, which was soon found to have few facilities for leave. According to William Hope,

The currency on board ship could not be spent ashore, so a nearby
American military base sent a fleet of Army trucks to collect our
liberty-men, and take them to their base where everything was laid
on for our benefit, drinks, food, cigarettes and entertainment; in
return the officers of the Belfast gave a quarter-deck cocktail party
for our hosts.

Boyd was aware of the difficulties with money and that British
sailors were unable to return hospitality. He asked for a supply of
dollars to be available at favourable exchange rates, commenting,
'As the object of sending these ships is partly to give ship's companies
a change in colder climates it is necessary for them to use U.S. dollars
if they are to be able to take advantage of their visit.' He and his staff
were put up by Major General Swing, commanding the US 11th
Airborne Division, which occupied the area. He inspected a guard of
honour from the division and watched a march past of 187 Glider
Infantry Regiment. Entertaining was on a modest scale: just a
luncheon party for four US army officers on the 28th and a dinner
party for General Swing and seven others on the 30th.

They sailed on to the British base at Kure where they arrived on
4 September, and Boyd met Lieutenant General Robertson, the
British Commander-in-Chief. As to naval operations, he concluded
that the effects of the war were receding and the naval shore party
could be reduced. There were four dinner parties for British and
Commonwealth naval and military officers, so the facilities of the
admiral's quarters were used to the full.

On 11 September they arrived at the American base at Kobe,
where Boyd called on local commanders. By this time he was
beginning to form views on the Japanese people after reading an
article in the July edition of the Monthly Intelligence Report which
claimed that,

it is all too easy to conclude that the uneducated Japanese are dazed from the exposure of their leaders, and deprivation of the former stimulus for their efforts and mode of life would probably be tractable to strong leadership from amongst their own people. It is however, in my view, impossible to formulate, in the absence of any form of fraternisation, a reliable assessment of the outlook of the educated and more influential Japanese.

* * * * *

The next stage was to visit the ports of China. On 18 September they arrived at Woosung, which was familiar to the long-standing members of the crew. They took on two Chinese pilots for the passage 215 miles up the Yangtze to Nanking, the capital of the Nationalist-held country from 1927 until the Japanese occupation. Boyd found that the pilots had 'great experience of the river in pre-war years' but were 'ignorant of the latest changes in the channel'. They relied heavily on the navigation skills of Captain Ellison and the navigating officer J. A. Meares, though it is not clear where they got their information. In any case they arrived safely to make a very noisy entry. The *Belfast* fired a 21-gun salute in honour of China while the gunboat *Yung Sui* replied with 15 guns as the appropriate number for a vice admiral, to which the *Belfast* in turn replied with another 15 guns. They soon found that Chiang Kai-shek was unable to see them and had to be content with meeting other officials and diplomats. The entertainment programme was now in full swing, starting on the 20th with a cocktail party for 283 guests including the British ambassador, the representatives of the British prime minster and American president, the heads of the Chinese navy and numerous diplomats. On another night Boyd and his staff went ashore for dinner with Chinese officials. General Pai Chung-hsi made a speech that, to Boyd's amusement, was badly translated, ending with 'the somewhat startling toast to King George, Sir Stevenson, and Colonel Boyd!'

There was a great shortage of motor transport in the city, but Boyd had brought a Rolls Royce, which was disembarked and in his opinion proved invaluable as it 'made a considerable impression in a community, many of whom had not seen before a British car of this quality'. He climbed 393 steps in pouring rain to lay a wreath at the tomb of the Nationalist leader Sun Yat-sen. They put together a cricket team captained by the admiral himself but lost by four wickets to a team under Australian leadership.

All this time Boyd and his men were trying to push the idea that the British should train the men of the Chinese navy, which would greatly increase their standing in the area – no one mentioned the effects of training the Japanese navy in the early years of the century. Boyd thought that the leaders of the Chinese navy made a good team. The Commander-in-Chief, General Chen, was often on his travels, so work was delegated to his deputy, General Kwei, who was 'forceful and exuberant' and was delighted to be nicknamed after General Blake, the British commander who had made the transition from land to sea warfare in the seventeenth century. His chief of staff was Rear Admiral Chow, who spoke good English and 'alone had any understanding of naval matters and problems' but lacked the personality and political skills of his chief. Boyd raised the matter of naval training and was pleased to find that the Chinese 'set great store by British naval training' but found it difficult to move away from what the Americans were offering. The ambassador reported, 'All these authorities stressed their wish to have the benefit of British naval training and discipline and expressed the opinion that they were superior to American methods.' The ambassador was delighted when a leading writer from the *Belfast* wandered into a police training school. Perhaps his peaked cap caused him to be mistaken for an officer, but he was invited to talk to the cadets. 'This he did for upwards of an hour, expatiating on the British Empire and on conditions in Germany, both of which countries he had recently visited.'

They sailed downriver and on 25 September arrived in the more familiar surroundings of Shanghai. Boyd fumed that the British buoys were still occupied by American ships but did not feel the matter was worth raising. By this time even the super-fit admiral was becoming overwhelmed with the constant engagements, and he commented, 'There was no easing off at Shanghai in the tempo of the programme and indeed sometimes arrangements almost overlapped.' There was a luncheon party on the 25th for four guests including the British consul, followed by a cocktail party for 210 that evening. There was a dinner party on the 26th, a cocktail party for 208 on the 28th and a buffet supper and cinema show for 25 guests on the 29th.

Boyd received news that Chiang Kai-shek would now be available to meet him in Nanking. The Americans provided a Piper Cub light aircraft, and he and his chief of staff flew to the city, where they had a very courteous reception, a 25-minute interview and an invitation to dinner with Chiang and his formidable wife. Boyd noticed that, 'A large painting of Hong Kong island on the dining room wall helped to make the British guests feel at home!' – only the exclamation mark suggests that he saw the irony, that the Chinese were asserting their claim to the colony. Boyd raised the question of the training again and thought he had found a way to the Generalissimo's heart when he discovered that as a boy he had wanted to go to sea. The Generalissimo apparently suggested that he might visit Hong Kong and dine with Boyd on board the *Belfast*, but such a visit would have huge diplomatic implications and in in the car afterwards the translator, a 'nervous little man', claimed that actually he had meant *Belfast* to visit Nanking again.

On 2 October, Boyd flew back to rejoin the ship, which was now at Tsingtao (Qingdao). At Chinwangtao [now Quinhuangdao] from 5 October there was the usual embarrassment over the crew's inability to pay for anything. 'There are unfortunately no canteen facilities accessible to British sailors, nor can the local cafés and restaurants be used.' From Chinwangtao Boyd flew to Peiping (as Beijing was known then) in another Piper Cub for a two-day visit in which he and some of the *Belfast*'s officers visited the Summer Palace of the emperors. Back with the ship, he joined a party to celebrate the Chinese National Day, 10 October: 'toasts were enthusiastic and frequent. The wine with which these were honoured was of a new and more vicious brand with the happy result that the use of interpreters became less and less necessary as the meal proceeded.' Boyd formed the opinion that Chinwangtao and Peitaho would be useful bases to escape from the summer heat of Hong Kong, if the Chinese agreed. On 15 October they arrived back at Hong Kong. Boyd concluded optimistically, 'I feel this cruise to have been of the greatest value and I have benefited immensely from the opportunity of meeting responsible Chinese authorities from CKS downwards, and American naval and military officers.'

The *Belfast* was in Hong Kong for Christmas, and according to Hope,

The youngest rating changed rig with his captain. The officer-of-the-day was carrying out the duties of the quarter-master, he piped the call, 'All hands who haven't done so and wish to do so, may do so now.' Minutes later a very drunken rating staggered onto the quarter-deck and proceeded to urinate over the side. Needless to say he found himself quickly on Jimmy's defaulters list.

But Hope's amusement did not last long. All men were screened for the rampant disease of tuberculosis, and he was the only one from the *Belfast* found to have it. Looking at the possibility of death, he made the best of it: 'My mess-mates tried to make sure that I went out happy, my wake turned into a celebration, out came treasured stores of ship's rum, the next day I was dispatched to hospital still in an alcoholic daze.' He was sent home and survived, but it was 1960 before he could work again.

Jake Jacobs left early in 1947 to spend two months at HMS *Terror* with very little to do except take part in a very violent football match during which his jaw was broken. He was sent to the P&O liner *Ranchi* for the voyage home with 4,000 troops on board and about 50 naval personnel. They refused to obey the army sergeant major's orders to mount sentries and were generally rebellious until the captain threatened to put them ashore at Aden. They arrived in England in April, and Jacobs went to Portsmouth Barracks to await demobilisation.

* * * * *

The *Belfast* carried out more visits flying Boyd's flag during 1947. From 24 January to 10 February she visited Jesselton (now Kota Kinabalu) in what was then the British colony of Borneo, and Sandakan further along the coast, followed by Manila, the capital of the Philippines. She was on more familiar territory from 21 February to 24 March when she went to Kure, Shanghai and Tsingtao. In April she entered the King George VI dry dock in

Singapore and left on 10 May. By now the Malayan 'Emergency' was in progress as the minority Chinese began a guerrilla war. The *Belfast* patrolled off the coast and visited ports such as Penang and Malacca, but her heavy guns were not called on to fire on any rebels and she had a relatively quiet summer.

At 1045 on 19 August 1947 the crew assembled on the quarterdeck and Admiral Boyd gave a farewell speech then hauled down his flag. The ship was almost ready for the voyage home. Various ratings joined, hands serving sentences of detention ashore were returned to the ship, and next morning the orders that had signalled her sailing from Portsmouth eight years earlier rang out across the decks – 'Special sea dutymen ... guard and band ... clear lower deck ... hands fall in for leaving harbour ... obey telegraphs ...' At 1030 the buoy was slipped and the ship made 'speed as necessary for leaving harbour'. Soon she was heading through the main passage and the band was disembarked. A programme of exercises began that evening with tests of steering from the after position at 2151. There was a heavy rain squall at 0545 next morning, and then the crew settled down to scrub the decks and clean the ship, which would remain routine for the rest of the voyage. On the 22nd the crew rigged derricks to exercise the procedure for ammunitioning at sea and then they carried out close-range firings. By noon on the 24th they were between Singapore Strait and the Andaman Islands and they entered the harbour on the 25th to moor up to No. 13 buoy just after nine in the morning. There was plenty of leave in port. Lieutenant (E) Woods was married, a reception was held on board and the crew had a general payment. On 3 September the ship went into Admiralty Floating Dock No. 31 and the crew spent the next hours cleaning her bottom until the dock was flooded again at 0910 on the 4th. More officers and ratings joined for passage to the UK and mostly for discharge from the navy. She sailed on the 11th.

There was a brief stop for water at Aden on the 23rd to the 24th, then she passed through the Suez Canal, meeting the liner *Empress of Scotland* on the way. She arrived at Malta at the beginning of October, and four Chinese ratings were transferred to the cruiser *London*, which would take them back east. She left for Gibraltar on 5 October, meeting many ships in the crowded waterways – names such as *British Hope*, *Clan MacGillan*, *British Courage*, *Royal Baltimore*, *Cheshire* and *Empire Aid* reminded them that the nation's merchant marine was still a major force in the world. They moored alongside the mole opposite the Rock on the 9th, and patrols were landed to help police the seamen on leave in this lively naval port. There was some work in painting the side of the ship to enhance appearance on arrival home, then they sailed on the 11th, meeting many more British ships in the Straits and outside. They were off Cape Finisterre at the north-west corner of Spain late on the 12th, and in sight of the French island of Ushant by dawn two days later, signalling that they were entering the English Channel. At 1342 they sighted Lizard Point in Cornwall, for some the first view of the homeland for several years, then passed some once-familiar landmarks – Eddystone Lighthouse, Berry Head, Portland Bill and St. Catherine's Point just after midnight on the 15th. They rounded the eastern end of the Isle of Wight and by 1341 were passing HMS *Dolphin*, the submarine base at the entrance to Portsmouth Harbour. They moored alongside the North Corner Jetty, and at 1500 the ship was opened up to relatives of the crew, for long-awaited reunions. Over the next few weeks men were discharged, the ship was slowly de-ammunitioned, and the old and new navy moved in and out of Portsmouth Harbour –

the battleship *Nelson* came out of dock on the 17th, the aircraft carrier *Illustrious* was in and out, and there were constant submarine movements.

* * * * *

An official report on the early part of the commission claimed that the ship and her crew 'had played some considerable part in the rehabilitation of the interests of the British Empire in the Far East'. But on a larger scale they were swimming against the current of rising nationalism and British decline, which would be followed by a great tidal wave that swept across eastern Asia in the next year or two.

WARS IN THE EAST

AT THE *BELFAST*'S LAUNCH IN 1938 it was suggested that the policy of naming ships after towns and cities might help to 'establish special interest between each city and a particular vessel of the fleet', but of course this had not been fulfilled due to the circumstances of war and a Far East deployment. One outstanding issue was the bell that the City of Belfast had subscribed for in 1939, as there had been no opportunity to present it. By May 1947 the City Corporation was aware that the ship would soon return to home waters and wrote to the Admiralty. They were informed that she would be back in October and would pay off into the reserve immediately. 'As she will have spent 2½ years on foreign service the ship's company must be granted leave as early as possible.' A visit to Belfast was out of the question, but the Admiralty offered the possibility 'that the gifts be retained until HMS *Belfast* re-commissions' (which was not likely before the end of 1948) or that a deputation be sent to England to make the gift. The Corporation chose the former, but in September 1948 the Admiralty informed them that the *Belfast* was being brought forward for service in the Far East Fleet and could visit the city in October. Despite the short notice, the City agreed. It was planned that the ship should arrive in the harbour at 3 p.m. on the 20th, when the tides were right, and enter the Dufferin Dock on the north bank of the Lagan, across the river from where she was built.

Her new captain, E. K. Le Mesurier, however, pointed out that 'we will not have our full crew, or anywhere near it. We are going out with a scratch crew, plus reliefs for the East Indies and China Station, and we will take over the bulk of the crew of another ship on the China Station, that ship being brought home by our scratch crew. There will, however, be about a hundred men who will stay on in the ship as the *Belfast*'s company, and nearly all the officers will stay, including, I am glad to say, myself.'

After her arrival in the city on the 20th, the officers of the *Belfast* were entertained at a reception in the City Hall, while the lower deck were invited to the Floral Hall, Hazelwood, for a dance. The next day (which incidentally was Trafalgar Day) was a busy one for Captain Le Mesurier: he had to call on the Prime Minster of Northern Ireland at Stormont Castle, the chairman of Belfast Harbour Commissioners at his office, and the Lord Mayor in the Victorian splendour of the City Hall, before having a luncheon with the city dignitaries along with two dozen of his officers. The ship was open to the public in the afternoon, while the sailors were invited on a tour of the city, and in the evening there was a dance for officers at the Ulster Yacht Club and for ratings again in the Floral Hall. Others were offered free entry to five cinemas and two dance halls. Next day the captain's calls were returned and at 1145 the bell was presented on the quarterdeck. Captain Le Mesurier accepted it gracefully and referred to the Belfast Blitz in April 1941: 'It is just over nine years since the ship left her birthplace and she has suffered, in the words of our Naval Prayer, the "dangers of the sea and the violence of the enemy". Your city too has suffered the violence of the enemy, but we are both now as tough as ever and fighting fit.' This was the third Harland & Wolff ship he had served in, and 'there are no better shipbuilders anywhere than the men of Belfast.' At 6.15 in the evening the Royal Marine Band played *Ceremonial Sunset* while members of the council, Harbour Board and the Ulster Club and their ladies gathered for an 'at home' with the wardroom officers – and ratings who had any energy left were invited to a further dance in the Floral Hall. They prepared for sea next morning and at one in the afternoon left for the long voyage to Hong Kong.

* * * * *

She arrived in December. George Oliver, a telegraphist and ex-*Ganges* boy, was drafted to the *Belfast* at Hong Kong and saw her as she was delivered by a steaming crew. 'We watched the arrival with some misgivings as she was not at all smart in appearance, and was painted in drab home waters colours. Nevertheless, we all agreed that she had good lines and looked every inch a modern cruiser bristling with firepower.' But, 'Soon HMS *Belfast* was looking smart in the light blue/grey paint scheme of the Far East Fleet, and the crew had adjusted to the new equipment.' Soon Oliver regarded *Belfast* as 'MY ship', though he had his difficulties:

> No-one expected a young TO [trained operator] to have yet reached the top of his proficiency, and I was having a bit of a thin time in terms of reading the Hong Kong broadcast with the required efficiency. The broadcast was getting busier and the speed of the Morse broadcast was increasing … at this stage I had to face the chief telegraphist a couple of times and was told to pull my socks up. Paradoxically, he would temper his criticism with praise for other work I did, especially for my willingness to go aloft and work on the main spread of aerials, which needed a good head for heights.

The newly formed crew of the ship was tested early, when on 12 January 1949 an RAF Vampire fighter force-landed in disputed

Chinese territory. The *Belfast* arrived in Bias Bay and sent a party ashore in boats, then inshore to salvage the aircraft. It was hauled on to a pontoon, which was towed out by the ship's boats and hoisted on board with the *Belfast*'s crane.

* * * * *

On 20 April the sloop *Amethyst* was heading up the Yangtze to Nanking to protect British nationals – perhaps unwisely, as it was known that Mao Tse-tung's communist forces were advancing in the area. She was draped with Union flags, but there was no guarantee that the insurgents would recognise them, and even less that they would respect their neutrality. She came under shellfire, which caused several fatal casualties and damaged the ship, and she ran aground and was trapped. Negotiations to release her continued for several months with no result, as the remaining crew began to suffer from shortage of supplies.

Admiral Sir Patrick Brind was another remarkable officer. He was 6 feet 2 inches tall and had been known as 'Daddy' ever since his days as a midshipman. He was later described as having 'the naval officer's refreshing way of meeting problems and people', but, 'He was not an ordinary naval officer, he had knowledge of people and was a friend of people.' He was much in demand as a lecturer, and when the crisis began he was attending a course at the Royal Naval College, Greenwich. He flew back to take overall command of the *Amethyst* situation, mostly flying his flag from the *London* until he hoisted it on board the *Belfast* in July. Communication with the *Amethyst* was insecure, but her new captain, Lieutenant Commander J. S. Kerans, signalled, 'Request advice on my action if menaced by a typhoon.' Brind replied with a strong hint that he was to be encouraged to escape. 'The golden rule is to make an offing and take plenty of sea room.' Oddly enough, Kerans did not understand this until very late in the day, but he made plans for an escape in any case.

Brind held a dinner party for about a dozen guests on board the *Belfast* on 30 July. He knew that something was likely to happen, but this was an excellent cover. He addressed his guests: 'Ladies and gentlemen, I should like you to think with me at this moment of His Majesty's Ship *Amethyst*, and I give you the toast, "HMS *Amethyst* and all who sail in her."' As the admiral's guests were ushered ashore at around ten, George Oliver and his shipmates were surprised that the party seemed to end rather early, and he was called to duty: 'The wireless office was fully manned and my watch had been allocated the middle watch [midnight until 4 a.m.]. The leading telegraphist in charge told me that I would be able to stand down as he had plenty of operators available. I was a bit surprised when I was called for the watch. When we got to the office, the chief telegraphist was there and told us that this would be an important watch as HMS *Amethyst* was about to attempt to escape from the Yangtze. I was allocated the broadcast channel and had to read the Morse messages that would report progress and were addressed to the admiral.' The dining cabin was cleared but the officers were still in formal dress as they monitored progress during the night. Admiral Madden joined and the two admirals settled down with the commander-in-chief's flag captain, staff officer operations and flag lieutenant in white 'mess undress' rig.

There were Sitreps (situation reports) from the *Amethyst* as she escaped by following a brightly-lit river steamer and was fired on from the north bank with minor damage. Then there was a quiet period followed by a report that the sloop was approaching the boom across the river. To Oliver, 'This was a tense time' until they received the signal that the *Amethyst* was through, and eventually at dawn the *Amethyst* met the destroyer *Concord* and sent the much-quoted signal, 'Have rejoined the fleet south of Woosung. God save the King.' Brind replied,

> Welcome back to the fleet. We are all extremely proud of your most gallant and skilful escape and that endurance and fortitude displayed by everyone has been rewarded by such success. Your bearing in adversity and your daring passage tonight will be epic in the history of the navy.

It was indeed regarded as an example of how sailors should behave under pressure, but it also signalled a serious setback to the British naval presence in the region, as well as marking the advance of communism in China.

* * * * *

On 21 October the fleet received a typhoon warning, and Captain Le Mesurier followed Admiral Brind's policy of getting plenty of

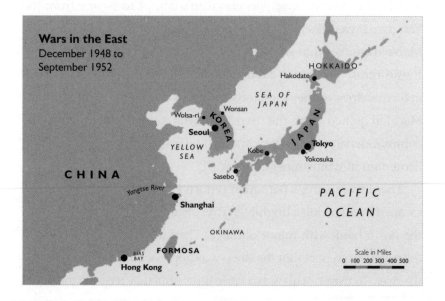

sea room, slipping the mooring in Hong Kong and heading out to sea. That night there was a distress signal from the Chinese merchant ship *Taipeh* 120 miles to the south-west, and *Belfast* was the nearest ship so she headed towards her, but it was soon cancelled and she went back to Hong Kong. A week later there was another message that would bring the ship closer than ever to the effects of the civil war in China. The tank landing ship *Cheung Hsia* had sailed from Canton with 600 refugees on the 14th, including many officers of the Chinese navy and carrying 100 or 200 tons of dockyard machinery. On the 16th she ran aground on Pratas Reef in the northern part of the South China Sea and lay there at an angle. The passengers were taken ashore in batches by sampan and junk at the rate of 60 or 70 per day and were living on the supplies issued to the local meteorological station. On the 30th *Belfast* was instructed to help and took on a medical officer and two sick berth attendants, a Mr. Francis Lee of the Tahing Shipping Company, who was fluent in English and Chinese, and an officer claiming to be Commander Chow of the Chinese navy; but he was soon discovered to be Lieutenant General Chou Li-Huan of the Nationalist Army. He had been trained in armoured warfare by the Germans before the war, fought against the Japanese and spoke no English, but a 'a tri-lingual exchange of information' was arranged between the general, Lee and the British officers.

The *Belfast* had a stormy passage out, with monsoon swell hitting the ship beam on, and anchored off the island to begin 'an exasperating exchange of signals' with the refugees. It was decided to leave those still on board the LST, who were supplied with food and were in no immediate danger. Instead General Chou, who was 'an efficient, forceful and pleasant character' went ashore to organise the refugees there. They were mustered on the beach and put into the ship's pinnace and two motor junks to go on board the *Belfast*. Eventually 226 people were embarked, including 82 marine and naval officers, one of whom carried a suitcase full of silver dollars, which he tried to hide from the others, while another had 'quite a large sum in US dollars'. The 17 most senior were put up in the gunroom and the others in the cinema. The 113 petty officers and ratings squatted in columns of four on the starboard waist while 12 women and 15 children were put up in the boys' messdeck, which had its own toilets. Apart from the officers they presented 'a picture of hopeless apathy'. The crew of the *Belfast*, according to the captain, 'turned to with the usual cheerfulness and humanity of the sailor', while the passengers 'settled down with oriental calm to await the future'. The voyage back was slightly less stormy than the one out, but nearly all the women and half of the children were violently sick. Eventually they were transferred to a merchant ship, which was to pick up the rest of the survivors and take the party on to Formosa, their original destination. Captain Le Mesurier commented, 'It is questionable whether – if the Communists eventually launch an attack on Formosa much resistance will be made.'

* * * * *

On 23 January 1950 the *Belfast* was put into dry dock at Singapore to have her bottom scrubbed and boilers cleaned. One of her outer propeller blades was found to be chipped, perhaps having been damaged during the rescue operation off Pratas Reef. New tachymetric directors were fitted to make the 'pom-pom' guns far more accurate, and the forward range-finder was removed as it was superseded by radar. For the crew, showers were fitted throughout to replace baths, more refrigerators were added and the sick bay was given air conditioning. She floated out on 25 March, and Captain Sir Aubrey St Clair-Ford took command. He was a wartime destroyer captain and, according to Peter Cardale, the navigating officer, he was 'a splendid chap ... rather like an overgrown schoolboy – redfaced and bouncy, and with a great sense of fun, and fortunately I got on extremely well with him.' The crew nicknamed him 'Sir Strawberry Cadillac Ford'. After working up, the *Belfast* was in Hong Kong by 12 May, where Rear Admiral W. H. G. Andrewes hoisted his flag as second-in-command of the Far East Fleet. There was no rest: the ship went out immediately on fleet exercises followed by visits to Japanese ports.

The *Belfast* moved out of Hakodate harbour on Saturday 24 June and anchored in the bay to avoid the effects of Typhoon 'Elsie'. It passed eastwards over Japan and the ship re-entered early on Sunday morning. That evening Admiral Andrewes began to receive disturbing news – South Korea had been invaded by the forces of the communist state to the north, and war was imminent. Since it fell directly on the fault-line between 'East' and 'West', between communism and capitalism, there was no telling where it would end. The *Belfast*'s gunnery officer, H. G. G. Ogilvie, was on duty that evening and winding up after the Sunday cinema show. He saw the admiral walking up and down the deck with Captain St Clair-Ford, 'undoubtedly discussing the grave situation which had arisen when the North Koreans had invaded South Korea that morning, and all the implications for us in the Fleet'.

Ogilvie was right. The admiral was indeed considering his options. The *Belfast* was the only Royal Navy ship in north Japanese waters, and Andrewes decided to move south so that he could concentrate his ships if necessary. It would also make it easier to intervene in southern Korea where action seemed likely, and it would be the best place to be if the Soviet Union intervened. Ogilvie overheard him say, 'You had better raise steam as soon as possible and prepare to sail as soon as you can. See that the ship is darkened.' The order to prepare for sea was given at 2300, and the ship was under way two hours later, heading down the east coast of Japan in bad weather. Soon they received a signal from the commander-in-chief, Far East Station, that they should be ready to take action under the United Nations charter. The United Nations Security Council met, boycotted by the Soviets, and authorised a force for Korea. Meanwhile the *Belfast* arrived at Yokosuka on the 27th and Andrewes was driven to Tokyo to find the American commander, Admiral Joy. He was in conference with General MacArthur and his chief of staff was 'not in the picture' according to Andrewes. He was about to leave when Joy arrived. 'He told me that he took a serious view of the situation on land in Korea.' Andrewes' offer to evacuate British and US civilians was not considered necessary, and the American commander, with Pearl Harbor fresh in his mind, was anxious not to have too many ships in Japanese ports in case the Soviets struck. It was agreed that the *Belfast* should take on fuel and provisions and then join with other British forces south of Japan. Andrewes was driven back along the 'long dull dusty road', and the *Belfast* sailed about 1700.

When the force eventually assembled it was 'an impressive sight as the *Belfast* led the British Fleet into Okinawa'. However, the British aircraft carriers were equipped only with obsolete piston-engined aircraft, and the *Belfast* had a reduced peacetime complement, which meant that only three of her four turrets could be manned. In the meantime, according to Ogilvie, 'We carried out the preparations for action so familiar to some of us on board, but a new experience for the young members of the crew ... We had a fine, well worked-up ship's company who had been in commission for 18 months with few changes.'

The *Belfast* went into action for the first time in this war on 6 July, and according to Ogilvie,

> Thereafter we bombarded the advancing North Korean troops for many days and nights, answering calls for fire from the hard pressed army. We carried out indirect bombardments when mostly under way, and the fall of shot was spotted sometimes by Forward Observers on shore, and sometimes by aircraft. The aircraft were either British or American and we quickly became accustomed to working with either. Sometimes we carried out a direct shoot but usually it was indirect, at a range of 20,000 yards. Several times we bombarded at our extreme range of 24,000 yards.

Unusual shoots included firing at moving trains on the coastal railway, usually with the 4-inch batteries, although, 'Sometimes we would illuminate a train with starshell and let fly at it with the six inch as it appeared out of a tunnel.' The *Belfast* was proud of its reputation for rate and accuracy of fire and 'the Americans found it hard to believe that our 6 inch triple turrets were hand operated'.

* * * * *

The *Belfast* was in need of a refit, and she had a reduced crew on board, so she was sent home. On 6 August, Admiral Andrewes came on board to say goodbye, and the ship sailed from Sasebo soon afterwards. She was in Hong Kong two and a half days later, but her stay was short and there was no time for official entertainment, except for a small cocktail party and a party given by the colonial secretary who was administering the colony in the absence of the governor. Chinese stewards were given leave and were to re-join the ship in Singapore before she sailed from there, which earned their gratitude. She sailed on the 11th and passed the cruiser *Ceylon* heading towards the battle zone. They carried out a night encounter exercise with the destroyer *Concord* and took on board one of her petty officers who was suffering from chronic toothache. They arrived at Singapore and the *Belfast* was taken into dry dock. The crew moved into shore accommodation in HMS *Terror*, for 'in the climate of Singapore, living conditions onboard any ship in dry dock are unacceptable ... There is no doubt that the well planned accommodation, playing fields, swimming pool and sailing facilities are very beneficial to both officers and ship's company.'

On 8 September there was an official farewell cocktail party, and guests included Sir Patrick and Lady Brind as well as other admirals, their wives and dockyard officials. Meanwhile the commander flew back to the UK to make preparations for the ship at Chatham. After a farewell by the C-in-C, she sailed in the afternoon of the 9th. She oiled at Aden, where the captain made arrangements for mock air attacks with the local RAF commander, and both watches were allowed three hours' leave.

In the Red Sea the ship met large numbers of oil tankers and the P&O liners *Chusan* and *Stratheden*, carrying the England cricket team. Captain St Clair-Ford was concerned about etiquette in passing through the Suez Canal in convoy. 'I would recommend ships arriving the regulation hour and a half before the schedule time of departure of the convoy (0600 & 1800 from Suez, 0000 1200 from Port Said. However, from the information given by the pilot, it is probable that [a] ship arriving even two hours after the schedule time will catch the convoy, but naturally under these circumstances a warship could not expect to have her normal place at the head of the convoy.' The *Belfast* duly entered at 0615 on the 24th leading a small convoy of three ships. She anchored in the Great Bitter Lake for two and a half hours, but even the senior naval officer in the Middle East and General Sir Brian Robertson, the army C-in-C, were not allowed to board due to lack of notice but were able to lie off in a barge and greet the ship. The passage was completed and the ship headed for Malta in perfect weather, during which 'opportunity was taken to pipe hands to bathe during the dog watches'. The *Belfast* entered Grand Harbour, Valetta, at 0830 on the 27th. It was almost empty, as the fleet was out exercising, so the crew had the bars and other entertainments almost to themselves for two days until they sailed again. On the way to Gibraltar they met the 1st Cruiser Squadron and the carrier *Glory*, and at Gibraltar they found the new battleship *Vanguard* with cruisers and destroyers. There was excellent weather and 'glorious sunshine' as the ship sailed north across the Bay of Biscay and east along the English Channel, to anchor in the Thames Estuary at 2030 on 2 October in what one of the *Belfast*'s men called 'the gray dark oggin just around the Nore'.

A salute was fired for the commander-in-chief at the Nore in the morning of the 6th, and the ship proceeded up the Medway estuary, with the crew only too glad to get away from the exposed anchorage to a buoy about a mile from the dockyard. Cardale was delighted that his wife and family were able to greet him from afar. 'Thelma and the two children were standing waving as we passed Garrison Point, Sheerness. A wonderful welcome for me, and a great achievement for them to be there at that time, especially as Thelma was expecting Tom in about a month's time. They came on board at Chatham and in the afternoon we drove to Liss for leave.'

In view of the urgency of the war situation, the *Belfast* had been given special permission to enter a dry dock with her ammunition still on board, but it was a time of neap tides, which would not lift her over the sill of the dock, so the laborious task of removing the ammunition had to be carried out over the weekend before the ship could dock on Monday 9th. This was the first return of a warship that had been in the Korean operational area, and Captain St Clair-Ford was warned to expect press interest, but he was still surprised when about 50 reporters, newsreel and even television cameramen arrived as soon as the ship was secured. He was far less happy with the quality of the coverage: 'in spite of all this, the subsequent press reports were very scanty … I had taken great pains to emphasise to the press the excellent work that was being put in by large numbers of British and Dominion ships … It appears … that the views of the youngest boy onboard and the news value that one of my officers plays the bagpipes is of far greater interest to the British public who still remain ignorant of the great effort that is being made by our naval forces …' Meanwhile we can infer that the crew did not find autumnal England congenial, and the ship's commission book later described a time 'when the rain is weeping out of the skies and Chatham looks even drearier, when the gay blacks and daring browns of the Island Race seem more bedraggled than ever, when the bus or tram or train is full of complaining voices, sniffling noises and wheezy coughs spreading a million bacteria, when in the name of equality among men, the bus conductor snaps your head off or the waitress throws your meal at you …'

The policy of sending the commander back by air soon began to pay off, for it was not just the ship that had to be renewed. The commander 'was able to make the detailed arrangements by personal contact between the ship and the drafting office, and Chatham was completely ready for us'. The ship was given a full war complement of more than 900 men, including reservists who had been called up and men who were retained although their time was about to expire. As to the ship, a spare pump was replaced, the jamming of the port cable holders was investigated, and the recreation space was converted into a messdeck. By 16 October she was ready to sail with her new complement. Two days later she went over the degaussing range at Portland then sailed for Gibraltar, where she arrived on the 31st to disembark four scientists who were joining the Home Fleet. Though she had carried out many drills on the way south, she proceeded to Malta to complete working up. In just over two weeks the ship carried out four fire-control exercises with the 4-inch guns and five firings at sleeve targets. There were five exercises with the close-range anti-aircraft weapons as well as starshell firings, sub-calibre practice by day and by night, and night encounter exercises with the *Bermuda* and the First Cruiser Squadron. Exercises were carried out with submarines, torpedoes were fired, and there were numerous air plotting and tracking drills. Captain St Clair-Ford thought it was 'a most valuable period for all departments in the ship'.

She sailed for Port Said on the 17th, still carrying out air exercises on the way, and on the 19th she joined the midnight convoy through the Suez Canal, led by the French cruiser *Jean d'Arc*. St Clair-Ford was aware that the ship might have to 'gare up' or approach the narrow waters on the side of the canal when meeting ships going the other way, so he ran the two inner propellers only to avoid possible damage. He felt vindicated at four in the morning when a northbound convoy of sixteen ships was encountered. Out in the Red Sea, the arrangement made on the way home for exercise with aircraft was implemented and more drills were held. The crew was allowed leave at Aden as the ship was ahead of schedule, a party was arranged for the local British community, and games were organised for officers and crew. The ship arrived back at Singapore on 4 December, exactly twelve weeks after

leaving. On the 9th she sailed for Hong Kong, arriving on the 14th, to
continue working up over Christmas – 'What a party!' noted the ship's
commission book. One of the ship's company described the colony:

> There is contrast here by day; the commercial enterprise with all its
> display of wealth, as set against the water people living simply in
> small boats, and using everything that no one else has thought to
> use again. By day the city is a city; by night, the Chinese people come
> into their own. The main streets sound to the unforgettable clatter
> of wooden sandals in the distance, the rattle of a Mah Jong game,
> or a merchant calculating gain or loss on his abacus. More quietly,
> in the shadow, sits the bank guard, idly nursing an enormous rifle.
> In small shops, the ivory carver, the makers of sandal-wood chests,
> the basket makers – all the thousand and one skilled craftsmen – sit
> at their work of sleep nearby.

* * * * *

The war situation had changed drastically while *Belfast* was away.
At the beginning of September the North Koreans had begun an
offensive that drove the UN forces back until they held only Pusan in
the south-east. Then General Macarthur led an amphibious landing
at Inchon just west of the South Korean capital, Seoul, and soon they
were heading well into North Korean territory, until China intervened
to drive them back. By the time the *Belfast* rejoined in December, the
line was beginning to stabilise around the 38th parallel.

The *Belfast* was back in action off the east coast by 19 February,
when she bombarded Wonsan with 127 rounds of 6-inch and 27
rounds of 4-inch. The fall of shot was spotted by aircraft from an
American carrier. The ship then fell into a routine of bombardment
followed by rest and replenishment. As her commission book put it,
'Most of war is boring; and the few moments of excitement too

intense for recognition', and it is not necessary to describe every bombardment in detail. During this commission the ship fired 7,816 rounds of 6-inch ammunition and only 538 rounds of 4-inch, for most of the gunfire was at long range. Cardale recognised the importance of some targets but later wrote, 'Sometimes I felt that the bombardment targets we were given were hardly worthy of a 6" brick.' There was a constant threat of enemy air attack, and the ship was covered by a Target Area Combat Air Patrol with aircraft from British or American carriers, or occasionally from the US Air Force, US Marines and the South African Air Force. Five main supply routes south were identified – ships and junks off the east coast; the road and railroads in the east, which were largely coastal; the western land route; coastal shipping along the west coast; and Chinese shipping across the Yellow Sea. The United Nations blockade stopped up the three maritime routes, while it was claimed that a cruiser and two destroyers were needed to stop the coastal rail and road route.

As navigating officer, Lieutenant Commander Peter Cardale found the work challenging and rewarding. 'I got more satisfaction from my job as navigating officer in *Belfast* than any other ship during my career. Pilotage in Japanese waters was interesting, and it certainly was on the west coast of Korea, where the charts were from very old surveys, and we sometimes had to proceed up rather obscure creeks. On one occasion, I had to do a quick survey in the approaches to the Han River to see where we could get to. I was not proud of it, but it sufficed.' During the second commission he had use of Type 268 radar which was

> quite suitable for pilotage and navigation, though not designed as such … it was to prove invaluable on the west coast of Korea, and enabled me to take *Belfast* into many estuaries and creeks in fog, or

in the dark, which would not otherwise have been possible. On a least one occasion, we went up the thirty mile approach to Inchon amongst islands and sandbanks at 22 knots in thick fog, using radar alone, a pioneering feat of blind pilotage, though not as rash as it sounds, as we knew the estuary well, and there was no traffic. As a bonus, in some of the extremely cold weather, I frequently found it convenient to navigate from the warmth of the bridge plotting room where the one and only display was situated, rather than from the freezing open bridge!

As a further bonus, Captain St Clair-Ford was 'most generous' in allowing Cardale to handle the ship, 'although very capable when doing so himself'. Cardale worked closely with Ogilvie, the gunnery officer, who was 'a very likeable and modest, though somewhat fiery fellow … He and I had been a good bombardment team and we got on very well together. Sometimes when working his bombardment spotting disc during a shoot at anchor, he would become apoplectic with rage and throw away his chinagraph pencils, or other accoutrements, and it was then my job to recover them, or if necessary to work his disc for him!'

* * * * *

Most of the time the *Belfast* was based at Sasebo, a large natural harbour at the south-western end of Japan that had been fitted for naval use by the Imperial Navy. With Japan's new peaceful role in the world, a referendum had only just been held about converting it to a civilian port, but it was the closest harbour to the southern end of the Korean peninsula and that was soon overtaken by events as the United States, Commonwealth and other Allied navies began to use it. According to the port history, 'On the commercial strip from Matsuura-Cho down the main street new curio stores, cafés, cabarets, and dance halls sprouted like mushrooms after rain to serve the United Nations troops. Pedicabs jammed the streets.' In addition there were said to be 597 brothels. The men of the *Belfast* had their own take on the port, which they visited 25 times during the conflict:

> You'll not forget the upthrusting hill on the left as you come in, named after the characteristic curve of a famous film-star – and a remarkable likeness too. You'll not forget that two-funnelled monster that puffs and blows its way round the harbour (and did anyone discover what it really did?) You'll not forget the archway at Fleet Landing and its tribute to the modesty of the US Marine Corps. You'll not forget the Black Market Street and its offshoots, or those tiny ships bursting with the most incredible merchandise. You'll not forget the bustle, the blaring music, the tin-pot taxis, the people, the puddles, the chaos; and especially near the alleged river, the smell. Someone told me that Sasebo made him think of this hell-bent, rip-roaring towns you read about in the old Wild West.

Cardale was not impressed. Sasebo was 'a dreary place, and apart from walks, boating picnics, the US club, visiting the Hirita china factories, there was not much to do. Fortunately we never spent much time there, going to Kure instead when any base maintenance was required. Though Kure itself was little improvement on Sasebo, it was in a beautiful setting in the inland sea. There were good walks and scenery, and visits to the sacred shrine of Myagima [Myajima], which was a lovely spot.' Some of the sailors could not help noticing an ominous work ethic among the Japanese – 'To witness their love of industry and pride in workmanship and to wonder – to wonder perhaps uneasily – about or own modern ways at home.'

There were other excursions, for example at Yokosuka in the autumn of 1951, when a trip to Tokyo was arranged – 'a sprawling and not very distinguished city. We did see the principal Buddhist and Shinto temples, and the massive Diet [parliament] building, heavily monstrous without, but a monument of functional achievement within. The Imperial Palace needed a special permit which unfortunately we did not have.' During a stop at Kobe in June 1952, visits were arranged 'for intending travellers to Kyoto, for tourists to visit the Dunlop Rubber Factory, or the Girls' Opera at Takarazuka; for dancers wishing to attend the Mission to Seamen's party; and for a host of others who wished to take advantage of the generous private invitations. Nearly 200 visited the Girl's Opera, which turned out to be a sort of *Folies Bergère* without the major undressing, extremely well staged on one of the biggest stages in the world.' It was the only non-naval port visited during the commission, and to Cardale it was the most memorable. 'Everyone, both officers and ratings, were made most welcome and much entertainment and events were laid on, and Japanese swarmed all over the ship.' The passage out through the Inland Sea of Japan was 'a most wonderful scenic passage through many islands', but it was not without its navigational hazards. Power cables were not fully marked on the charts: 'As we approached one, it did seem to be horribly low, so we stopped the ship and with the aid of the sextant and radar range, I calculated that it was just all right, and actually the mast cleared by a good margin.'

The *Belfast* refitted in Singapore from 12 May to 17 August 1951, while the crew moved into HMS *Terror*. To Cardale, who shared a cabin with his volatile friend Ogilvie, 'The buildings were cool, and well laid out in pleasant gardens, and with good facilities for games, and a swimming pool, a sailing club, a naval club with ten-pin bowling alley ...' She left on 18 August, and there was a bizarre accident when the Chinese canteen manager bumped into a torpedo tube which had been set outboard instead of the normal fore and aft for an exercise. He fell overboard as the ship was sailing at 22 knots. The alarm was quickly raised, the ship turned round, and he was lucky to be picked up over the starboard bow. Back on the west coast of Korea, it was noted, 'It hadn't changed a bit.' That was not just a geographical matter, for the war had now descended into a stalemate. The crew had to adjust to great changes in temperature, some of which recalled the service in the Arctic.

> 11 or 12 degrees Fahrenheit [minus 12 degrees Celsius] is not a comfortable temperature in which to do much else than bemoan your fate in having to suffer it. In February/March of '51 we had quite a lot of it, and it wasn't comfortable. Those of you who were unwary enough to place an ungloved hand on a guard-rail quickly realised that burning does not come from heat alone. So in the kindness of your hearts spare a thought ... for the people who had to keep watch on such places as the bridge and the GDP.

Summer heat was even worse in a sense: 'You can do something about cold; normally you can get out of it. But without air-conditioning there is nothing you can do about heat: it follows you inexorably and wherever you go ... our metal construction was no place to endure it. So, if you have any kindness left, spare another thought for the Engine Room.'

But that was not the worst of the weather. In October 1951 Typhoon 'Ruth' was in the neighbourhood and again the ship put to sea.

> By early Sunday morning it looked as if she was going to pass unpleasantly close, and along with the other ships we weighed anchor and made for the broad open spaces. On that morning ... we sailed out in as gentle a wind and sea as ever was seen. But by the

time we were only a little way out there was already a fresh breeze, and a little over an hour later almost a full gale and steep seas.

According to Cardale, 'it was already blowing a full gale by the time we cleared the land, and shortly afterwards some 6" shells broke loose in a shell-room. However, some brave souls managed to secure these, without damage, or injury to themselves ...' Soon they were feeling the full force of the typhoon.

> That night of the 14th October was quite a thing. The best solution was to heave to and ride it out, keeping the wind about 20 degrees on the starboard bow. An official document – always a master of understatement – refers to the seas as 'terrific'. The ship rolled up to 35 degrees, and the seas filled the waists to a depth of 3 or 4 feet. Certainly to stand at the level of our Flag Deck, and look at wave-crests higher than you are, is a situation in which no one of God's children should ever want to find himself.

The writer of the report in the ship's commission book mused on 'just what a weak, puny and impotent thing we are in the face of this comparatively slight phenomenon of nature ...' However it was soon over. 'The speed with which the typhoon hit us was only equalled in surprise by the speed with which it disappeared.' To Cardale it was 'the severest storm I have ever experienced ...' However, 'We had lost seven Carley rafts, and there was quite a lot of damage to upper deck fittings, but I never felt there was any cause for alarm.'

* * * * *

As the last and largest of the pre-war cruisers, *Belfast* still had high-quality accommodation aft as well as good signal and plotting facilities, so she was nearly always in service as a flagship – Rear Admiral Scott-Moncreiff replaced Admiral Andrewes in 1951. The ship attracted a number of VIP visits including by President Syngman Rhee of South Korea and Alben Barkley, one of the lesser-known vice presidents of the United States in November 1951. They often arrived by helicopter, which was a relatively new phenomenon, and one sailor joked that ceremonial would have to be modified: 'Now we'll have a pipe; "Attention on the upper deck, face upwards".' There was another kind of ceremonial on 4 February 1952 when news arrived of the death of King George VI, and the ship fired a 56-gun salute. Four months later, at Kure again, she staged a parade to mark the birthday of his daughter, now Queen Elizabeth II.

Despite the demands of active service, in naval tradition the ship kept up a sporting programme. She was reasonably successful at soccer, the sport of the lower deck, winning 60 matches, drawing 6 and losing 14. The hockey team was even better, winning 27 matches out of 34. The rugby XV was less successful, losing 11 games out of 21, but it was claimed, 'Rugby is essentially team-work demanding constant practice: and we did a lot of sea time.' Cricket was only played 'spasmodically', and again it was claimed, 'A sea-going ship must always be a disappointing place for the cricket enthusiast: the game takes up so much more arrangement and time.' During the refit at Singapore there was swimming, water polo and athletics, and there was an enthusiastic boxing team. At sea, deck hockey was played on the quarterdeck, 'ad infinitum – and in the opinion of many ad nauseam. Looking at this remarkable game, one wonders whether it is a game at all or just an excuse for letting off steam.'

* * * * *

The *Belfast* operated mostly on the west coast of Korea, which unlike the east coast had hundreds of islands, demanding careful navigation. The map published in the ship's commission book was greatly simplified in that respect and only showed about twenty of them, including ones where the ship saw action. On 15 July she was on the way to refuel when she received an urgent signal that North Korean forces had landed on the nearby island of Chagni-Do. This was part of a group including Paengyong-do on the same latitude as Seoul and at the western end of Korean territory. They were useful to United Nations forces as a jumping-off place for agents on the northern mainland. The loss of the smaller island might well lead to the capture of the larger one, for it was believed that 300 North Koreans had landed in rubber boats. The *Belfast* arrived off the coast at 1000, 45 minutes after receiving the message. It was the beginning of an engagement that brought elements of the crew, if not the ship itself, far closer to the action than the shore bombardments of Normandy or Korea. They linked up with the *Amethyst*, 'not after all, up some river or another at the time', as the ship's commission book put it later.

> As we came in, we sighted a small boat idling a mile or so off shore, and promptly lowered the [landing craft, personnel] to investigate. The boat, we found, contained three South Koreans who during the night before had gone off on a reconnaissance of the mainland. When they returned, they had known from their reception from the beaches that these were not their life-long friends whom they had left on the island the night before. Their luck changed when we arrived to pick them up.

Then both ships sent armed boats towards the shore to capture any invasion craft that might be found on a beach to the west of the island. To try to get information they steered towards caves on the beach where civilians could be seen sheltering but were fired on from a cliff above, Marine Coffin being wounded in the leg. As they retreated, the *Amethyst*'s boat picked up a naked North Korean whose operations had been disturbed by the invasion. Air strikes were called in and both ships opened fire. The *Belfast* came under fire when, 'Another battery to the east began firing on us! Indignantly taking advantage of our larger guns, we got out of their probable range, and let them have it. The conditions, the Gunnery Officer said, were almost ideal. There was an obliging green slope up to where the flashes were coming from, and our first ranging shot made a nice brown mark, showing exactly where the shell had landed.' Then the *Belfast* used *Amethyst* to spot the fall of her shells on a battery on the other side of the island, and all the enemy guns were silenced. That night the island was re-invaded by South Korean guerrilla forces under American leadership; attempts to tow junks and sampans inshore failed, and the landing was 3½ hours late, but the enemy was confined to hill postions, which were bombarded by the warships and by air strikes. Eleven Korean casualties were brought on board including one woman, but the *Belfast*'s medical team were not understating their case when they claimed, 'the [Sick] Bay was strewn with stretchers and the blood lay thick'. As more naval forces had arrived, the *Belfast* was able to continue to her refuelling rendezvous. The operation was judged a success.

* * * * *

On 29 July 1952, the *Belfast* suffered her first casualties on board in this war when a 76mm shell from a battery at Wolsa-ri struck her, fracturing a steam pipe, which caused a Chinese rating to be scalded to death in his hammock and wounded four others. But the war was already winding down, and the *Belfast*'s final patrol ended on 27 September 1952, the day the war officially finished, though police actions continued. She was superseded by the *Newcastle* and began the long voyage home. On 4 November the Belfast returned to Chatham, after having been away for two years and eight days. Thelma Cardale was on Garrison Point again, now with three children. After de-ammunitioning, the ship 'proceeded up river and through the lock at Chatham to a great welcome from the awaiting families, who of course swarmed on board as soon as the ship was alongside'.

Again she seems to have been a very happy ship. Cardale wrote, '*Belfast* was the best ship I ever served in, particularly the second commission, and I had many good friends in the wardroom.' Ogilvie agreed: 'She was the best ship I served in in my 36 years.' She was now to be to be paid off into Class III reserve, one of a great fleet of more than 200 ships that were kept in and around the naval ports ready to be mobilised for the next war. Few of them would ever see service again.

12

RECOVERED FROM THE RESERVE FLEET

THOUGH THE RESERVE FLEET WAS A GRAVEYARD for many fine vessels, the *Belfast* was not finished yet. The battleship was in rapid decline, and attention was focused on aircraft carriers, submarines and anti-submarine warfare, but the cruiser was not entirely disregarded by the navy. The name ship of the Soviet *Sverdlov* class appeared in British waters, and this raised the prospect, in a new war, of surface raiders, which had done a great deal of damage in the last war. The 6-inch guns of cruisers such as the *Belfast* were considered part of a counter-strategy against them. Meanwhile the only new cruisers under construction – the *Lion*, *Tiger* and *Blake* – had languished unfinished in Clyde shipyards since the end of the war. Each had four redesigned and highly efficient 6-inch guns, but these ships did not enter service until the end of the decade, and they did not compare favourably with ships of other navies. In the meantime, the older cruisers had to continue showing the flag and carry out any other roles that might be found for them.

Considering the *Belfast*, *Swiftsure* and *Superb* in March 1953, it was remarked, 'All three ships compete in the era of new guns and the control systems which will be fitted in the *Tigers*. The director of gunnery would have liked to see the three older ships fitted to that standard but had to accept that it was impracticable in view of the structural alterations necessary.' In April 1955 it was suggested that the main role of the *Belfast* should be to attack large enemy warships, to protect aircraft carrier groups from surface and air attack, to operate independently in defence of trade, and to provide flank support for the army, as she had done in Korea. However, in January 1956 it was decided that the *Belfast* should not have a full modernisation as originally proposed, but only an 'extended refit' according to plans drawn up that spring, which left her with an eclectic mixture of old and new.

As to armament, she was to be refitted to the standard of the cruiser *Birmingham* of 1936, which had recently been rearmed. This was defined as 'able to defend themselves against present-day air attack in all conditions and other ships to a limited extend in blind fire.' The torpedo armament was to be removed. Her 6-inch guns would be retained, but the fire control improved, her close-range anti-aircraft armament would be upgraded. Her main engines were reckoned to be good for another ten years: endurance would be reduced, but it was already greater than that of the new *Tiger* class. Her generator capacity (always a weakness) would have to be accepted as it was, partly because of a national shortage of electrical draftsmen to map out the changes. The possibility of fitting the ship to operate helicopters was considered – the most ambitious plan was to operate up to three of the new Westland Whirlwinds, which would involve accommodation for five officers, 12 senior rates and 23 junior ratings. This proved impracticable without the removal of gun turrets, and instead a 25-foot square was cleared astern for helicopter landing, but there were no facilities for storing or maintaining them.

The navy could not be unaware of the new and terrifying weapons that might be used against it, and the first Atomic, Biological, Chemical Defence (ABCD) manual was issued in 1959.

The dangers of radiation had only recently been discovered, and the title of the manual implied that in a sense it was already outdated in that it did not take account of the new and far more devastating hydrogen bomb. The manual did not deal with the effects of a bomb blast in the vicinity, and there was no real answer to that; it tended to augment existing procedures of damage control, wearing of suitable gear, prevention of flooding and dealing with casualties. It did, however, state the necessity of equipping each ship with suitable ventilators and filters so that it could operate in a radiation environment.

The old admiral's cabin survived the refit with just some rearrangement of the staff cabins forward of it, so as a flagship she retained something of pre-war style for entertaining. The officers still lived aft of the engine room, though in more modern ships they were accommodated closer to the bridge. The living quarters for the crew, however, were completely changed, for in 1956 the Admiralty had bowed to pressure and adopted the American policy of having the men sleeping in bunks and eating in central cafeterias. The alterations to the *Belfast*'s accommodation were to be 'the largest improvement to the ship', for now they ate in dining halls rather than their messes. The chiefs and petty officers had theirs on the port side of the old hangar space. Senior rates – chiefs and petty officers – lived in separate messes but ate in the same compartment, on the port side of the old aircraft hangar. As a break with tradition, the branches were mixed for senior rates, except in the case of officers' cooks and stewards. They were allowed to choose their bunks, in order of rank, length of service badges and age. The junior ratings' dining hall was on the port side of the deck and could be converted to a cinema. Even more important, most of the crew were now to sleep in bunks rather than hammocks, and in smaller messes.

It was not possible to find bunks for all the men in such an old ship, so sleeping accommodation was provided on the basis of 60 percent of the ratings in bunks and 40 percent in hammocks; chiefs and petty officers were not normally expected to use hammocks. According to the orders of around 1960, bunks were to be filled before hammocks were allocated, though if possible some settee bunks were to be left unoccupied in each mess to provide recreation space. As was tradition, the boys, now known as 'juniors', were to be kept separate 'to make supervision easier', and their mess just aft of 'B'-turret support had its own bathroom. The marines and some petty officers' messes were now situated aft of the engine room just forward of the officers' quarters – though mutiny was no longer the threat it had once been. The improvements were made possible 'by reductions in the complement and by building in a large portion of the upper deck, which latter has been possible because of the removal of the torpedo tubes.' The largest of the messes, just before the engine room on the upper deck, was interrupted by the ABCD (Atomic, Biological Chemical Defence) headquarters but had room for 77 bunks, 2 settees and 29 hammocks. It was used by the Quarterdeck division of seamen. Forward of that was an engineers' mess for up to 97 men, then one for the supply and secretariat branch for 82, then one for watchkeepers with 37 bunks, 4 settees and 11 hammock spaces. The next mess was placed round the support of 'B' turret and was used for petty officers and stores. The mess round 'A'-turret support was for the Top division of seamen and had 12 bunks, 3 settees and 13 hammocks, but more men were accommodated in forward areas such as the capstan machinery space.

Externally, the most noticeable difference in the new *Belfast* as seen from a distance was that she was fitted with lattice masts to support the increasing amount of radar equipment. This included

Type 277Q, part of a combination of radar sets used in aircraft warning and height finding. It demanded a large and prominent parabolic reflector mounted on the mast. Type 992 provided 'a very high data-rate video-signal' 'to facilitate accurate and reliable auto-following of fast moving targets'. Seen closer, the biggest change was in her new bridge structure, in which both captain and admiral would command from enclosed spaces, which was essential in the days of possible nuclear radiation. The lowest level of the bridge structure, O1, was mainly taken up with petty officers' messes, now with fixed bunks and no provision for eating. Above that, level O2 had the admiral's bridge forward, the admiral's and captain's sea cabins, wireless offices and platforms for Bofors guns outside. O3 had the compass platform for the captain, and the Action Information Organisation (later known as the operations room) from which the weapons were controlled. It also had the chart room and facilities for the navigator. Level O4 above was open and could be used in good weather. By now it was policy to fit air conditioning in new ships, including the 'Tribal'-class frigates, which were largely intended for use in the Persian Gulf, but *Belfast* only had it in selected compartments. Apart from that, she was ready for almost anything, including an Arctic store in the bows. With all the changes she now displaced 15,000 tons – fifty percent more than the planned figure of 1936.

* * * * *

By the late 1950s the navy was resisting huge cuts imposed by the Defence Minster, Duncan Sandys, who believed that it had no great relevance in an age of nuclear warfare. The admirals managed to convince him that the navy might fight on after the homeland was devastated, and that in any case amphibious forces and a naval presence were essential in the Cold War. However, the reserve fleet was no longer relevant if the ports were to be destroyed by nuclear attack, and it was cut to 75 ships by 1962–3. The *Belfast* was to avoid this cull by being sent on active service again.

As the *Belfast* languished in reserve or was torn apart under refit, the navy was undergoing great changes. The system of officer training was being reformed, and midshipmen no longer spent long periods at sea as part of the complement of warships on active service. Instead they would spend shorter periods in ships dedicated to the purpose, and at one stage the *Belfast* was considered for this role. As to ratings, conscription was still in force but was little used by the navy after the Korean War. It only had 6,700 national servicemen in 1953 compared with 133,700 regulars and 5,200 women, who of course did not serve at sea in those days. However, National Service made the services unpopular generally. As one naval captain put it,

> For ten years since the end of the war elder brothers have been called up, done their time, and come out. A national attitude to this service has developed among the young: for the large majority, it is that they hate the prospect of it, they would go to great lengths to dodge it – some of the tricks to fail the medical are most ingenious – and, once in, although they like it better than they expected, they long for it to be over.

The stock of wartime reservists had declined, and with affluence and full employment ashore it was no longer so simple to recruit boys for long service. The Royal Navy was always highly skilled at keeping the outward form while reforming the substance, so the crew that assembled at Portsmouth in November 1959 did not look very different from the men who had formed the complement twenty years earlier. The dress uniforms of officers, petty officers and junior ratings were identical from a distance, but there were subtle distinctions. Accountant and engineer officers no longer wore colours between their gold stripes to set them apart; there were now four electrical officers, though they were indistinguishable from the others. There were no warrant officers, for those who had risen through the ranks were now commissioned as special duty officers and could only be identified by their age. All petty officers now wore the fore-and-aft rig uniform, and all junior ratings, including cooks, clerks and stewards, wore square rig, apart from a few who had entered before the changes and continued to wear the older dress. The square rig itself had been greatly simplified with a zip front, and it was only worn for formal duties such as commissioning and parades. Men working on deck usually wore dark blue trousers and light blue shirt, while civilian clothes were allowed when going ashore. Most of the ratings still joined as boys, including those in the engineering and electrical branches, but they were now known as 'juniors' – not to be confused with 'junior rates', which meant all ratings below petty officer. They were taken on for an initial term of nine years instead of twelve, for the Victorian ideal of long service was no longer relevant, and twelve years of continued employment was not as attractive as it had been in the hungry 'thirties. Recruitment had been quite successful in the last few years with 8,200 taken on from 1957 to 1958, enough for a navy of less than 100,000 men, especially as older men were often prepared to re-engage.

The British navy still considered it had an important role 'East of Suez'. Besides the rise of communist China, the situation in the Far East became even more threatening in 1954 when the French were forced out of Vietnam, leaving a communist state in charge in the north and a vulnerable one in the south. The South-East Asia Treaty Organisation (SEATO) was formed in September that year for collective defence, though it only included three Asian countries – Pakistan, the Philippines and Thailand. The dominance of the United States, United Kingdom, Australia and New Zealand led to the suspicion that it was a continuation of colonialism by other means, though the fear of communism was sincere enough. Much of the *Belfast*'s activity in the region would be in support of SEATO.

* * * * *

The *Belfast* was ready for service by May 1959. Captain J. V. Wilkinson was appointed to the command, and at 1015 on the 12th her new ship's company marched from the barracks at Devonport and arrived on board 15 minutes later. The Lord Mayor of Belfast came on a visit and was joined by the commander-in-chief. They were saluted with a march past. The commissioning ceremony was at 1100, and 23 minutes later the jack and ensign were hauled up to signify the ship's operational status. In the afternoon the men began to strike down their baggage and draw their bedding.

In the wardroom, old traditions were maintained and regulations enforced, according to the rules of May 1959. Officers paid £3 per month for messing, and there was a set dinner or a guest-night dinner once a week. Ladies could be entertained in the wardroom in port on Sundays after church and in the evening after cinema, from 1900 to 2300; an empty cabin was to be set aside as a 'powder room' for them. Visitors were to be treated with attention: 'Any officer sighting a stranger looking vague, lost, pointedly unconcerned, unusually interested in a rivet head, is to move rapidly and apparently happily to his side before he begins to stand on one leg.' Officers could only wear civilian clothes just before or just after shore leave. 'Sweaty athletes' were allowed to call briefly to collect mail but were not to linger. Members were not allowed to treat one another at the bar as that might hide problems of alcoholism or debt. They were warned that the bar should not be 'unduly hampered by using its purely secondary function of bodily support', and at busy times they were 'requested to swallow their drinks away from this source, allowing other even more thirsty officers to be served'. Officers had to provide cleaning materials for their stewards, whose valeting duties included shoe polishing, laying out forenoon and evening dress and making up the laundry. Their cabin duties were to make up the bunk daily and convert it to a settee when possible; to clean the cabin and brightwork and wash the paintwork, and make up the bed in the evening. Officers were not to complain loudly about food or service but to have a quiet word with the petty officer steward or mess secretary. They were never 'to vent their wrath upon the individual steward serving them nor address the mess to gain moral support while still at table'.

The ship was ready for the Navy Days from the 16th to the 18th and attracted 5,102 visitors on the last day. On the 24th she dressed overall for Empire Day. She spent summer working up and was in Plymouth for more Navy Days during the August Bank Holiday, when she attracted up to 11,604 visitors a day, and Master Stephen Richard Greig, son of the ship's communications officer, was baptised on the quarterdeck. On 19 August she put to sea for trials, including tests of the auto-boiler control, and next day she set sail for the first stage in a journey to rejoin the Far East Fleet. She arrived at Gibraltar on the 23rd, exercising on the way, and at Malta on the 26th, where the crew enjoyed the traditional pleasures of the port. After her arrival at Singapore she hoisted the flag of Rear Admiral Varyl Begg, second-in-command of the Far East Station and a future

First Sea Lord. The crew was accommodated in HMS *Terror* for much of the time while the ship was at 48 hours' notice for steam. She was in Hong Kong from 19 December 1959 to to 2 January 1960. Then she sailed to Sandakan in north-east Borneo and was visited by W. K. C. Wookey, the Resident and the Governor – for the colony did not become a part of independent Malaysia until 1963. She went on to Madras in India, where she entertained a party of 130 children from local orphanages, and then to Vishakapatnam, 400 miles up the coast, where she was open to visitors and conducted rowing and sailing races; one of the dinghies capsized. She returned to Singapore at the end of February, then began an Australian cruise.

* * * * *

Captain Wilkinson drafted a very detailed set of orders on how the ship was to be run. The first lieutenant was responsible for the cleanliness of all messdecks, with divisional officers for their own groups. Linoleum was to be 'treated carefully as it is most expensive and difficult to replace'. 'Adequate shielding' was to be placed behind dartboards to protect the paintwork. Ratings were restricted to their own messes, except when visiting individuals, there on duty, or passing through as a gangway. Officers passing through in this way would normally remove their caps so that the ratings were not expected to show 'appropriate marks of respect' by standing up and ceasing conversation. Bunks and hammocks were to be stowed by 0645, and settee bunks were to be 'rigged as settees' during working hours. Though dining was no longer done in messes, each mess was still to provide a number of cooks, who were to prepare tea for their messes during stand-easies and were to 'square up' the messes between 1215 and 1310 as well as to work in their messes for ten minutes after stand-easy before joining their part of the ship. Men's gear found 'sculling around' the messdecks would be taken to the regulating office and put in the traditional 'scran bag', which was opened once a week, and items could be redeemed from it at a cost of 2*d* [c.1*p*] each. Evening rounds were conducted by the captain at 1030, and messdeck rounds by the commander at 1930. There were two standard routes for evening rounds, selected by the senior officer, who was accompanied by the master-at-arms and the bugler.

The ship carried a number of Chinese ratings for domestic duties – two chief petty officers, five steward petty officers, nine leading stewards and twenty stewards were listed along with five cooks. A separate list, presumably of non-regular men, showed a petty officer cook, a leading cook and a leading steward and three cooks. Accommodation was provided in two compartments on the upper deck just aft of the engine room and close to the marines. One for chief and petty officers seemed to be well provided with 18 triple bunks, though it was only listed as having nine men in bunks and one on a settee. An irregular-shaped compartment had room for 39 men in bunks, settees and hammocks. Chinese ratings were allowed one cubicle in the junior ratings' heads.

Amid the port visits and ceremonial duties, it was never possible to forget the possibility of war, and detailed plans were drawn up. Items such as the children's party gear, the admiral's car and two Land Rovers were to be landed, along with all records more than a year old to reduce fire risk. The complement was to be increased by 7 officers, 13 chiefs and petty officers and 66 leading rates and below, which would bring most of the hammocks into use. Timber for shoring-up damaged areas was to be taken on board, and all men were to be issued with lifebelts. They were to land their civilian clothes at the first opportunity and be prepared to wear action dress.

Even a thin layer of clothing can make all the difference to life or death by minimising the burning effect on the body of flash from conventional or nuclear explosions. Clothing is also a great life preserver to those thrown into cold water as it helps to retain the body's temperature. It also affords protection from the sun's rays to those who may find themselves in an open boat in tropical climates.

During full 'action state' each man was to be fully clothed and have his trousers tucked into his socks with sleeves rolled down. Anti-flash gloves and helmets were to be worn, but only those on the upper deck had to wear steel helmets. Everyone was to wear lifejackets and carry gas masks. Most of this still applied in 'normal state' except that anti-flash gear could be carried rather than worn. 'Relaxed state' was only to be adopted when specifically ordered, but the men could strip to the waist while keeping their gear close. Six first-aid posts were to be set up, in the capstan flat, petty officers' mess, CPOs' bunk space, shipwrights' workshop and in two officers' cabin flats.

There was always an ideological element in the Cold War, which would continue if it became 'hot', and enemy agents were considered a serious threat. 'Everyone is to be on the alert to prevent sabotage. Saboteurs may be civilians, men or women dressed in uniform or even a member of our own ship's company.' There were plans for dealing with prisoners, and the captain's secretary was to keep a list of all officers and ratings with knowledge of enemy languages – they might be selected as guards in the hope of overhearing conversations. But they were not to initiate interrogations, for if done unskilfully it would prejudice the process. It was a fine line. Men might talk out of shock or anxiety immediately after capture, and this was to be encouraged.

The ship could carry troops for up to four days at a time to a maximum of 24 officers, 23 warrant officers, 48 sergeants and 330 other ranks. Accommodation was arranged for the 'worst possible case' in which the exposed decks were not available for sleeping, but up to 750 camp beds might be deployed about the messdecks, making life very cramped for crew and passengers. Soldiers were to wear shoes rather than boots on board, to preserve the decks as well as their own balance. With Gurkha troops, naval officers were not to issue them orders directly as they would not respond and would answer only to their own officers. They were considered to be very bad sailors, and buckets were to be carefully set out for them.

* * * * *

As part of the commitment to SEATO, the *Belfast* took part in many joint exercises with the navies of the other nations. International tension was extraordinarily high during these years and was exacerbated by civil war in the former Belgian Congo and the shooting down of an American U2 spy plane on 1 May 1960. The split between Soviet and Chinese communism did not become fully apparent until the end of the year. In the meantime, the SEATO allies feared some kind of communist demonstration on the anniversary of the Korean War and put on a show of strength. Back in Singapore on 12 April, the ship's company of the *Belfast* was addressed by Captain Wilkinson, for she was about to begin the most intensive part of her commission. On the 21st a staff officer transferred from the British aircraft carrier *Albion* for the purpose of Exercise 'Sealion', a joint exercise by the United States, British, Australian and Philippine fleets.

The ship sailed for Manila on the 23rd in company with the Australian carrier *Melbourne* and an escort of seven destroyers and frigates. There were many exercises on the way including one in electronic warfare, a mock attack by Sea Venom aircraft, which was 'broken up' by Bofors guns, rocket firings at a towed splash target, and an anti-submarine exercise in the evening of the 26th. They arrived at Manila on the 28th to host a staff conference on board. There was a little rest before they sailed on 2 May for the first phase of 'Sealion' proper. Next day there were gunnery shoots, tracking exercises and a helicopter transfer from the American carrier *Yorktown*. Then they returned to port, and the hands cleared the quarterdeck for a critique of the exercise by group commanders and operations officers. Phase 2 of the exercise started on the 6th, and the approaches to the harbour were swept for mines to allow the exit of three carrier groups. The *Belfast* was part of Task Unit 320.1.2, Rear Admiral Begg, which in turn was part of Task Group 320.1. She would spend most of the time escorting and supporting the carrier *Albion*, which meant following her movements when she turned into wind to fly off or land her aircraft, for example on the 9th, when flying was conducted early in the morning and again after 0930. She headed back to Singapore on the 11th at the end of the exercise. A press conference was held on board on the 13th.

On 26 May she left Hong Kong to sail to Inchon, the site of the decisive landings in 1950. She was in company with the *Albion* and other ships, arriving on the 30th to join American and other SEATO forces to commemorate the start of the war and perhaps deter any further aggression. There was a full round of events including visits by the ambassador, while the marine band played ashore. She sailed on 5 June to visit Kobe in Japan, where they celebrated the Queen's official birthday on the 11th, and prepared to move out to cope with Typhoon 'Mary' – but in the event it passed further south than expected, and she did not have to move. In June they were back in the old haunt of Sasebo, though it is doubtful if many people on board could remember her numerous visits a decade previously.

There were more visits and exercises before the ship arrived back at Singapore in September. On 13 October she entered the King George VI dry dock for a longer repair, and her crew was paid off and flown home to end the commission.

* * * * *

A new ship's company was assembled in Portsmouth. Most of the ratings mustered at HMS *Victory* in November 1960. Some were then sent home to await flight instructions, and the Royal Marines went to Eastney Barracks nearby for pre-embarkation training. Then they went out in eleven flights by Britannia aircraft of RAF Transport Command, arriving to feel 'the hot breath of the tropics on their necks'. During the changeover period the regulating department worked out the system – 'if you were sun-tanned you were leaving and if you had a white skin you were arriving!' The *Belfast* was recommissioned on 31 January 1961 under the command of Captain Morgan Giles. The ship's commission book reported, 'The parade, in the heat of the day, was mercifully short and was followed by a service on the quarterdeck.'

The programme of SEATO exercises was just as intense as before, and there were only three weeks to work up before the ship was due to take part in Exercise 'Jet 61' in February. During firing and tracking exercises a Sea Vixen fighter from HMS *Hermes* crashed in the sea twenty miles from the *Belfast*, and wags joked that the ship's gunnery department had been effective for once. An oil slick was found, and the ship's whaler picked up some wreckage; then an RAF Shackleton spotted the pilot and observer, the former smoking his pipe in a life raft. They were picked up by a naval helicopter and landed on the *Belfast*'s quarterdeck. In the wardroom visitors' book, the pilot wrote, 'Glad to be aboard … !'

Exercise 'Pony Express' consisted of 'an amphibious assault landing exercise of brigade size, featuring vertical envelopment'. It was to be preceded by 'anti-submarine and anti-air warfare events during the movement phases, a rehearsal and advance force operations'. It was intended to restrain the activities of Lotus, 'a strong military power which adheres to the Circle Trigon Political Philosophy, along with its ally Bellicus'. The *Belfast* was the only cruiser in the British contingent, alongside a commando carrier equipped with helicopters, a conventional aircraft carrier plus submarines, destroyers and frigates. The forces assembled in the Philippines and Singapore, and mock landings were to be conducted in North Borneo. The *Belfast* carried Rear Admiral Michael le Fanu, who was deputy exercise director. The ship was not much involved in the early stages apart from the occasional arrival of unexpected visitors by helicopter. 'Our big moment arrived on the 17th April when we were detached to lead the FIREX group and bombard an island off North Borneo called Balam.' There was another aeronautical accident that afternoon when a Scimitar from HMS *Victorious* crashed. The pilot ejected and was picked up (but later died), and the *Belfast* searched for wreckage.

Replenishment at sea (RAS) was one of the standard features of modern naval life, especially in the broad waters of the Pacific, Indian Ocean and South China Sea. According to the *Manual of Seamanship*,

> For a fleet to operate for long periods away from shore bases it must be replenished from specially equipped ships, and sometimes larger ships must replenish the smaller ones. Standardisation of the method of connecting the gear has made replenishment at sea between ships of the NATO [and SEATO] countries speedy and efficient, and sometimes quicker than when a ship replenishes in harbour.

It could be done to transfer goods such as food and ammunition, personnel including senior officers and, most importantly, fuel. It might be done by a tanker trailing a line astern, but mostly it was done with the ships abeam and by rigging light or heavy jackstays. This revived the ancient arts of the seamen in several ways: steering had to be very accurate during the transfer, as the two ships might interact and collide. Old-fashioned deck seamanship was still needed even in the electronic age, for casting lines across and rigging the derricks and tackles. The *Belfast* carried out 283 RASs during this period.

A trip to Korea was cancelled, and the ship visited Japan at the end of May. Nagasaki was 'dreary', but visitors could see 'the purported ground Zero of the atomic bomb burst', the original 'Madame Butterfly house' and a peace statue. They learned that 'True Geisha girls are NOT, as many imagine, high priced "call girls" but first class entertainers.' Those who resorted to real 'call girls' were impressed that they shared their beer with their clients, unlike the girls of Hong Kong who charged huge prices for coloured water. They reached Kure on 1 June and found themselves some distance from the town – they had to use buses with very limited leg room, unless they could afford taxis. Then they headed for Tokyo through the Inland Sea, with expectations that at last they were going to a big city with money in their pockets. It was not enough. Prices in the capital were very high, and many sought entertainment out of town. Those who stayed could see the massive walls of the Imperial Palace, but it was only open to the public on two days a year. They left Japan on 14 June.

Though they shared many experiences in common, each of the ship's departments had its own highlights and low points for the commission, and as the engineering mechanics noted, 'The usual

friendly rivalry and comments between departments soon developed
…' For the gunnery department, 'Each man had a Surface Action,
AA Action, SU Defence, AA Defence, AA Cruising etc, etc station. At
first the majority were wrong but in a few days people were reaching
the right place … For a little over a fortnight the gunnery rates were
here there and everywhere and eventually we could fire the 6"
without forgetting to put the SA/QF gear to SA, and the 40/60,
providing a certain Able Seaman, bearded and now departed, was
not closed up!' The radar plotters jokingly reported their
consumption of stores in the commission book: 'Pencils used – 9873.
At least 92% of which immediately disappeared to mark gauges,
shale boards, notices, the multitude of stateboards in the gunnery
office and several bulkheads. Tracing paper – 13,648 yards. We used
847 of these – the paint sprayers had the rest.' For the
communications department, 'Wearing the flag of the Flag Officer
Second-in-Command Far East Station has of course not gone
unnoticed in the signal world, even if it only meant the arrival of
those extra hands.' To the forecastle division of seamen, 'Throughout
the commission we've had our fair share of rust; we've no idea how
many times we've rigged the jackstay.' Their colleagues on the
quarterdeck lamented that their area was not as sacred as it had
once been. 'Why is the quarterdeck so popular? Why must every
rating wearing oily shoes choose to walk all over it? If a fuel pipe
bursts, why must it be aft? Why must helicopters land on it? Why
must we tow aft from the quarterdeck?' The Top division, according
to their report in the commission book, were only interested in sport
and relished beating the petty officers at cricket, though they had to
admit that, 'The Division has not performed outstandingly at Soccer.'
The small diving team enjoyed many experiences, including 'some
of the most beautiful coral reefs in the world'.

The Royal Marine detachment was smaller than in the past, with two captains, two colour sergeants, three sergeants, two corporals, three buglers and 25 marines. 'Ceremonial duties have naturally been one of the main occupations. In addition to the routine duties, the detachment joined up with the marines from HMS *Loch Alvie* to provide a guard for the Independence Day celebrations in Dar-es-Salaam. In spite of only one rehearsal, both detachments gave a very creditable performance.' The supply department had many duties besides clerical work and storekeeping. 'We have "Scribes" and "Dustys" who are accomplished TCB operators, damage control enthusiasts and who number among the special sea dutymen. Our chefs almost made a 4" gun's crew but instead have devoted themselves to first aid, action working parties, fleet bakers, as well as being specialists in cafeteria action messing.'

In an era that saw the first gas turbine propulsion and nuclear power, the engine room artificers and mechanicians, or 'trogs', were confused by the old machinery. 'A quarter of a century ago (sounds even longer than 25 years) she was designed and troglodycally speaking we are basically the same; slightly more sophisticated from the control angle of course but it is still a new thing to most of us and will remain a black out for some time yet!' Their colleagues, the engineering mechanics (as stokers were now known), noted, 'Members of other departments were notably reluctant to visit machinery spaces in the tropics. It was even suspected that the communications department purposely included cigarette tins and other incombustibles with their waste in order to be banned from entering the boiler rooms!' The electrical department was now quite large, with four officers and 89 ratings, few of whom had any experience in cruisers. 'With the commissioning ceremony over, life became real and earnest. We had three weeks to get to know where all the knobs and switches were before we plunged into Exercise Jet 61.' The carpenters, or 'chippies', regarded themselves as the handymen of the ship and regretted that their duties would soon be taken over by the engineering branch.

A new generation of sailors experienced the delights of Hong Kong for the first time:

> As *Belfast* nosed her way in on that misty morning of May 8th, the muted roar of the traffic mingling with the chirpy hoots and sirens of the harbour vessels filtered through to the ship's company fallen in on deck for the ceremonial entrance … Here at anchor lie the most varied assortment of ships imaginable; from stately passenger liners carrying their wealthy globe-trotters in 5 star luxury to ports all over the world, warships and cargo vessels down to Liberian tramps and the intriguing centuries-old sampans and Chinese junks with their characteristic fan-like, tattered multi-coloured sails, sadly conceding however to the march of progress with their powerful diesel engines. And of course everywhere, like water-beetles flitting across a lake, move the water-taxis, the wallah-wallahs, business like in their unceasing activity.

There was a break from the usual activities in November, when the ship sailed from Hong Kong to take part in the independence celebrations of Tanganyika, one of many African colonies that set up its own government at this time, as the great bulk of the British Empire was wound up. The commander-in-chief's Royal Marine band was embarked at Singapore, then there was a stop at the RAF island base of Gan in the Maldives, where the ship's divers removed some obstructions in the harbour. The ship arrived at Mombasa in Kenya on 4 December to take on board Rear Admiral A. A. F. Talbot. The crew went ashore to collect such souvenirs as wood carvings and native drums, but longer visits had to be cancelled due to flooding. They sailed with the frigates *Rhyl* and *Lochalvie* to arrive at the Tanganyikan capital Dar-es-Salaam at 0600, to be welcomed by many Africans and Europeans. The ship, dressed overall and illuminated at night, was visited by the governor-general and by the incoming Prime Minister. The Duke of Edinburgh arrived next day for the formal celebrations, which centred on a flag-raising ceremony in the town's stadium at midnight, attended by many of the *Belfast*'s company. The country was later merged with Zanzibar to become Tanzania.

On a visit to Australia in August and September, Melbourne did not find favour with the crew. It was too much like home – 'not Pompey [Portsmouth] or Guz [Devonport] but some residential Midlands town, not very interesting architecturally'. Like their predecessors in 1945, they were introduced to the custom of bars closing at 6 p.m. Sydney was much better, right from the entry as they passed the Heads in 'the most perfect morning imaginable' then went ashore in a city that was 'much more vital and interesting than Melbourne'. Mrs. Morgan Giles invited the crew to a ball at the Trocadero attended by an equal number of the 'belles of Sydney', and they adapted the words attributed to the Prime Minister, Harold Macmillan, at a rally in 1957 – 'We had never had it so good.'

In this commission the sporting activities were not interrupted by war, though as usual they had to take second place to operational needs, which was often used as an excuse for lack of success. The soccer team had 'not lived up to the promise shown early in the commission' but had 17 wins and 4 draws from 36 games. In athletics, 294 men entered for the 16 events of an inter-divisional athletic meeting during docking in Singapore. They were beaten by the Royal Marines, and the Eighth Destroyer Squadron edged them into third place by two points. In basketball they were unsurprisingly trounced by the USS *Princeton*, but the team, including a Chinese tailor, steward and chief petty officer, won seven successive games after that. As to boxing, opportunities were very limited and only AB McKee entered the Fleet Open Championship, in which he won the light middleweight division. For rugby, 'The 13 month season has seen our transition from the mud of the UK to the hard grounds and fast open rugby of the Far East. This all took some time to become accustomed to but after several trials and our first 3 games (all lost) we settled down to play some very constructive rugby.' The water polo team could only attract seven players including five chiefs and petty officers and had an average age of 35. Interest was lukewarm and the players complained of 'the supporters we never had'. Sailing was conducted by 'a small nucleus of sailing enthusiasts', and there were regattas during intervals in the major exercises. The final of these was during 'Jet 62', when the captain came fourth in dinghies and Surgeon Lieutenant Taylor fifth, with Radio Operator Felton sailing the whaler. The cricket team took on 'the mighty HMAS *Melbourne*' and was defeated by an innings and 130 runs. After 'a drastic revision of tactics and teamwork', they had more mixed success. Hockey, a traditional naval sport, suffered from the posting of the star centre-forward PO Verral and the 'pillar of defence' Sub-Lieutenant Smith, while 'the second eleven made up in energy what they lacked in skill'.

* * * * *

On 26 March 1962 the ship left Singapore for the last time to voyage home across the Pacific. They stopped in Hong Kong for two days, when, 'The ship's company used all available time to scour the local shops for rabbits [gifts] and staggered to and fro like a column of ants, laden with all sorts of unlikely objects. Wicker-work chairs, camphor-wood chests, children's toys, radios, cameras, typewriters and tape recorders soon littered the decks ...'

In Hawaii they encountered the might and history of the United States Navy. 'As we entered Pearl Harbor we were surrounded on all sides by massive carriers, guided missile ships, conventional and nuclear submarines and hosts of smaller ships. We sailed past the famous 'Battleship Row' where seven battleships were sunk or damaged by the Japanese attack in December 1941.' Socially the islands did not live up to their reputation: 'dusky maidens seemed to be in short supply' and expensive hotels were no substitute – but the crew had many invitations and entertainments. They sailed on 22 April, Easter Sunday, for a 2,400-mile voyage to San Francisco. On the way across a search revealed 50 pounds of opium and heroin intended to be smuggled into the USA. The would-be smugglers were put in the cells, and there was concern that the American authorities would search the ship further on arrival and perhaps put her in quarantine for several days. They were relieved when no further action was taken. It was warm and sunny and 'many of us concentrated on getting brown for the Americas and England. Every lunch-time and make-and-mend *Belfast* looked like a plague ship, with unmoving figures in various states of undress littering the decks.'

The ship entered San Francisco Bay. 'From the moment we passed under Golden Gate Bridge, through a crown of white-clad sailing boats, and saw the city laid out in the hills and valleys of San Francisco, we suspected this was a city we would never forget.' Very few of the sailors had visited America before, and the experience was overwhelming. Ashore, 'The hospitality of the natives was tremendous. Bus and car tours were provided by residents to enable us to see and appreciate the scenic beauty of the city. Invitations poured in from all sides covering every possible activity from a trip to Las Vegas by private aeroplane to equally private supper parties.' The local press reported, 'Usually when any of the larger vessels tie up at strange ports there is resentment of one sort or another that leads to at least a little misunderstanding. The crew of the *Belfast* conducted themselves in such a manner that no-one had anything but good to say of them.' By the time the ship left, the crew was exhausted and the decks were strangely empty as they caught up on sleep.

The next stop was Seattle, where the World Fair was in progress with the theme of 'Man in the Space Age' – though an ageing cruiser from an earlier generation of naval warfare might seem a little out of place in such an environment. Dozens of sailors volunteered to stand guard at the British Pavilion, and eventually four sailors, four marines and two sergeants were chosen to stay behind when the ship sailed and rejoin her later. On 11 May the ship headed north for Vancouver, where there was a cocktail party for the officers and a dance for the ship's company. There was a particularly full sporting programme, including sailing, cricket, hockey, water polo, rugby and soccer. The crew complained, 'We invariably had the best available side fielded against us ... we usually did well for the first five minutes at least, then the consequences of training, on wine, women and song began to tell.' They sailed for Victoria, where they were visited by the High Commissioner for Canada. They took part in the city's centenary parade which was 'in the traditional American style lasting some two-and-three-quarter hours and was complete with the armed services, service and college bands, dance troupes, cheer leaders, majorettes, floats and so on ...' They left on 22 May for the Panama Canal.

The final visit of the commission was to Port of Spain in Trinidad, where for the first time on the voyage home they were unable to moor alongside, and some of the men were deterred by the twenty-minute boat trip. Those who did go ashore enjoyed limbo demonstrations and steel bands. On the way across the Atlantic they were called to a merchant ship on which a crewman had had a serious accident, but he died before they got to him. The *Belfast* reached Portsmouth on 19 June 1962, having travelled 73,500 miles with the expenditure of 38,345 tons of fuel. The ship's company had been paid just over a million pounds and eaten nearly two million pounds of food.

* * * * *

While the *Belfast* was away the navy had changed yet again. In 1960 the *Vanguard*, the last of the navy's battleships, was scrapped without ever seeing active service. In the same year, the first of the nuclear-powered submarines, the *Dreadnought*, was launched; but unlike her namesake of 1906 she was not in the vanguard of progress and relied on an American reactor. New building concentrated on eight guided-missile destroyers, which at 6,200 tons were as big as an older generation of frigates; on the *Leander* class frigates, which were mainly for anti-submarine work but were able to carry out many of the tasks that the *Belfast* and her sisters had done in earlier generations; and on large numbers of small minesweepers, which were in fact used for many other roles. No new aircraft carriers were built and the CVA-01 being designed would never see service. Instead the older ships, going back to the wartime *Victorious*, were modernised as far as possible on hulls that were often too small for modern supersonic aircraft. Amphibious warfare had largely been neglected for ten years after the war, until the Suez Campaign of 1956 (though a disastrous political failure) showed new possibilities. These included the use of helicopters for 'vertical envelopment'. This offered some hope for the old cruiser's revival, with a plan 'To provide a troop lift with amphibious landing capability in the shape of HMS *Belfast*.' She would be equipped with four assault landing craft on davits, each capable of landing a platoon of troops. 'Y' turret would be removed along with part of the after superstructure, and she would be given 'provision for operating as many Wessex-type helicopters as possible including limited maintenance facilities commensurate (for each helicopter) with that provided in a frigate'. But a study showed that it would take considerable time, and both 'X' and 'Y' turrets would have to be removed to provide adequate hangar accommodation. Removing 'Y' turret and providing a Wessex platform would only be 'a gesture' and its value would be 'almost negligible'. It would be much better to refit the existing command carriers, ex-aircraft-carriers, *Bulwark* and *Albion*. The idea of using her as the Dartmouth training ship was revived in 1964 but came to nothing. A handbook of 1966 suggested that old classes of warship were obsolescent and put the *Belfast* and the other surviving cruisers among the '2nd rate gun support vessels', implying that their only real role would be in support of the army, which was indeed what the *Belfast* had done in her last two periods of war service. Another classic cruiser role began to end in the late 1960s, when the government decided to withdraw from 'East of Suez' – though that decision would take some years to implement. The *Belfast*'s sea service was not completely over – at the end of 1962 she visited Amsterdam, and in August 1963 she was commissioned under the Admiral Commanding Reserves and with a reserve crew for Exercise 'Rock Haul' – but she would never be in the front rank again.

With concentration on the nuclear deterrent, anti-submarine warfare in the North Atlantic and amphibious operations, even the more modern cruisers, *Tiger*, *Lion* and *Blake*, were struggling to find a role, and two of them were converted to helicopter carriers with their after guns removed. In 1965 *Belfast* was reduced to an accommodation ship in Portsmouth for sailors of the reserve division, men awaiting ships and for sea cadets. It was a humble enough role, but it had unintended consequences. In April 1967 a party from the Imperial War Museum, led by the director Noble Frankland, came to the port to look at the cruiser *Gambia* of 1940, with a view to preserving one of her gun turrets. But, 'We found her, a pitiful figure lying in "death row". Age and vandalism had reduced her to a travesty of her wartime splendour.' Peter Simkins of the Museum suggested it might be possible to preserve a whole cruiser, and they could see the *Belfast* at anchor nearby. They accepted an invitation to lunch by her Captain, T. E. B. Firth, and even as they boarded Frankland began to see that her preservation was possible. 'There was no rust to be seen and, in place of the evidence of vandalism on *Gambia*, there was the gloss of naval spick and span. Captain Firth and the officers showed us all over the ship and we noted much equipment we thought we might be able to remove and preserve. My thoughts, however, were now consumed by the idea of preserving the whole vessel.' A committee was set up, including the director of the National Maritime Museum at Greenwich and naval officials. In 1968 it concluded that preservation was possible under the auspices of the two museums. It would still require great efforts to persuade the navy to hand the ship over rather than profit from her scrap value and for the Department of Education and Science to authorise the museums to man her.

One advantage was that her former captain, Morgan Giles, now a retired rear admiral, was an outspoken Conservative Member of Parliament, and he became chairman of the *Belfast* board. The attitude of Lord Louis Mountbatten, cousin of the Queen and former chief of Combined Operations, Viceroy of India and Chief of the Defence Staff, was less helpful even though Frankland was cooperating on a documentary about his life. Mountbatten was somehow convinced that the *Belfast* was rusted through and conveyed that impression to Prince Phillip. The National Maritime Museum pulled out, and Frankland was out of the country in the spring of 1971 when his deputy, C. H. Roads, began to establish a charitable trust to preserve the ship. They raised £170,000 to repair her in a dry dock at Tilbury on the Thames and then bring her upriver to the Pool of London opposite the Tower – the largest ship ever to enter the area, which was traditionally a merchant rather than a naval harbour but was now little used apart from tourist boats. The journey was completed on 15 October 1971 when the ship passed under Tower Bridge and, as a wartime Swordfish flew overhead, was moored on a permanent site at Hay's Wharf. She was opened to the public six days later, on Trafalgar Day, though visitors only had access to her open decks.

A problem with any preserved ship, especially one that has seen several decades of constant change, is what stage to represent in its display. The *Victory* at Portsmouth is shown as she was under Nelson at Trafalgar, though that was only one stage in her long and active career. The *Great Britain* in Bristol is restored to her original condition as built by Brunel, though it might be argued that she had a much more successful and longer life with different engine, rig and accommodation on the Australia run. The *Cutty Sark* in Greenwich is represented as a tea and wool clipper, which was definitely the most distinguished part of her history. With the *Belfast*, the policy was 'not to restore the ship to any one particular period of her history but instead to present one compartment in the condition of one period, another in another and so on with the object, which we ultimately achieved, of showing all of the *Belfast*'s development over the whole period of her life from the time of her commissioning to our acceptance of her'. This had the advantage that it did not require major structural work to restore her to a particular period. Some features of the ship including the engines and main armament have changed little over the years. Others, such as the electronics and messdecks, have altered radically, though one messdeck is displayed as it would have been in wartime, with hammocks. The most striking post-war features – the bridge and the lattice masts – are shown as they were in her last years of service. Externally, she is painted in the disruptive pattern camouflage of 1942–4 – purists have complained that this is inappropriate with fittings from the 1950s and 1960s.

* * * * *

In 1978 the *Belfast* was incorporated in the Imperial War Museum, part of a policy of expanding beyond the South London galleries, which Frankland regarded as claustrophobic, that included the acquisition of an airfield at Duxford. With a prime site in the centre of the city, perhaps the most prominent of any preserved ship, she attracts about a quarter of a million visitors a year. Frankland was rather disparaging about the *Belfast*'s history, claiming that she 'was not the most distinguished of the Royal Navy's Second World War cruisers' and that she 'could not, for example, rival the battle honours and the fame of HMS *Sheffield*'. This perhaps underplayed her role in the *Scharnhorst* action and the Korean War.

The *Belfast* represents the million men and women who risked their lives in the Royal Navy during the Second World War, and whose numbers are sadly reduced seventy years after the end of the conflict. It also represents important stages in British history – one of the first casualties of war in 1939, enduring the Plymouth Blitz in 1941, the frozen horrors of the Russian convoys, a key role in the Royal Navy's last big-gun action and participation in the Normandy invasion. It offers a unique perspective on the dawn of the nuclear age as seen by those on board the ship, whether well or ill-informed. It experienced at first hand the visible decline of British sea power in China in 1945–6 and its subordination to the United States. It was on the fringes of the Chinese Revolution, which changed Asia and the Pacific for good or ill, and played a more active role in the Korean War. It was affected by the social changes ashore, which gradually penetrated the navy in the 1950s and early 60s.

The *Belfast*'s preservation, like that of most historic ships, is largely a matter of chance. Britain has the greatest ensemble of preserved ships in the world, led by the *Mary Rose*, *Victory*, *Great Britain*, *Warrior* and *Cutty Sark*. But the country did not do well, compared with the United States, in keeping the warships of the more recent age. Most of the warships left over from the Second World War were scrapped in the late 1950s and early 1960s, as a long-term conflict at sea seemed increasingly unlikely in the age of the hydrogen bomb. Britons were still concerned with the sea at that time but seemed to seek modernity in the age of the affluent society, and the ship preservation movement was weak. No aircraft carriers or battleships were preserved, in contrast to the United States, which has several. The only British wartime destroyer is the *Cavalier*, which was launched in 1944 and saw little wartime service. The only submarine, the *Alliance*, was launched in 1945, and her appearance was drastically altered later in her career. There is no escort ship from the Battle of the Atlantic in this country and very little in the way of amphibious warfare vessels. This leaves the *Belfast*, which had a much longer active service record than any other, despite a gap in the middle. Of course, the experience of the crews of aircraft carriers, destroyers, escorts, submarines, minesweepers and coastal craft was very different for that on cruisers and battleships, but in a sense Belfast has to represent all of them.

As this is being written, the *Belfast* is firing a gun salute to mark Queen Elizabeth II's reign as the longest-serving British monarch. It is to be hoped and expected that she will remain at the heart of national life for the future.

BIBLIOGRAPHY

IWM   Imperial War Museum
ADM   Admiralty papers in the
       National archives, Kew

GENERAL

General History

Angus Calder, *The People's War, Britain
1939–45*, St. Albans, 1982
Norman Longmate, *How We Lived Then*,
London, 2002
A. J. P. Taylor, *English History, 1914–45*,
1965, reprinted Oxford, 1975

Naval History

Corelli Barnett, *Engage the Enemy More
Closely*, London, 1991
Eric Grove, *Vanguard to Trident*, London,
1987
S. W. Roskill, *The War at Sea*, 4 volumes,
London, 1954–61

Books and Pamphlets on HMS Belfast

Richard Johnson-Bryden, *HMS Belfast,
Cruiser, 1939*, Barnsley, 2013
John J. Hole, *HMS Belfast: An Illustrated Tour
of the Machinery Spaces*, Ashford, 2011
Imperial War Museum, *HMS Belfast*, 1991
Ross Watton, *The Cruiser Belfast*, (Anatomy
of the Ship), London, 1985
John Wingate, *HMS Belfast*, 1971. This
contains many useful documents,
including the accounts by Brooke Smith
and Ogilvie which are cited below

PROLOGUE: MINED

Personal Accounts

ORAL HISTORY
Lawrence Conlon, IWM 26748
John Harrison, IWM 21103

Peter McSweeney, IWM 27451

MANUSCRIPTS
William Crawford, IWM Documents 1998
J. A. Syms, IWM Documents 11556
George A. Thring, *A Sailor's Reflections,
1939–43*, Royal Naval Museum
William F. Read, IWM Documents 65/35/1

LOG
ADM 28/107731, November 1939

REPORTS:
ADM 358/3058, missing personnel, including
death of Stanton the painter, 1939
ADM 267/66, 267/139, reports on damage
ADM 267/111 reports on damage to ships,
1939–40

1. THE BIRTH OF A CRUISER

Printed Books

Robert Gardiner (ed.), *Conway's All the
World's Fighting Ships, 1906–1921*,
London, 1985; *1922–1946*, London, 1980
Norman Friedman, *British Cruisers*,
Barnsley, 2010
Michael Moss, *Shipbuilders to the World:
125 Years of Harland & Wolff*, 1986
D. K. Brown, *A Century of Naval
Construction*, London, 1983
George E. Finch, *Tiffy: The Autobiography of
a Naval Engineer*, London, 1991

Periodicals

Newspaper reports of the building and
launch in *The Times* and the *Belfast
Telegraph*

Manuscripts

LOGS
National Archives, ADM 53/107728, August
1939

SHIPS' COVERS

Ships' covers in the National Maritime Museum are the main source for the design and building of the ship, though according to D. K. Brown, a naval constructor himself, 'They may be "the Truth and nothing but the Truth" but they are not "the whole Truth".' The volume on the *Belfast* class is No. 566. It includes items such as correspondence of design proposals, comments of different branches such as engineering and gunnery, legend of particulars, extracts from Admiralty Board minutes, armament statement, details of accommodation for crew, schemes of complement, quarter bills and many other details

SHIPS' PLANS

The original plans of the ship and the *Edinburgh* are also to be found in the National Maritime Museum. The larger ones are rolled and in the ADR series. For the original building of the ships, these include: NPA 6715, inboard profile; NPA6716, forecastle deck; NPA6717, upper deck; NPA6719, platform deck; NPA6720, hold; NPA6721, cross sections; NPA6722, bridge etc.; NPA6723, side armour; NPA6724, rig; NPA6725, lines; NPA 6726, cross sections of hull; NPA6727, sketch of rig; NPA6728, outboard profile and 'top down' view; NPA 6759, inboard profile. Most of these can been seen in low resolution on the museum's website

The ADF series includes folded plans, which show many features in great detail. These include plans of many of the individual compartments with their fittings, including radar and radio offices, shell rooms, catapult arrangements, course of anti-aircraft ammunition on the 'scenic railway', voice pipes, galleys, bakery, etc. The 1936 specification for the class is to be found in the same archive

2. PREPARING FOR SEA

Printed Books

Admiralty, BR 827, *A Seaman's Pocket Book*, 1943
Richard Hill, *Lewin of Greenwich*, London, 2000
Louis Le Bailly, *The Man around the Engine*, 1990
Roderick MacDonald, *The Figurehead*,
Bishop Auckland, 1993
Navy Lists, 1936–9
Charles Owen, *No More Heroes*, 1975
P. M. Rippon, *Evolution of Engineering in the Royal Navy*, volume 1, Tunbridge Wells, 1988, volume 2, London, 1994
John Whelan, *Home is the Sailor*, London, 1957

Periodicals

Roderick Macdonald, 'Riddle of the Sound', in *Naval Review*, October 1991

Manuscripts

Confidential Reports on Officers:
Lister, ADM 196/148/588
Scott, ADM 196/92, 196/127, 196/144
Thring, ADM 196/149/250

LOG
ADM 1/15676

Personal Accounts

Already cited; Conlon, McSweeney, Syms, Thring

MANUSCRIPTS:
Francis Allen Lister papers, LIS/1 in the National Maritime Museum

3. WAR WITH GERMANY

Printed Books

Admiralty, *North Sea Pilot: Part II, North and East Coasts of Scotland*, seventh edition, 1914
Admiralty, BR 224, *The Gunnery Pocket Book*, 1932
Brian Lavery, *Hostilities Only*, Greenwich, 2004
Rory O'Conor, *Running a Big Ship*, Portsmouth, 1937
D. A. Rayner, *Escort*, London, 1955

Manuscripts

Administrative Orders and Ship's Instructions for HMS Belfast, IWM Documents 9037. Catalogued as 'c 1960', but one of the volumes is clearly from 1939

REPORTS, ETC.
ADM 199/362, Rosyth War Diaries, 1939–40
ADM 1/9989 *Belfast* proceedings, including capture of *Cap Norte*, 1939
ADM 1/10169 *Edinburgh* and *Belfast*, report of proceedings, 1939
ADM 1/9928 Home Fleet, initial operations in war 1939

ADM 116/4204 Home Fleet tactical instructions, 1936–9, including recommended speeds and rpm
ADM 199/393 Home Fleet War Diary, 1939–41
ADM 116/5782, 5783, 5784, Prize Money; Correspondence and Papers
National archives HCA 57/14, Prize Money Papers for the *Cap Norte*

Logs
ADM 53/107728 to 107731, August to November 1939

Personal Accounts
Already cited; Crawford, Harrison, Lister, Syms, Read

Manuscripts
John Campbell, IWM Documents 9036
George E. Finch, Report on the *Cap Norte* in NMM LS/1/8

4. REPAIR

Printed Books

Robert Burgess and Roland Blackburn, *We Joined the Navy*, London, 1943
K. G. B. Dewar, *The Navy from Within*, 1939
Martin Gilbert, *The Churchill War Papers*, volume 1, London, 1993
Alec Guinness, *Blessings in Disguise*, London, 1985
Derek Howse, *Radar at Sea*, Basingstoke, 1993
Brian Lavery, *In Which They Served*, London, 2008
J. Lennox Kerr (ed.), *Wavy Navy*, London, 1950
Winston G. Ramsey, (ed.), *The Blitz Then and Now*, 2 volumes, London, 1987
Navy List, 1942–3

Periodicals

The Times, November 1939
Daily Telegraph, 29 July 2008, 'Andy' Palmer, obituary

Manuscripts

Confidential Reports on Officers:
Dathan, ADM 196/148/571
Parham, ADM 196/147/574, 196/124/3, 196/93/143

Logs
ADM 53/115417, 53/115418, November–December 1942

Ships' Covers
No. 566 as above, including: proposed completion programme, scheme of war complement, straightening of keel

Ships' Plans
These include: NPA6737, inboard profile; NPA6738, forecastle; NPA6739, upper deck; NPA6740, lower deck; NPA6742, hold; NPA6744, bridge etc.

Reports, etc.
Mass Observation Archive, University of Sussex, reports 886, 887
ADM 199/655 Plymouth Command War Diary, 1941

Personal Accounts

Already cited; Finch

Manuscripts
Wilfred Lindop, IWM Documents 92/27/1
James McCarthy, IWM Documents 13288
Richard John Mc Moran Wilson, later Lord Moran, IWM Documents 2115

Oral History
George Burridge, IWM 25217
Leslie Coleman, IWM 27228
Arthur 'Larry' Fursland, IWM 26746

Letters
J. G. B. Powell, IWM Documents 15776

5. RUSSIAN CONVOY

Printed Books

Naval Intelligence Division, *Iceland*, 1942
Navy List, 1943
Oxford Dictionary of National Biography, Robert Burnett

Manuscripts

Logs
ADM 53/117009 to 117011, January to March 1943

Confidential Reports on Officers:
Burnett, ADM 196/127/205, 196/144/210, 196/92/95, 196/51/230

Reports, etc.
ADM 199/73 Reports on convoys JW53 and RA53
ADM 199/77, North Russia Convoy Reports, 1943–4

Others
Louis Le Bailly, *Some Hints for Officers About to Go to Sea*, Churchill College, Cambridge LEBY/3

Personal Accounts

Already cited; Burridge, Coleman; Fursland, Wilson

ORAL HISTORY
Lancelot 'Lance' Tyler, IWM 28765
Denis Watkinson, IWM 27461

6. THE WAR IN THE NORTH

Printed Books

Admiralty, BR 16, *Engineering Manual*, 1939
Admiralty, BR 224/45, *The Gunnery Pocket Book*, 1945
Admiralty, BR 827, *A Seaman's Pocket Book*, June 1943

Manuscripts

LOGS
ADM 53/117012 to 117020, April to December 1943

CONFIDENTIAL REPORTS ON OFFICERS:
William Hawkins, ADM 196/150/189

REPORTS, ETC.
ADM 223/4, intelligence papers, 1943, results of carrier attack
ADM 182/15 Fleet Air Arm complements in Admiralty Fleet Orders, 1943
ADM 182/133, 134, radar complements, 1942, in Admiralty Fleet Orders
ADM 1/11784, question of retention of catapult aircraft, 1943
AIR 10/2081 Supermarine Walrus manual
ADM 220/81 report on radar, Belfast. 1941-6
ADM 1/19272 Home Fleet Technical Orders, 1943
ADM 234/188 BR945, 6-inch turret drill 1940
ADM 239/307, Radar Manual 1945
ADM 259/360 Type 149 radar, tried on *Belfast*
ADM 234/57 handbook for 4-inch guns, 1944
ADM 1/11260 Esmonde citation

Personal Accounts

Already cited; Coleman, Fursland, Tyler, Watkinson, Wilson

MIDSHIPMEN'S JOURNALS
R. L. Garnons-Williams, IWM documents 7687
Herbert Smith, IWM Documents 1829

MANUSCRIPTS
K. J. Melvin, IWM Documents 16004

Video etc

Catapult Ships, 1940, in IWM, *The Royal Navy at War*, *Fleet Air Arm*

7. THE *SCHARNHORST*

Printed Books

A. B. Cunningham, *A Sailor's Odyssey*, London, 1951
Brian Lavery, *Churchill Goes to War*, London, 2007
Brooke Smith in Wingate, *HMS* Belfast, pp 110-11
John Winton, *The Death of the Scharnhorst*, Chichester, 1983

Newspapers and Periodicals

Naval Review, February 1944, 'Banderillero', *Battle of St. Stephen's Day*

Manuscripts

LOG
ADM 53/117020, December 1943

REPORTS, ETC.
ADM 1/16676, recommendations for awards, including Hawkins, Meares, Mountifield, Dathan, Day, Fursland, Mason, Yeo
ADM 234/342, staff history of the sinking of the *Scharnhorst*
ADM 199/913, sinking of the *Scharnhorst* 1943
ADM 220/214 Type 271 radar operating procedure

Personal Accounts

Already cited; Fursland, Wilson

ORAL HISTORY
Parham, Churchill College, Cambridge, PARM

LETTERS
E. Palmer, IWM Documents 3763

Video, etc.

IWM, *Royal Navy at War: War in the Frozen North*

8. TO NORMANDY

Printed Books

Sarah Bradford, *George VI*, London, 1989
Ken Ford, *D-Day Commando*, Stroud, 2003
Paul Lund and Harry Ludlum, *The War of the Landing Craft*, Slough, 1976

Sir Bertram Ramsey, *The Year of D-Day*, Hull, 1994

Manuscripts

LOGS
ADM 53/118693-118969, January to June 1944

Confidential Reports on Officers:
Dalrymple Hamilton, ADM 195/52/231, 254, 144/574
Richard Tosswil, ADM 196/150/83

REPORTS, ETC.
ADM 199/941, Operation 'Tungsten'
ADM 199/1661, report on Operation 'Neptune' by Dalrymple Hamilton
ADM 179/263 report on re-ammunitioning ships of bombarding force, 1944
ADM 1/12555 training and organisation of bombardment units
ADM 199/1562 Eastern Task Force orders 1944
ADM 1/16160 review of system for control of bombardment, 1944
ADM 199/1559 Force J, orders and memoranda
DEFE 2/370 bombardment plan
DEFE 2/1319, Combined Training Centre, Precis of Lectures,

Personal Accounts

Already cited; Brooke Smith, Fursland, Herbert Smith, Parham, Watkinson, Wilson

ORAL HISTORY
Austin Baker, IWM 31328
David Jones, IWM 25240
Charles Simpson, IWM 24907

LETTERS
D. Withers, IWM Documents 13040

9. TO THE EAST

Printed Books

G. C. Connell, *Jack's War*, London, 1985
Sir James Eberle, *From Greenland's Icy Shore*, Durham, 2007
Peter Hodges, *British Warship Camouflage*, London, 1973
Brian Lavery (ed.), *The Royal Navy Officer's Pocket Book*, London, 2007
Louis Le Bailly, *From Fisher to the Falklands*, London, 1991
George Melly, *Rum, Bum and Concertina*,

London, 1977
Oxford Dictionary of National biography: Royer Mylius Dick

Manuscripts

LOGS
ADM 53/118968 to 111869, June to July 1944
ADM 53/120958 to 120966, April to December 1945
ADM 53/122644, January 1946

Confidential Reports on officers
Dick, 196/93/152, 196/120/66, 196/146/493
Reginald Servaes, ADM 196/127/243, 196/145/456, 196/93/7

REPORTS, ETC.
ADM 1/18686, report on mission to Shanghai
ADM 1/19332, report of proceedings, December 1945

Personal Accounts

Already cited; Simpson, Watkinson

MANUSCRIPTS
R. M. Dick, National Maritime Museum DCK/27, DCK/29. DCK 32

MIDSHIPMEN'S JOURNALS
J. F. W. Mudford, IWM Documents 11360

ORAL HISTORY
Jake Jacobs, IWM 27045
Archie Jarvis, IWM 33724
Bob Jones, IWM 27229
James Maas, IWM 25202
Bernard Thomson, IWM 27489

10. SHOWING THE FLAG

Printed Books

British Commonwealth Occupation Force, *Know Japan*, Victoria, Australia, 1946
Eric Grove, *Vanguard to Trident*, London, 1987
Patrick A. Moore, *The Greenie*, Stroud, 2011
Oxford Dictionary of National Biography: Denis Boyd
Ogilvie, in Wingate, *HMS Belfast*

Manuscripts

LOGS
ADM 53/122644 to 122655, January to December 1946

CONFIDENTIAL REPORTS ON OFFICERS
Denis Boyd, ADM 196/144/696, 196/127/257, 196/96/8

REPORTS, ETC.

IWM Documents 7263, correspondence on church fittings, 1947-50

ADM 199/1457, British Pacific Fleet and Eastern Fleet, Commander-in-Chief's dispatches, 1945–6

ADM 1/20311, allocation of cruisers to British Pacific Fleet, 1946-47

ADM 1/20301, release of doctors, 1946

ADM 202/332, *Belfast* marine detachment, 1945

ADM 1/19332, British Pacific Fleet, report of proceedings, 1945–6

ADM 1/21707, report in provisions in Home Fleet, 1946

FO 369/3449, internment camps, Shanghai, 1946

Personal Accounts

Already cited; Dick, Jacobs, Jarvis, Jones

ORAL HISTORY

Frank Briggs, IWM 27340

Bob Shrimpton, IWM 21735

11. WARS IN THE EAST

Printed Books

HMS Belfast, 1950–1952, the Record of a Commission, copies in Imperial War Museum and Royal Naval Museum

Anthony Farrar-Hockley, *The British Part in the Korean War*, two volumes, London, 1990–5

C. E. Lucas Phillips, *Escape of the Amethyst*, London, 1957

Oxford Dictionary of National Biography: Patrick Brind

Manuscripts

LOGS

ADM 53/124515 to 124577, October to December 1948

ADM 53/125515 to 125526, January to December 1949

ADM 53/127579 to 127590, January to December 1950

REPORTS, ETC.

ADM 116/5778, 1/23537, 23549, 23547, routine reports on naval activity, Korean War

ADM 1/28083, ship's bell in Belfast

ADM 1/21806, report of proceedings, 1949

ADM 1/22518, report of Proceedings, 1950

ADM 1/21806, rescue of Chinese landing ship, 1949

ADM 234/546, summaries of data of radio equipment, 1950

PERSONAL ACCOUNTS

Manuscripts

Peter Cardale, IWM Documents 368

George Oliver, IWM Documents 23618

12. RECOVERED FROM THE RESERVE FLEET

Printed Books

Admiralty, *Ship ABCD Manual*, volume 1, 1959, in the National Maritime Museum

Brian Lavery, *All Hands*, London, 2012

Brassey, 1959

Commission Book, *HMS Belfast, 1961–1962*, copies in Imperial War Museum and Royal Naval Museum

Admiralty Manual of Seamanship, 1967, especially volume II

Noble Frankland, *History at War*, London, 1998

Oxford Dictionary of National Biography: Morgan Giles

Manuscripts

The cover for the 1956–9 refit is No. 839. Plans include: NPA6753, inboard profile; NPA6754, upper and lower decks; NPA6755, decks; NPA6756, sections of hull; NPA6757, bridge, etc.; NPA6758, hold; NPA6760, upper and lower decks;

LOGS

ADM 53/150747 to 150754, May to December 1959

ADM 53/152933 to 152944, January to December 1960

ADM 53/155111 to 155122, January to December 1961

ADM 53/157281 to 157292, January to December 1962

ADM 53/159377 to 159385, January to September 1963

REPORTS, ETC.

DEFE 5/112 Exercise 'Pony Express'

ADM1/24887 reduction of *Belfast* to Class III Reserve, 1953

OTHERS

HMS *Belfast*, Wardroom Mess Rules, 1959, IWM K03/2274

Administrative Orders and Ship's Instructions for HMS Belfast, 1959, IWM Documents 9037

INDEX

HMS Belfast

Exploded deck view after modernisation refit, 1959

Drawing by Ross Watton